Job Interview

This Book Includes:

Guide, Questions and Answers, Preparations And Winning Interview

This content is provided with the sole purpose of providing relevant information on a specific topic for which every reasonable effort has been made to ensure that it is both accurate and reasonable. Nevertheless, by purchasing this content, you consent to the fact that the author, as well as the publisher, are in no way experts on the topics contained herein, regardless of any claims as such that may be made within. As such, any suggestions or recommendations that are made within are done so purely for entertainment value. It is recommended that you always consult a professional prior to undertaking any of the advice or techniques discussed within.

maybe is a legally binding declaration that is considered both valid and fair by both the Committee of Publishers Association and the American Bar Association and should be considered legally binding within the United States.

The reproduction, transmission, and duplication of any of the content found herein, including any specific or extended information, will be done as an illegal act regardless of the end form the information ultimately takes. This includes copied versions of the work, both physical, digital and audio

Table of Content

Job Interview Guide

A Complete Guide And Success Tips For Job Interview Preparation. Preparation Tips and Question Answering Techniques. Winning Guide To Answering Even The Toughest Questions.

unless express consent of the Publisher is provided beforehand. Any additional rights reserved.

Furthermore, the information that can be found within the pages described forthwith shall be considered both accurate and truthful when it comes to the recounting of facts. As such, any use, correct or incorrect, of the provided information will render the Publisher free of responsibility as to the actions taken outside of their direct purview. Regardless, there are zero scenarios where the original author or the Publisher can be deemed liable in any fashion for any damages or hardships that may result from any of the information discussed herein.

Additionally, the information in the following pages is intended only for informational purposes and should thus be thought of as universal. As befitting its nature, it is presented without assurance regarding its prolonged validity or interim quality. Trademarks that are mentioned are done without written consent and can in no way be considered an endorsement from the trademark holder.

Introduction

In everyone's professional life, we must learn how to seek out and prepare for our ideal job. We spend time and money obtaining educational degrees and/or technical training, not to mention professional experience in lower-level jobs, internships, and volunteer work. The reward for investing our personal resources in all of this is, ultimately, to secure that ideal job in a career of our choosing. The final barrier to obtaining that dream is to secure an interview—and employment—with the right company. Here you will find a guide to help you do just that.

From learning how to put together the best resume and cover letter to understanding and preparing for the toughest interview questions, this guide will take you step by step through the process of obtaining and successfully completing a job interview. You will also learn how to do important research on a company prior to the interview, as well as how to maintain professional standards at the highest level. The guide will also review some common mistakes to avoid, and take you through customary post-interview follow up and etiquette. The final chapter will give you a thorough overview and a quick checklist to follow from the start of your search to the completion of your interview.

Now is your chance to secure the job of your dreams. With some careful planning, preparation, and practice, you are well on your way to accomplishing the best job search and interview possible. Use this guide to begin your path to financial, professional, and personal success!

Chapter 1: The Typical Interview: An Introduction to the Process

The process of securing and performing well in a job interview can be challenging, but it is ultimately one of the most rewarding endeavors on which you can embark: securing your ideal job is one way in which to gain entry into whatever elite group you've always wanted to be a part of. While there is no truly typical job interview—the experience encompasses too many variables (candidate, employer, field, and so on) to be wholly predictable—there are some common elements that occur in most interview situations. Understanding the basics of interviewer's categories of questions, as well as honing your ability to answer clearly and cleverly, can give you a significant advantage in the interview process. The importance of a job interview really cannot be overstated: this simple act is the culmination of your years of hard work, focus, and energy. You may have paid tens of thousands of dollars for a higher education or special training just to get to this point; you may have spent your entire life dreaming of this particular job in this particular field; you may have an inkling that this job might be able to propel you to success and security in ways you have heretofore only dreamed of.

Job interviews are complex enterprises, as well. You are selling yourself, of course—your set of skills, your personality, your professionalism—but you are also hoping to present your ability to be part of a larger team or company. Indeed, part of the process of interviewing requires understanding subtle and psychological cues; you are not the only person involved, of course, and you need to be able to "read the room," as it were. While there are no specific set of rules for any given situation, as each situation will be markedly different, there are some general ideas about how you can prepare yourself for any eventuality that you might happen upon in an interview. This is what this guide is for, to help you review the heart of the interview process, the kinds of questions you will likely be asked, along with how you might best answer them using particularly tested techniques.

Attending a job interview is a potentially life-changing event, so it should be approached with great deliberation and care—as well as the knowledge that the interview is far more important to you than it is to the interviewer. Having been made aware of that, however, it also behooves you to know something about the interviewer—when possible—and certainly to do research on the company itself. Armed with more information always makes you appear to be a better candidate, well-informed, and eager to join this new group.

Thinking about what kinds of questions the interviewer may ask, and preparing some possible answers to potential questions is some of the most valuable research you can conduct. Certainly, you cannot predict every question the interviewer will ask, but you can anticipate some basic ones, based on the job requirements, your own resume, and the knowledge of standard questions frequently asked.

Be sure to review your resume and cover letter before the interview (and, by all means, do bring these with you for reference, of course). It is likely that the interviewer will ask you specific questions related to one or more of your past experiences. The better you know your own resume, the stronger a candidate you will seem. Also think about specific experiences in past working relationships that you might mention or highlight in the interview; the resume lists your experience and your accomplishments, but it doesn't give a clear sense of how you interact with superiors or colleagues in a working situation, and it would be prudent of you to have some stories prepared detailing some of those experiences. Listing your skill set, including both hard and soft skills, will help you to highlight what it is about your professional and/or educational experience that sets you apart from other candidates.

You should also be very clear on what the duties and expectations of the position that you are applying for are: what, specifically, does the job require and how best will you be able to fulfill those expectations? A job advertisement will sometimes give you just a few lines of explanation; at other times, it will have a lengthy description. Either way, make it your responsibility, prior to the interview, to find out all you can about the position itself so that you can directly address how your past experiences and present skills can best be suited for said position.

Beyond the position itself, it is always important to understand the broader working culture of the company as a whole. This ensures that you can demonstrate that you are a good fit, not only for the specific job but for the company in general. This includes understanding whether the work environment is collaborative or highly individualized; this difference alone will determine how you will respond to questions asked by the interviewer, as well as whether you are, ultimately, a good fit. Obviously, when you study the company, look into its working practices and traditions. Notice, as well, when you submit your resume or attend your interview, how employees appear to interact and work. This kind of observation can give you a sense of job satisfaction and collegiality in any workplace. It can certainly give you the information needed to make a final decision about which job to take, assuming that you have more than one offer or the resources to make your decision only when you are certain that you are a good fit.

In addition to knowing yourself, your interviewer, the job requirements, and company culture, you should also be prepared to ask or ascertain the potential for growth that is inherent to the position. That is, understanding what is required of the specific position is crucial, but knowing what opportunities might exist beyond it is also a way to impress your interviewer that you have even more to offer. In addition, this information is crucial to your personal decision-making process: depending on your age at the time of the interview, it may be very important that you move beyond whatever position you are applying for at the current time. Indicating that you are prepared to learn more or to take on more at the very beginning gives the impression that you are eager to integrate into the company from the start.

Certainly, it is also the case that you should be prepared to ask about salary and benefits if such things were not made abundantly clear before the interview. This kind of information is obviously important for your own decision-making process, but it is also crucial that you make clear your expectations from the start, as well. When asking about salary and benefits, already have prepared what you will be satisfied to take; that is, don't ask the question without having your own answer ready, as many interviewers will respond by asking you what your expectations are.

Finally, the importance of attitude cannot be overstated: in the end, if you are enthusiastic, prepared, and knowledgeable, this will go a long way towards presenting yourself as an ideal employee. Throughout this guide, you will gain tips on what to do before the interview—building a resume, creating a cover letter, researching the company, outlining your story, and reducing stress—as well as how to develop particular interview skills that will give you that winning approach to interviews for success every time.

Chapter 2: Pre-Interview Preparation: Resume and Cover Letter

Obviously, before you can secure a job interview, you must prepare a winning resume and, typically speaking, write an engaging cover letter. These two elements are the most significant documents you will ever create in your quest for the ideal job. The two sections below will take you through both processes with some basic guidelines and handy tips for how to stand out from other applicants, securing that all-important interview.

Building the Best Resume

Building your resume is, really, a two-part process: first, you have to acquire education, experience, and skills that are appropriate to put into a resume; second, you have to understand how to assemble that information in an impressive, professional, and attractive manner. In the first case, think about your experiences and skills in the broadest manner possible: clearly, educational accomplishments are important, but other activities and experiences can also apply to a variety of job requirements. Especially if you don't have a wide variety of experience yet, think of how even minor things that you have done could be applicable to certain skills attractive to a job market (leadership, independent thinking, and teamwork). In the second case, there are numerous tips and techniques that you can follow in order to build the most impressive, most readable, and most successful resume.

- First, if the sincerest form of flattery is an imitation, then flatter some successful job seekers out there and review some examples. You need not build your resume completely from scratch; the internet provides a plethora of samples for you to review and to adjust according to your own needs. Be sure to review samples that are relevant to your field, as different fields have different standards.

- Second, if you are feeling apprehensive about creating your own resume, especially if this is your first attempt, then use a template. Again, the internet is awash with templates (most of them are free) that can help get you started. Do be aware, however, that the template is just the base on which you build: customize it to fit your specific experience and personal   story.

- Third, consider the format of the resume, as well as the field. Resumes can be organized chronologically (this is perhaps most common), listing educational and professional achievements and positions in the order at which they occurred, from most recent on down. However, there are other types of resumes: a functional resume, for instance, lists skills and abilities with relevant examples, rather than a chronological work history; a targeted resume is one that is "targeted" specifically to one particular position so that it lists only skills and work experience relevant to the specific job itself. A combination resume would do some sort of mixture of the aforementioned.

- Always include contact information, though this no longer means that you need to provide a physical address (with so many workplaces themselves not adhering to one particular physical address and the growth of remote work, this has become moot). Do include a phone number at which you can be reached, of course, as well as an email address—a *professional* address, not butterflykisses22@gmail.com. It's fine to use Gmail, as long as the address is professional;

create a new account if you have to. You should also include links to other professional sites at which you are associated, such as LinkedIn or other social media that you utilize for professional purposes.

- Relevant to the above point, you can create your own website for professional purposes: if your resume feels agonizingly short—and most employers prefer shorter resumes—then creating a personal, professional site is one way in which you can tell more of your story before landing the interview itself. Provide a link to this space on your resume, and allow your prospective employer to peruse it at will. This has become ever more important in the "gig" economy.

- Back to the resume itself, be sure to make it as "skimmable" as possible: while we all want to believe that each prospective employer reads our hard-won accomplishments with great care and thoroughness, they probably do not, especially for highly competitive fields. Some ways in which you can make your information easily readable are as follows:

- o use a basic font, such as Times New Roman or Arial;
- o don't justify your margins, which creates odd gaps in formatting;
- o keep dates and other numbers aligned to the right;
- o use digits when employing numbers (10, rather than ten);
- o avoid entering any information;
- o use boldface to highlight either the company for whom you worked or your respective roles at previous workplaces, but not both;
- o avoid all caps;
- o when using bullet points, keep it to two lines or less;
- o employ a separate section for skills, so prospective employers can read through quickly;
- o and be consistent in formatting throughout your resume, leaving some white space for ease of reading.

- Always start with the most recent relevant work experience and work your way backward chronologically. Typically speaking, you should only include the last decade of work experience (up to fifteen years is acceptable) and only work experience that is relevant to the position to which you are currently applying. That said, be sure to use space wisely: you may have done a college internship that is more relevant to the current position under consideration than your previous work experience. Customize thoughtfully.

- If you don't necessarily have a lot—or any!—work experience in the field to which you are applying, you need not give up. This is the occasion to create a functional resume, wherein you list relevant skills and activities you have acquired and experienced that fit with the job. This is also the occasion to write a strong cover letter that will detail why you are, in fact, a good fit for a job in which you have little professional experience (see the following chapter for advice on creating strong cover letters).

- While the most effective resumes will showcase your "soft skills"—such as good communication and strong leadership—they will do so in a direct and active manner. That is, don't simply state that you have effective communication skills, formulate a bullet point under a relevant work experience that demonstrates how you employed effective communication skills or strong leadership on the job. Specificity is key, and it allows you to stand out far more than fancy fonts or colorful graphics.

- Also remember that work experience doesn't always have to indicate traditional, paid employment: if you have volunteered for years at a facility or for an organization that has relevance to the job position, then, by all means, consider including this experience in your work history. This is part of what will make you an effective employee and a passionate contributor—in fact, this kind of work often showcases your passion to a greater degree.

- Next, move onto the education section of your resume and keep it in reverse chronological order, with the most recent first. Also, you should always list your work experience first, unless you have just graduated from college or other educational institution. Work experience will almost always be more relevant to your current job search than your college education.

- While numbers can be important to work experience— showing how long you were employed at a particular job, or revealing a particular salary range—it is less important in an educational experience. When you graduated is not as relevant as the fact that you did graduate, and your GPA is less important than your achievements and honors along the way.

- You might also consider listing special skills or achievements in a separate section, space permitting. This is your opportunity to show that you have excelled in particular areas (such as learning a second language or getting an award for achievement in your field) or that you have acquired specialized skills (such as knowing HTML or Java).

- Finally, be sure to address any red flags or gaps in your resume: these are fine to discuss within the interview itself, of course, but you should be aware of them and prepared to discuss them in honest detail.

Creating a Compelling Cover Letter

Along with the resume, the cover letter is the most significant part of the pre-interview process: a cover letter showcases who you are and why you would be the best fit for this particular job. Not every job application requires a cover letter, but most professional level positions do—even if they don't require it, it's often a good idea to prepare one, just in case, as it can often help you organize your thoughts when preparing for an interview. Many people dread writing a cover letter—there are overwhelming numbers of examples online—but it can be both beneficial to you and to your potential employer. In fact, some employers rely on the cover letter more than the resume to decide who to select for the interview process; it is an equally important part of your desire to land that ideal job.

- One of the most fundamental bits of advice that anyone could receive regarding writing cover letters is to craft an individual and specific cover letter for each job application. While this might sound like a lot of work—and it potentially is—it is the only way to ensure that you are perceived as someone who is knowledgeable and passionate about this particular position. Address the cover letter to your interviewer, hiring manager, or potential employer, when possible, and customize the letter to address the requirements requested and the skills you possess that will allow you to thrive in the job. Some research into the company (this is addressed in the following chapter) may also help you in crafting the perfect cover letter for a particular company.

- Having said the above, it is still appropriate to use a template to get started or to recycle a handful of words or phrases for each cover letter. The trick is to avoid sounding generic: like using "To Whom It May Concern" or "I am applying for a position (rather than noting which) at your company"—these are vague and reveal a lack of interest on your part.

- If you don't know the name of the person to whom you should address the letter, then resort to something else more specific than "To Whom It May Concern." For example, you could address the letter to "Department Hiring Manager" or "Executive Search Committee," again specifying which department or position that your search would fall under.

- One of the first mistakes you must avoid when writing a cover letter is a rehashing ground that is already in your resume. The cover letter is the place where you can expand upon the basics of employment position and time period and allow your accomplishments and personality shine. When thinking about how to construct a cover letter that reveals a fuller portrait of you as an employee, ask yourself some pointed questions: choose a particular activity mentioned on your resume, and ask yourself how you approached implementing this task, what skills it called upon; ask yourself what specific details are important to understanding how you accomplished a particular task or landed a specific job; finally, ask yourself what parts of your personality were key in how you landed and handled a specific job and/or task. These kinds of questions not only help you craft a stronger cover letter, but they also prepare you for the interview that will surely come.

- Be sure to focus on the skills and experiences you have that are directly relevant to the position—and to the larger company. Avoid suggesting how wonderful the job would be for *you*—certainly, any hiring manager will be aware of what is at stake for a potential hire—but do mention what you would bring to the company, the department, and/or the group.

- The cover letter is also the place wherein you can make the case that you are the ideal fit for a particular position—even if you don't necessarily have the employment history to back it up. That is, you can really showcase your skillset here, to show your potential employer exactly what it is that you have to offer, even if your resume is either thin or disparate from the exact position you're aiming to get.

- In terms of tone, there is a balancing act to strike: on the one hand, you are writing a professional piece for a professional purpose; on the other hand, you are trying to come across as a personable and pleasant person who will fit in with a larger team or company. Excessive formality makes you seem stiff and distant, while too much conversational personality can appear sloppy or flippant. You want to appear approachable and   professional.

- This is also a moment at which the research you've done on the company (see the following chapter for more on that) comes in handy: craft your cover letter using the style and lingo of the company to which you're applying. Read their web site and absorb some of their keywords and phrases—beware of overdoing this, as it can sound sycophantic, but it does show that   you   would   be   a   good   fit.

- Edit carefully, proofread thoroughly: a cover letter with errors is a blatant dead end. Have someone else read it if you fear your writing skills are not quite up to par. Last, this is one of the single most significant pieces of advice that you can get for any piece of writing you are doing: READ IT ALOUD before your final edit and submission. Reading aloud can help you capture the tone (is it too stiff and formal? Too conversational?) and flow (is it too rambling? well organized?), as well as alert you to mistakes (if you're gasping for breath at the end of a sentence, then it probably needs some editing). By the time you are called in for the interview, you should know your cover letter like your own reflection—because, indeed, that's what it is, a reflection of who you are, and will be as an ideal employee.

Finally, be sure to keep a master list of all the jobs for which you have applied, as well as copies of the particular resumes and cover letters that you ultimately send out. Always keep your basic template in place, but save versions of the basic resume and cover letter that are customized to each particular job search.

Chapter 3: Pre-Interview Preparation: Company Research

Another surefire way in which to ensure that you are one of the best—if not *the* best—candidate for the position is to demonstrate how well you fit with the company and its culture. This requires that you not only understand exactly what the job is requiring (read and re-read that job description) but also what the company as a whole does and how it conducts business as usual. Showing that you know a good deal about the company—its founding and history, its corporate structure, its products and results, its overall culture—lets the interviewer know that you are a serious candidate with enthusiasm for working at this particular company. This is one of the ways you can set yourself apart from other candidates and set yourself up for success. You want to have a clear understanding of the practical workings of the company, as well as a sense of how workers are expected to behave and produce.

- Obviously, review the company's web site thoroughly. This will reveal many truths about a company, from the most basic information to the mission statement to overarching themes that seem to run throughout the organization. You should know all the basic information about a company, such as its history and size. Be sure to read the "About" page on the web site, as it will give you the bottom line regarding a company, but also pay attention to keywords and phrases that come up throughout the site, which will give you greater insight into the corporate culture and specific goals of this particular organization. In addition, the web site's very structure and organization, as well as the quality of its design and writing, will speak volumes about a company—such as whether clear communication or flashy graphics are more important.

- The same process applies to a company's social media presence: a lot can be inferred about a company based on its presence—or lack thereof—on social media. If there isn't a social media presence, then you can be reasonably confident that the company considers itself traditional or artisanal in some form or fashion. If there is a social media presence, but it is not professionally or consistently run, then you can infer that either the company needs assistance in this area or that its public image is poorly distributed. This is helpful information for you personally, as well as professionally. It would be imprudent to go into an interview with a detailed critique of a company's social media presence, but it might, under cautious circumstances, be a place for you to suggest your worth.

- LinkedIn, of course, is the most prominent social media spot for companies and professionals. Do take a glance at that, as well, and if you know the interviewer's name, also be sure to peruse his or her profile in addition. This can give you valuable insight into their specific role within the company and how you can speak directly to that. It can also help with breaking the ice, as well: perhaps you have something in common with the person (school or colleagues, other activities or interests).

- Glassdoor is another invaluable site, especially with regard to the interview itself. They offer sets of interview questions and responses that you can peruse, as well as providing reviews from former candidates with information about how interviews were conducted or how companies were operated. These reviews may not always be perfectly accurate—

disgruntled employees can certainly vent on this site—but it will allow you to form an overall impression of company culture and practices.

- You can also do a quick Google search (Google News is even more pinpointed) to see what is currently going on in the company at large. This is especially valuable if you are applying to a smaller subsidiary or segment of a larger, international company. Basically, you are researching to find out what has been in the news regarding their development and activities in recent months.

- Once you've conducted some of this practical research, you can start to spend some time formulating some secondary impressions of the company to give you a sense of how you will fit in and how important this particular job interview is to you. Occasionally, what you might discover in your research will be disconcerting, and you may decide to devote more effort to another position or company armed with that knowledge.

- Barring that, be sure that you feel well-informed about the company's strengths. This will be an excellent way to ensure your interviewer that you are enthusiastic about the progress of the company, as well as give you the ability to showcase how your skills dovetail with their strengths.

- Take a minute to discern how financially healthy a company is—especially if you are applying to work at a start-up or other emerging company. This allows you to be a better decision-maker, as well as potentially making you an impressive candidate. Knowing some details about the financial dealings of the company can be an advantage in certain cases.

- Reinvestigate social media sites with a different goal in mind: how does the company interact with the larger community? Updates about goals and progress, welcoming new customers or divisions within the company, reports about upcoming promotions and events: all of these things will give you a stronger sense of how engaged the company is with the local community, with employees, and beyond. This kind of review can also give you insight into how a company responds to complaints or delays or other problems.

- A way to get to know a company in-depth is to seek out someone who works there or once worked there: they will be able to provide direct advice on company culture and goals. Be sure to conduct yourself professionally when undertaking such an attempt—this is for a job interview, not for personal gossip—and know who you are talking to. A former employee may not have the most recent, relevant information, and an unhappy employee may not provide the most accurate   assessment.

- Do some specific research on the company's history and its top employees, such as the CEO, CFO, and other top management. Name-dropping in an interview can be inappropriate, of course, but you may discover an interesting tidbit that fits perfectly with your own experience. On some occasions, interviewers might expect you to have a working knowledge of a company's founder or historical development. It can't hurt to come prepared.

- At this point in your research, you should have been able to glean some information regarding the company's values and how they align with your own. This becomes important with how you will approach certain topics within the interview or hiring process. For example, the subject of work-life balance is always an important one but a sensitive one that should be handled with care. If you notice that the company's values are skewed toward production and shareholders, then you must be willing and ready to put in a long and devoted work week. If the company is devoted to sustainability, then you should be aware of how you present yourself (plastic straws are probably frowned upon). Basically, when you agree to work at a particular company, you implicitly agree with the company's values; be sure that you feel comfortable with and knowledgeable about these core concerns.

- While you may not be able to bring up everything you discover in an interview, doing company research has the benefit of preparing you for what to expect, not only during the interview but also when you are successfully hired. Certainly, be prepared to talk about a company's history, mission, and major players, as well as any major achievements that have recently been made. The more that you can present yourself as an already well-informed employee, the better you demonstrate how well you fit into the company culture and its overarching goals.

- Last, it also makes perfect sense to spend a little time researching the industry as a whole: knowing what the competition is doing and how they operate can offer ideas as to how you might be able to position yourself as the ideal employee with a breadth of industry-wide knowledge. It can also significantly impress an interviewer if you gain some insight into how your company is responding to particular competition and how you see your presence in that initiative.

Chapter 4: Pre-Interview Preparation: Details of Your Story

Most questions you will be asked to answer during a typical job interview will be behavioral style questions (see Chapters 7 and 8 for more on interview questions), and the best way of preparing for these kinds of questions is to think of your previous professional (or educational) experience as an opportunity to put together a kind of story. The best interviews are ones that incorporate stories within a clear framework of what you have to offer to the position and to the company. As such, you should always be prepared when an interviewer asks you the simple (but potentially intimidating) question: what did you do when...? Or, how would you approach...? These open-ended questions practically beg you to tell a coherent story, rather than simply drop a set of vague characteristics that you might possess or amorphous hypotheticals that don't reveal anything specific about yourself or your abilities. These open-ended questions will inevitably crop up and being prepared for them requires you to think in advance about how you might present yourself in the story: preparing an outline and underscoring characteristics that reveal your value as an employee is a powerful way to impress an interviewer both with your skills and with your poise—as well as to reveal a cohesive narrative about who you are as a valuable employee.

As stated above, these kinds of questions are called behavioral interview questions ("Tell me about a time when you made a mistake"); they are designed to allow you to reveal behavioral characteristics that show strengths and abilities that can be applied to workplace scenarios. (For more on types of interview questions, see Chapters 7 and 8, or for an in-depth exploration of these themes, see my book *Interview Q&A*.) The best way to handle these kinds of questions is to be prepared in advance with at least a couple of stories that you have spent some time outlining. The interviewer wants a specific answer, not a meandering and vague recitation of how your leadership skills helped you out. Additionally, the interviewer is interested in your response to a situation—your behavior, your *actions*—rather than a passive recitation of generalized qualities.

Your first response should be concise and direct: "One of the most memorable professional mistakes I made was when XXX happened." Thus, you clearly indicate to the interviewer that you understand the question and give them a basis for following your story. Then, fill in the context: briefly indicate the background surrounding the event, what the consequences were, and then give details as to how you specifically handled it—and, ideally, what you learned from it, as well.

Always be certain to explain your role in the process honestly and thoroughly; there is no need to assign or deflect blame. The interviewer is trying to determine how you might respond to a difficult situation, not to assess your perfection or lack thereof. The more honest and genuine you are, the more you reveal the strength of character and a willingness to learn.

In addition, be certain that you provide some specific details: what exact steps did you take to remedy the situation, and what particular qualities in you did those actions reveal? The more detailed (though not long-winded) you are about your role, the more you address the specifics of your overall character and qualification for the position. In fact, specificity is truly one of the keys to conducting a successful job interview—or job hunt overall—and landing your ideal job. This applies to your resume and cover letter, as well; the more specific each component of your job search is, the more successful your candidacy. This means tailoring each component of your interview (and resume and cover letter) to each specific job applied for; this shows an enthusiasm that cannot be expressed simply via experience.

Elaborate on the end results of your story and, particularly, be sure to point out what you learned from the particular event. Especially if you are asked to recount a negative event from your professional history, like a mistake, you want to assure the interviewer that, rather than seeing it as a failure, you viewed it as a learning opportunity, one that allowed you to develop certain skills more fully. The importance of stories in any setting is that they reveal common ground among people and allow for emotional connection: the more familiar you are with the hero of your story (that would be you) and the motivations for your actions, the more genuine and emotionally personable you come across. For that reason, good storytelling requires some advance preparation and practice.

Before you begin to prepare your story, remember that the most effective stories in an interview setting will have the following qualities: the story should be simple and straightforward; it should be unique to you with an unexpected detail or two; it should be clear and concrete in its details; it should seem credible and genuine (this is *not* the time for fiction!); and it should create some sort of emotional connection.

Even if you feel skilled at answering questions "off the cuff," as it were, it will benefit you to spend some time with your story before an interview. Create an outline that would serve you for any number of stories:

- Give your story a name, which serves as an anchor of the overarching topic.
- Identify the problem or opportunity the story presents.
- Identify the players within the story. You should be the main character, of course, but clearly note who else was involved and how.
- Relay the central action of the story: what happened and why.
- Convey the results of the action: what followed from the central action and what was its impact.
- Identify what **competencies** this story reveals about its hero (you).
- Identify what **characteristics** this story reveals about its hero (you).
- Determine what about the story is **unexpected**.

- Competencies are skills that you possess that are valuable to the interviewer and employer. The most common competencies identified by prospective employers are that of leadership, problem-solving, teamwork, management or organization, communication, and customer-focused. Highlight one or more of these skills within the context of your story.

- Characteristics are traits that you possess that are valuable to the interviewer and employer. The most common character traits identified by employers are honesty, passion, confidence, motivation, reliability, and efficiency. Highlight one or more of these skills within the context of your story.

- The unexpected may be one of the hardest things to discover within your story, but it important to create some interest in the listener, especially considering that he or she has likely listened to more than one interview during the course of a day or a week; you want to stand out somehow. You can find unexpectedness in several places: the action itself could arise from something that is unusual

56

or unanticipated; the characters involved could be unusual (an outsider is somehow involved, or a quirky colleague); the response to the action could be risky or innovative; the result was surprisingly efficient or positive; or, the original approach was scrapped in favor of something new and daring. Finding the unexpected creates greater interest in your story—a hook, as it were.

o Consider using STAR guidelines to help you outline your story: Situation, Task, Action, and Result (see Chapters 9 and 10 for a more in-depth discussion of answering interview questions, including the STAR technique). This will keep you on track and focused on the importance of the story as a whole.

Even with all this preparation, you don't want to sound too rehearsed. First, you cannot anticipate the specific question that an interviewer might ask that would prompt a story, and if you answer with a canned response that doesn't quite fit the question, this is awkward and can seem disingenuous. This is why having two or three various stories that could be used to answer a variety of behavioral questions is most effective. Make sure you know the details and keep your story focused: practice so much that, instead of sounding rote, it rolls off the tongue like a spur-of-the-moment response. Don't write the story itself out and memorize a script; instead, memorize the outline and follow it to tell a naturally evolving story.

As with many aspects of your job search, certain components are somewhat consistent, such as the kinds of questions or prompts that frequently come up in interview situations. Again, this will be covered in more detail later in this guide, but here are some that are particularly well suited to putting together a cohesive story. Some particular kinds of stories that are always good to have ready to relay are as follows:

- Be prepared to "tell a little about yourself." Most people don't bother with spending any time with that, but it often leads to rambling and incoherent responses. Instead, use some of the ideas above to reveal something relevant about yourself in light of this position: the best idea is to keep it a short one-minute synopsis of what makes you the ideal candidate for the job.
- As in the example above, being asked to tell about the time you made a mistake is a classic interview question and can reveal a lot about you as a

candidate. Even a disastrous story wherein you learned a valuable lesson could showcase your tenacity, determination, and flexibility—as well as creative thinking and problem-solving.

- Prepare a story about teamwork: showcasing your ability to work with others in positive and productive ways is key in many, if not most, work situations. Support and teamwork are just as important, if not more so than leadership and individual initiative.

- Talk about a particular challenge you have faced in your professional life (or personal, if it can be made relevant) and how you confronted it and dealt with it. Overcoming obstacles is one of the core actions that reveal our deepest personality characteristics; additionally, these stories also offer a chance to make a lasting emotional connection with the listener.

- You might also relate a story about a time that you showed impressive leadership skills. Even if you are just now embarking on your career, you should be able to come up with a story wherein you took the lead in creating something meaningful or fixing a problem.

- Problem-solving also gives you an opportunity to reveal your professional and personal qualities. Tell a story about a time you resolved a complex problem and what skills you used in order to do so.

- There is also room in storytelling to reveal something more personal about yourself, especially in today's marketplace and within certain industries. "Tell me what you are passionate about" is a more common prompt than not in interview settings today. Find a way to tell a story about your passions and dearest interests that apply to the position for which you are interviewing.

- Finally, there are occasionally appropriate moments during which you can tell a story about what you do for fun, or for a hobby—things that are important to you personally. The purpose of telling such stories—and of the interviewer asking more personal questions—is to reveal particular traits that highlight who you are. For example, if you enjoy gardening, you could tell a story about the challenges and joys of overcoming weather and pests to harvest some homegrown food for your family. This kind of story says a lot about perseverance.

Telling stories about our experiences and ourselves is a way to humanize a sometimes sterile interview setting. Storytelling creates emotional connections and reveals more about you than the bullet points on your resume. Make these stories count by thinking them through and organizing them prior to your interview. If they are genuine, unexpected, and thoughtful, they will invariably become some of the most memorable things about you. Don't be afraid to be your genuine self, though always with a professional and practiced poise.

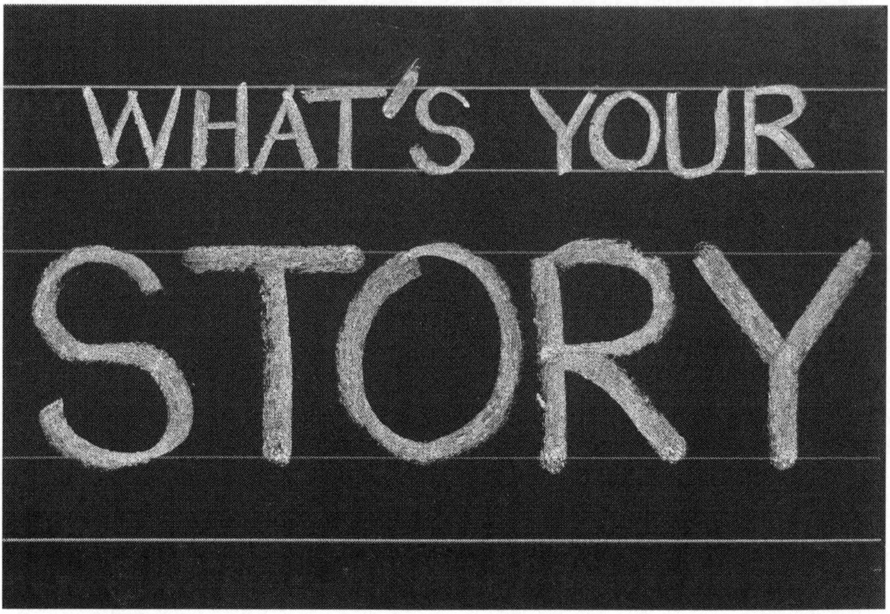
WHAT'S YOUR
STORY

Chapter 5: Pre-Interview Preparation: Professional Standards

Alongside the obvious ways in which you must prepare for a job search and interview—resume, cover letter, research, practice—you also have to consider the professional standards that are being asked of you in any given professional scenario. The research that you have conducted on the company should give you some sense of the standards of professionalism that the company will require—a tech start-up and an investment banker position will probably vary widely in what they expect. Nevertheless, it is always better, especially in an application and interview scenario, to err on the side of *more* professional rather than less. Professional etiquette is shown in how you present yourself, from the way you are groomed and dressed to the way in which you greet people and respond.

Some General Guidelines for Professional Etiquette

Certainly, any good job interview begins with an idea first impression, and that first impression is informed by how we look, particularly, how we are dressed and groomed prior to the interview. In recent years, the standards for what constitutes "business" dress have been changed and, for the most part, expanded. Still, a job interview is more than likely more formal than typical employee dress standards (especially when considering the proliferation of "casual Fridays" and tech start-ups jeans and t-shirts). Whatever the company for which you are interviewing, you should follow some basic guidelines to ensure that you are looking professional and making a smart first impression.

Looking Professional

- In doing your company research, you should have some broader knowledge of company culture, including how employees are supposed to present themselves in the workplace. Use that knowledge to base your understanding of how to present yourself at an interview: as stated above, an interview is likely a more formal affair than an everyday work look, but it gives you a starting point. Be sure to peruse any company photos, especially on social media, to get an idea of how employees dress when they are representing the company.

- While you are trying to look your best—professional and poised—you should also take into consideration your comfort level. That is, don't wear something that is too tight, too bulky, or too warm to an interview. The more comfortable you are in your professional attire, the more confidence you project. Be sure to take the seasons into the occasion, and wear layers if you tend to get warm during an interview; you can take off a jacket should you need to, if you are wearing a nice dress shirt or blouse underneath.

- Avoid wearing anything that is revealing, such as a sundress or low-cut blouse. This guideline doesn't at first appear to relate to men, but a vee-necked shirt or lack of socks might fall along these lines for men. The idea is not to look like you're going out with friends, but they are representing yourself professionally for a company.

- Be certain that your clothes are recently cleaned, especially if you plan to wear a suit or other truly formal attire, and check for stains, tears, or other signs of distress. If you do not have an appropriate outfit for an interview and lack the financial ability to purchase one quickly, there are many resources in communities, like Dress for Success, that will help you find something appropriate at a reasonable price—or for   free.

- Lay or set out your clothes the night before the interview. This ensures that you make a good inspection of everything (if you have pets, be sure to give yourself a quick roll before you leave the house) and that you don't have any last-minute delays. One of the worst things you can do is to show up late for an interview: give yourself plenty of time to get ready and   to   get   there   on   time.

- Finally, don't second guess yourself or overthink it. If you feel reasonably comfortable and have chosen a clean, pressed outfit that seems to meet the standards of the company, then you are probably going to be just fine.

Special Considerations for Men:

- In nearly every case of interviewing for a traditional company, a suit is required, regardless of standards for the everyday dress as an employee. Again, do your research, but always err on the side of being conservative when in doubt.

- According to most experts, a dark suit with a light-colored shirt is the most standard suit attire. Be sure that you have a matching tie, coordinated socks, and a nice belt, in addition.

- Again, if you do not own a suit, now is the time to invest in one—one that fits and is comfortable, not something that you had leftover from a cousin's wedding ten years ago. If you need assistance financially with acquiring a suit, check into local organizations that help people find employment.

- Beware of loud colors or overbearing ties; certainly, you want to avoid anything that seems overly whimsical or novelty (this is not the time to wear cartoon- or NFL-patterned ties).

- Of course, you want to appear neat and clean, but also be aware to avoid strong colognes or other scents; you do not want to trigger a reaction in an interviewer. Check your nails, too, as your hands will be noticed during an interview, from your handshake to handing out of documents and such.

- Avoid smoking before the interview, if at all possible. You don't want to bring in lingering smells of tobacco or other odors that might be unpleasant to an interviewer.

- Groom your hair nicely. Again, the rules for how to wear one's hair have changed dramatically over the last couple of decades, especially for men. Use your best judgment and follow what you see on the company's web site as a guide. An investment banking company will probably want to see short, conservative hair, while a tech start-up will likely not be bothered by longer or different styles.

- If you are called for a second interview, the best rule of thumb is to dress like your potential employer; this could mean being slightly less formal, but not always. At that point, you should have a good feel for the company in order to understand and integrate the culture.

Special Considerations for Women:

- Some of the same rules apply to women: you should probably wear some kind of suit, either with a skirt or pants. When wearing a skirt to an interview, you should always wear some kind of hose rather than presenting bare legs. Typically, you should avoid open-toed shoes or sandals. Again, do your research and peruse pictures of employees on social media. When in doubt, be more conservative than not.

- Remember to make sure that you are comfortable, and practice seeing how you feel when you are sitting down; an ill-fitting jacket has a tendency to gap when you are seated, and a tight waistband on pants or a skirt will cause discomfort. Most stores offer some sort of minor tailoring to have adjustments made to what you might purchase for an interview. If your budget doesn't allow you to purchase something nice for the interview, seek out local organizations that assist people in gaining employment. There are places that will help you find something appropriate, like the Dress for Success program.

- As with the advice for men, wear something that is darker in color, avoiding bright or flashy colors and embellishments, for the most part. A dark suit with a lighter blouse is considered the standard. Never wear low-cut blouses or sheer fabrics of any kind, and make sure the length of your skirt, if wearing one, is appropriate. Conservative interviewers often complain about the length of skirts; too short is inappropriate, while too long isn't professional. Stick to roughly knee-length skirts for interview occasions.
- If you must accessorize, then be judicious: don't cover your hands in rings or wear stacks of bracelets or long, chunky necklaces and earrings. Accessories are your chance to shine, really, if you employ them properly. With a conservative suit, one nice pendant or pair of pretty earrings can really pop and make you stand out.

- The same ideas above also apply to hair and make-up: be relatively conservative. Don't wear heavy eye make-up or drastically dark lipstick; these looks aren't considered wholly professional. With hair, keep it neat and tidy—be yourself, of course—and avoid overly stylized or trendy looks (such as lavender hair or faux beehive dos). Nails should be groomed, but avoid long, overly decorated nails, especially of the trendy press-on type. Not only do these appear flashy and lack professionalism, but they get in the way of your ability to execute daily business tasks.

- When it comes to shoes, avoid the kind of shoe you'd wear out on the weekend. Keep the heel to a minimum, and be sure that the shoes are closed both at the toe and the back. A basic pump style is always available, and these comfortable yet smart shoes will virtually never go out of style. It's a good one-time investment in a neutral color, such as brown or black.

- Match your hose to your skin color, rather than wearing colorful or graphically printed tights. Remember that the goal is to draw attention to your skills, not your style.

- Obviously, you want to be neat and clean for the interview, and be sure to avoid heavy perfumes or other scents that may be overpowering for others in an interview. Don't smoke right before the interview; if you can avoid it, smelling of smoke can be a negative trigger for many.

- As with the advice above for men, the guidelines for what constitutes professional dress have shifted and broadened over the last couple of decades. This is why doing your research into the company is important for you to have a clear sense of what would be the most appropriate attire. Still, it is doubtless best to err on the side of caution rather than flamboyance for an interview.

- If called for a second interview, follow the cues that you picked up while at first. Dress like your boss, perhaps a touch more conservatively, and you should be in line with what is expected.

Acting Professional

Acting professionally consists of any number of minor behaviors and skills of etiquette. As anyone who has worked with others in any capacity before well knows, the attitude one displays and the behavior one engages in speaks volumes about personal character and professional capacity. When embarking on an interview, it is understandable to be intimated by strangers who have some sort of control over your potential future. However, now that you have snagged the interview with your sharp

73

resume and descriptive cover letter, you need only to look—and act—the part. The following tips should help you develop your professional etiquette for the interview. See the next chapter for some other tips on how to put your best foot forward for any job scenario.

- Remember that one of the crucial tests you must pass when attending a job interview is the litmus test of whether you will fit into the culture of the company. In general terms, this means that you need to demonstrate professional etiquette and respect not only to your interviewer but toward anyone else you may encounter (other employees, like a receptionist or secretary or colleagues in your department or group). Your skills are rendered irrelevant if your behavior is boorish and rude.

- Consider your first impression; you must not only look the part but also act the part. A first impression can never be retracted, so it is important not to begin an interview on the wrong foot. From the moment you arrive at the company, be on your most professional behavior: for all you know, the person you greet in the hallway or ride in the elevator with maybe your future boss or colleague. Be enthusiastic and look happy—rather than apprehensive—to be there. Make eye contact and introduce yourself politely when appropriate, extending a handshake in most cases. When entering the interview space, be sure to accept instructions politely and strike and open—rather than defensive—posture.

- As mentioned above, be sure that the outfit you've chosen to wear for the interview is appropriate and professional, but also be aware of how it will appear when you are seated. You want to avoid the proverbial wardrobe malfunction (gaping blouse, popped button, overly hiked pants). Typically, you will be seated for most of the interview, so that's how you should test the comforts and utility of your chosen attire.

- Always remember to smile and appear interested in what the interviewer is saying. A smile (or, conversely, a frown) can speak volumes. If you appear smiling and approachable, then you are perceived as a team player with valuable character attributes as well as professional skills to bring to the company. A frown, on the other hand, can fluster or annoy the interviewer; it is difficult to know how to interpret the facial expression. Are you angry, annoyed, bored, frustrated, or otherwise unimpressed? This is not the impression you want to convey. Remind yourself that this experience, while somewhat nerve-racking, should be an amicable way in which to showcase your considerable talents and value. This would bring a smile to anyone's face.

- Body language, in general, reveals a lot about a person's feelings and character. Crossing your arms against your chest looks defensive, even hostile, while a lazy slump indicates a lack of interest or disrespect. Keeping your hands folded in your lap throughout the interview can have the effect of implying childlike anxiety. "Man-spreading" can look aggressive or arrogant. Again, maintain eye contact when answering questions and avoid sweeping hand gestures. You can hold a pen or pencil in your hand if it helps to center you, and this can come in handy should you wish to jot anything down. Basically, your body language should indicate that you are engaged and open, enthusiastic, and polite.

- When greeting others, be sure that you have a solid handshake, somewhere between limp and crushing.

A firm handshake reveals self-confidence and a courteous understanding of overall business etiquette. When meeting someone for the first time, it is considered polite to use an honorific, such as Dr. or Ms. or Mr. If the company for which you are interviewed is owned or operated by foreign nationals, then it would behoove you to do some research into the basic etiquette of the other country. Personal space is defined differently in different cultures, in addition to attitudes about how men and women behave.

- Addressing someone by their name is also a powerful piece of business etiquette that you can employ to curry respect. Everyone likes to be noticed and remembered, so try your best to remember and repeat the names of people that you meet. Should you be called in for a further interview, this considerate formality will inevitably be noticed. Still, don't sound sycophantic: continuously repeating the interviewer's name throughout the interview—"now, that's an interesting question, Dr. Jones. Let me see how I can answer that fully, Dr. Jones. Thank you, Dr. Jones"—can be annoying and patronizing.

- As you are seated for your interview—which you should be invited to do, rather than simply plopping down—place your personal items beside or underneath your chair. For everyone's sanity and to preserve your dignity, turn off your cell phone and any other device you may have carried with you. Have your resume and cover letter, along with a notepad or folder for notes, at the ready.

- If, for some disastrous reason, your phone should ring during an interview, you will be called upon to do some swift damage control. Do not dare look at the phone to check (unless you truly have a life-and-death situation on your hands); simply turn it off and apologize to the interviewer. You would have to be an excellent candidate to overcome this most egregious of etiquette breaches. It's better not to take your phone in with you if you have a habit of forgetting to switch it off. And off means *off*, not silent.

- When leaving the interview, be sure to restate your interest in the job and your pleasure at having met everyone. Shake hands again and repeat names, when appropriate. Be sure to thank the receptionist who showed you in, if relevant. Basically, just show proper manners on your way out the door.

- After the interview, it is customary to write a "thank you" note of some sort to the interviewer or interviewers to acknowledge their time and your opportunity. More on that will be covered in Chapter 12.

Chapter 6: Pre-Interview Preparation: Other Tips

In addition to following basic professional protocol, there are some very practical things that you must prepare in advance of an interview, as well. First, not only should you arrive on time and looking professional, but you should also anticipate practical preparations. Second, you should review your willingness to take on the job, as well as what that role entails. Third, you need to know how to prepare psychologically; dealing with pre-interview stress will ensure that you are relaxed and confident in your performance. Last, before you show up for your interview, spend some time thinking about potential questions and practicing your proficient answers, which will be covered in detail in the following four chapters.

Preparing for the Practical

Besides **looking at your best and arriving on time**, there are a few other practical considerations for how to function at your best at a job interview. As the old saying goes, nothing beats preparation in order to elicit the best performance. The better prepared you are, the more confident you will be, and the job you desire will be well within your reach.

- **Bring your resume and cover letter** with you to the interview. You will want to have a copy for yourself, as well as additional copies for the interviewer or interviewers. This is just in case you need to reference something in the course of the interview, or if additional interviewers end up coming to the session unbeknownst to you. This can also assist in future interviews so that others who might end up being involved in your hiring have copies of your credentials. Of course, the company can make additional copies, but it looks professional and organized if you happen to have a few extra copies on hand. Also, be sure to have a pen or pencil with you, examples of any materials that might be relevant to the position (portfolios, for example), and copies of a printed **list of references** with names, titles, company, and contact information. Most often, you don't need to provide this information with your resume, but if you get the interview, make sure to have this ready. Also, as mentioned before, *turn off* *your cell phone* before you go into the interview. Don't just silence it, turn it completely off.

- **Review your resume, cover letter, and job description** before the interview. While you will have a copy of at least two of those things on hand, you should be prepared enough not to have to reference them frequently or at all. If you're not absolutely clear on your employment history and duties that you have listed on your resume, then it comes across as inept (or even potentially inflated or false). Your cover letter should have included at least one or two more personal statements about your employment history, business ethics, or mission statement: be prepared to elaborate on anything that you have discussed there. As well, review the original job description that you used to respond to so that you are clearly able to anticipate how to answer questions that match your experience and skill set to what the company originally advertised.

- **Clean out your purse and/or bag** before you go to the interview. You don't want to waste time or to seem disorganized rooting around through your bag in order to locate any items you may need. Also, think about anything that you might need in the course of an interview for practical use—tissues, hand sanitizer, breath mints, eye drops, or other emergency toiletries—before or during the interview. It is always better to be prepared than not.

- **Use the product or otherwise familiarize yourself with what the company does/makes** prior to the interview. Get as much practical, hands-on experience as you can with what the company does overall, in addition to what you yourself have applied to do specifically. Understanding the product will allow you to be able to take the first steps toward learning how your role can enhance that product's viability or marketability. An interview isn't time for a critique, of course, but it is a time to show that you are aware of the product value and how your skills can contribute.

Skill and Requirements Review

In addition to the above practical considerations, you will also need to prepare some information that will undoubtedly come up during the interview. Being ready with these answers helps you to feel calm, confident, and fully prepared even before any questions regarding past experience are asked.

- **Know the job inside and out** before you arrive. That is, you should understand as fully as possible what the job requirements are for the position. If you have only a short description from the original advertisement, see if you can find out more detailed information from the company web site, social media, or a contact within the company. The more you understand what the ins and outs of the job entail, the better able you are to think about how to match your skillset to those requirements. Also, think about why it is that you *want* the job; that is, think about why you are best for the position, of course, but it is advantageous to display some enthusiasm about why it is that you are truly excited about the prospect of working in this particular capacity for this particular company. A little bit of genuine enthusiasm goes a long   way.

- **Know your audience** before you come to the interview, if at all possible. Find out who will be interviewing you and do some specific research on them, if available. The more you know about your interviewer(s), the better equipped you will be to anticipate what kinds of questions they will ask and what kind of expertise they are looking for. This information should give your confidence a boost, knowing (at least to a degree) what you are walking into.

- **Ask about the interview**, as different companies will employ different kinds of interviews: it could be a one-on-one interview with a boss or a human resources manager—knowing which it will be should help you know how to prepare. A direct supervisor will likely want to know more specific details on your specific skill set, while a human resources interviewer will likely ask more general questions about your fitness for the company culture and team structure. Other companies will employ committees or teams to interview you, which means that you should be prepared to answer a wide range of questions. Finally, it is completely fair to ask what kinds of questions might be addressed at the interview (see more on that below), so that you can be prepared with some potential answers in advance.

- **Review your skills** and be sure that you know how to elaborate on their applicability to the particular position. Be sure that you can adequately explain how a particular skill—effective communication, for example, or past leadership experience—connects with a specific job requirement. As with resumes and cover letters, throwing out these timeworn phrases is ultimately meaningless if you don't have any idea how they will connect with the real-time, practical demands of the job. For example, you might suggest that your effective communication skills will serve you in leading a team via clear, concise, and consistent email threads or will assist you in creating newsletters or memos for the department or will be crucial to your ability to generate efficient reports for management. Each skill that you listed on your resume should be applicable to a particular facet of the position for which you are interviewing. Those practical connections show that your skills have concrete value and make you a more memorable candidate.

Dealing with Stress

We all experience stress in our daily lives, being pulled from one task to the other, and trying to balance work with family, what we have to do with what we'd like to do. Add to that the stress of trying to find a new job, and you have some significant issues weighing on your mind and body. The problem now is: how do you relax and get enough sleep to be fresh and alert for the interview? Follow this advice on how to calm your nerves before and during the interview itself.

- It is never easy to put yourself out there for someone else to judge—especially in the context of what could be a life-altering job offer. The **stress and anxiety that you feel before a job interview are perfectly natural**; to acknowledge your nerves is to give you some control over how you respond. Some people even become so nervous that they are worried they might sabotage their own interview. The first step toward overcoming these kinds of nerves is to acknowledge your anxiety and to remind yourself that it is normal. Remind yourself that being somewhat nervous can also enhance performance, keeping you alert and ready for whatever question comes your way. Accept that a little bit of nervousness is just fine.
- In order to overcome overwhelming feelings of stress before an interview, there are some exercises you can

do to relax prior to the interview. For one, instead of just practicing your story or going over your resume, you can actually visualize the interview in your mind: conduct a **mental dress rehearsal** of how it will go, envisioning the most positive and powerful performance that you can give. Practicing this mental model will reassure you that you are capable of confronting anything that might come up. Boost your confidence by imagining the best possible outcome.

- Another way to prepare for an interview is to enlist **motivational tools**. You can create a playlist of motivational music to listen to while getting ready in the morning or working out at the gym. Or, you can find some motivational speakers (TED talks are an excellent resource) who will give you handy tips and tools for handling stress and anxiety. Also remember to look towards your greatest motivators: your support system of friends, family, and others who will motivate you to stay calm and focused.

- Give yourself a nice, long **pep talk**. Remind yourself that you have the skills, the ability, and the determination to get through this interview with grace and success. After all, you already were able to secure the interview; this means that the prospective employer already found lots to value in you, so remind yourself of everything that you bring to the table. The company would be fortunate to have you.

- **Watch** humorous and meaningless videos before the interview to calm and soothe your mind. Laughter releases stress, for one, and letting your mind occupy itself with something random shouldn't hurt at all if you are prepared and ready to go. In fact, it might sharpen your performance to allow your brain to relax a bit before the interview.

- **Exaggerate** your fears then dismiss them. Go over the worst possible scenarios you can think of, and then assure yourself that these will likely never even come close to happening. This is an excellent mechanism by which we learn how to confront our greatest fears, and in confronting them, let go of them. It is highly improbable that you will throw up or faint in an interview: imagining that, then, laughing at your exaggeration is one way to soothe your greatest (and surely exaggerated) fears.

- A lot of people's greatest fear is that they will **say the wrong thing**. To avoid this pitfall, remind yourself that this is actually quite a simple stressor to overcome. Keep it simple: avoid profanity or offensive language, and just be you. That's really all the advice you need to conquer that particular fear.

- While in the interview, if you need a moment to **compose yourself**, then take it. Ask the interviewer to repeat a question, or rephrase the question back to him or her to give you a chance to think about it before answering; take a sip of water; check in with the interviewer that you've fully answered a given question. There's nothing wrong with allowing yourself a moment of time to think. It's perfectly acceptable to say, "That is a really good question. Let me think about that for a moment."

- Remember, as well, that the interviewer is also in a stressful situation: **you are not alone**. It is difficult to conduct an interview with a group of people you don't know in order to choose for a competitive position. Recognizing that you aren't the only one in the room who may harbor some anxiety can be something   of   a   relief.

- Remind yourself that, ultimately, **you are in control** to a large degree. The interviewer only has a set of questions, while you are in control of the answers. This is *your* job interview; take ownership of it.

- If you tend to overheat or sweat when you get really nervous, then make sure you prepare for that, as well. Wear the most **comfortable** professional clothes you can find, and don't worry if your short sleeves seem out of place for the time of year. It's better to be as comfortable as possible. Looking professional is important, but not at the cost of feeling faint.

- Finally, the most important way that you can overcome stress prior to an interview is to **be prepared**. Have your resume and cover letter with you; practice your stories; look professional; be on time; demonstrate your skills; listen and follow up.

94

Chapter 7: During the Interview: Common Questions Part 1

Interview questions can be broken down into a handful of common types: credential and experience verification questions; opinion and behavioral questions; competency questions; brainteasers or other nonsense questions are the most frequent types of questions that are brought up in a typical interview situation. While perhaps the most important of these are an opinion and behavioral questions, we will start here with issues that deal with credentials and experience, as they are among the first questions that you will field at an interview. Knowing how to talk about your credentials, qualifications, experience, and other elements of your character is crucial to presenting yourself as the best candidate for the job.

Credential verification questions can do a couple of things in the course of an interview: first, they can allow for a breaking of the ice at the beginning, in order to allow both interviewer and candidate to warm up to the process; second, they can serve as a jumping-off point to elaborate on particular achievements in your educational or work history that will illustrate your fittingness for the job; third, they can give you the opportunity to explain away any gaps or unconventional issues with your resume.

First, credential questions can be a way to ease into the interview, allowing for everybody to settle in and relax a bit. Because these kinds of questions essentially ask you to review and verify your resume, be sure that you have a copy quick at hand in case you need to quickly look at something. Otherwise, you should be able to readily answer these kinds of questions without hesitation. The interviewer may ask a series of verification questions or just one or two that he or she is interested in; partly, this depends on how detailed your resume is in the first place. If certain credentials are of greater interest to your potential employer, then this serves as a way into broader issues, as follows.

Second, certain credentials might encourage interviewers to ask some follow up questions: for example, they might be interested in knowing why you stayed for so long (or so short) at a particular place of employment; or, they might be interested in knowing how certain kinds of coursework were relevant to your overall educational achievement. They might also use credential questions to prompt you to show a link between various activities and interests you've engaged with in the past: that is, you might be encouraged to show how seemingly disparate parts of your overall credential portfolio actually link together. Say you've been working as a graphic designer, and you also list that you volunteered at a food pantry: these credentials don't necessarily seem to have anything to do with one another. You should be prepared to show how you have learned skills from each that complement the other. Additionally, credential verification questions could lead to the interviewer following up on how these past credentials might serve the current position for which you are applying. That is, you might be asked not only how your credentials have reinforced your growing skillset through past experience but also how these credentials link to the requirements being asked of you for the current job.

Third, when an interviewer asks credential verification questions, he or she might be giving you the opportunity to explain or justify particular gaps in your resume. For example, if there is a gap in employment, then the interviewer might ask you what you were doing during that time and why the gap exists in the first place. In this case, be very prepared to answer honestly and thoroughly. For another example, the gap in your resume might be related to a particular set of skills. An interviewer can use a credential verification question to prompt you to expand on the kind of soft skills—leadership, effective communication, conflict resolution—needed to fulfill the requirements of a particular position. It can also be a prompt for you to expand upon a specific promotion or project. Finally, when reviewing your resume, an interviewer might candidly ask why certain skills seem to be missing. Be prepared to explain this, as well, and demonstrate how you intend to develop this skill or fill in your resume's gaps.

Beyond those opportunities, credential verification questions are also closely related to qualification questions. In this case, you are being asked to expand upon how your credentials and experience make you qualified for the position at hand. Your credentials reveal your qualifications in a concise and concrete way; however, the qualifications you possess represent more than mere credentials but also general work and life experience, in addition to the possession of a variety of soft skills that will assist you with any position you might want to tackle.

Some experience verification questions will simply ask you what particular, and concrete tasks did you perform during your past workplace situation. This might be something like "on your resume, you mention that you participated in Project X. What were you responsible for contributing?" This is an example of why it is so important for you to review your resume and have a clear sense of how you might explain each individual job position, task, or other events on it. These questions give you the opportunity to demonstrate that the variety of skills necessary to work on concrete tasks is valuable skills to any position to which you might be applying.

Experience verification questions also give you the opportunity to talk about past accomplishments, whether they be in the form of increased production and/or revenue, promotions, awards, or unique opportunities that you were able to take advantage of because of your exceptional previous performance. Oftentimes, an interviewer will simply ask you what your greatest accomplishments at a particular job or other experience might be. One effective way to prepare for an interview, in general, would be to keep a copy of your resume, wherein you take notes about particular talking points for each element of the resume: you may not necessarily have the space to list every accomplishment from every position, of course, but if you jot down notes about interesting accomplishments, the interview gives you the space during which to talk about a wider variety of successes than your resume can reveal. For example, if you worked on a particular project that received a significant amount of external attention and you were asked to speak to the media about it, this is an accomplishment that may not merit being listed on your resume but is certainly legitimate and strong enough to discuss in an interview. It reveals not only your expertise and dedication to a particular project but also your effective communication skills and flexibility to perform duties beyond the specific tasks required for production.

Another kind of experience verification question will ask how you handle difficult situations, in particular how you previously handled conflict resolution issues. Conflict resolution is one of those crucial soft skills that employers are looking for, especially in industries that prize teamwork and cross-departmental cooperation. Demonstrating that you have the ability to work with a diverse group of people, with varied skillsets and personality attributes, reveals that you are a valuable asset beyond the actual hard skills that you have been educated or trained to perform. Conflict resolution questions ask that you show a variety of attributes that allow you to resolve issues as they arise, including mediation, empathy, facilitation, creative problem-solving, and accountability. There are even entire positions within organizations that are dedicated to conflict resolution capabilities, but this is a valuable skill for any employee. Be sure to identify, prior to the interview, a particular instance at a specific job wherein you were called upon—or, better yet, simply took up the responsibility without being expressly asked—to resolve conflicts between staff members or between co-workers and management. Showing that you can handle conflict with poise and thoughtfulness reveals a lot about your worth as an employee overall. It also reflects your ability to understand and navigate a complex situation without creating more conflict. Be especially careful not to assign blame to others or to otherwise project negativity; focus on the attributes that you have, as well as the concrete actions you undertook, in order to resolve a difficult matter during previous work experience.

These are just a few of the kinds of credential, qualification, or experience questions you might be asked to relay during an interview: others might address what you consider to be challenging (this can allow you to speak to potential gaps in credentials or skills) or press you to justify how your experience and qualifications will impact the company's productivity and bottom line.

Chapter 8: During the Interview: Common Questions Part 2

As relayed in the previous chapters, some of the most important questions you will be asked have to do with opinion and behavior: these questions will likely make up the bulk of the interview and give you the opportunity to tell your various stories (as discussed in Chapter 4) highlighting both your experience (hard skills) and your expertise (soft skills). Hard skills are the technical and professional skills that are gained through specific education and training, while soft skills are the character attributes and personal qualities that a candidate brings with them to the position. Soft skills are also transferrable skills, appropriate in any workplace scenario, meaning that an employee with excellent soft skills is flexible and useful in almost any position. These skills are gained not through formal training, by and large, but via personal experience and self-awareness; soft skills demonstrate diversity and broadness of experience, as well as attention to detail and openness to others.

Many opinion questions will lead to a discussion of what you "like" or "dislike" about working styles or job preferences. These open-ended questions can be disconcertingly vague, so be sure that you have prepared a couple of specific examples of experiences in your past positions that were exceptionally positive and fulfilling, as well as examples of what didn't work as well for you. Again, remember to avoid the pitfalls of pointing accusatory fingers at others or dismissing particular ways of working as negative. You are here to present yourself in a positive light, so stay focused— even when asked what you might "dislike." Reflect on how you work best and run with that. Various areas in which you might focus are as follows: you might mention that you work quickly or efficiently with little error; this shows your style emphasizes speed and accuracy. You might talk about how your structure your day, which reveals that you like organization and routine or that you tackle tough projects first rather than last. You might discuss how much you prefer collaborative projects because you value a diversity of opinion and skill to create innovation. You might talk about how you work best if given a specific goal and deadline, then left to complete it on your own, which reveals strong organizational skills and self-direction. You might discuss that you prefer electronic communication to phone conversation because of its efficiency and precision; you can think through and answer more carefully in a written response than in verbal communication. All of these examples reveal something about your working style and, thus, how well you might fit into this company's culture. As with previous examples, always try to come up with specific examples and concrete descriptions to illuminate how your preferences affect your working style.

One of the most common—and potentially most dreaded—opinion questions is the alarmingly open-ended "tell me about yourself." This prompt encourages you to reveal something of your personality as well as professional strengths, often used as an icebreaker to allow both interviewer and candidate to settle into the interview. It is also a way in which the interviewer can gauge how quickly you think in a spontaneous atmosphere and allow you to show how comfortable you are in interpersonal communications. While it may not seem that you need to prepare for this question—after all, you know exactly who you are—it is important to anticipate the question and have some sort of prepared response. If you are thrown off by the question and have no particular idea of where you might focus, then you will inevitably get caught up in a rambling and/or irrelevant response that sets a wobbly tone for the rest of the interview. Instead, think about this question beforehand in light of the position to which you are applying, your relevant past experience and personality traits, and the company culture that you have researched. One simple way to prepare this kind of answer is to give a concise sketch of where you are now, personally and professionally, how you got there, and what you hope to accomplish in the future.

Oftentimes, behavioral questions, in contrast to opinion questions, will ask for a straightforward example of a time in which you did X. Not only do these kinds of questions give you a chance to highlight the kinds of hard skills you gained from educational or training experiences, but they offer a chance for you to emphasize the kinds of adaptable soft skills that you have used—and, presumably, will continue to use in the future—to handle various professional situations and personal challenges.

Behavioral questions will often be focused on problem-solving skills. Detailing a story in which you successfully confronted and eventually resolved a problem reveals a host of abilities that are applicable in virtually all workplace scenarios. Problem-solving includes a variety of soft skills that are necessary to professional success: the ability to analyze a situation showcases your ability to utilize logic and unbiased observation to generate possible responses to a specific issue. It also reveals your ability to evaluate which response will be most effective before implementing a coherent plan and assessing final results. When asked about how you solved a problem, use this formula to create a story regarding one specific instance at a previous workplace wherein you had to apply these important skills. Outline each element and formulate a concise and coherent answer, from identifying and analyzing the problem to generating and evaluating various responses. No matter what the position, problem-solving skills touch on virtually all of the most logical and significant of the so-called soft skills. This can allow you to prove that you are quick to respond and intelligent in your reaction.

Another kind of behavioral question that you might be asked to answer deals with goals: how do you show that you are goal-oriented; how do you specifically go about reaching goals. In the first case, your past behavior demonstrates that you are interested in and adept at striving towards productivity and success. In the second case, your story should outline specific and concrete steps that you undertook in order to reach the goals. These kinds of questions can take many forms: "give an example of a goal you set and how you achieved it"; "give an example of a goal that you failed to meet and why"; "why are goals important to your ability to perform?" These are just a few examples of how you might be asked to explain behavior that leads to achieving success and cultivating motivation. Prepare at least two examples of goals that you once had and met to varying degrees: you can showcase how you overcame obstacles or adversity to achieve your goals, for one example, or you can detail how you implement plans in a specific way to pave the way for your accomplishments. In any case, be sure to identify a specific goal that led to a concrete result, focusing on the kinds of skills that you needed in order to reach the goal. This might mean hard skills—you had to learn a new computer skill in order to reach the goal you set—or soft skills—you had to learn greater flexibility in order to overcome the obstacles presented before you can reach your goal. Ideally, you will able to detail both kinds of skills in showing that you are motivated by goals and—most importantly—able to demonstrate behavior that allows you to meet them.

Behavioral questions will also often involve a description of how you make decisions. Decision making is a key component of critical thinking overall and reveals an independent, well-informed, and decisive employee. For example, an interviewer might ask you simply how you make decisions in the workplace, and sometimes they will give you a particular scenario to work through. This requires preparation in terms of reviewing the concrete details of how you came to an important decision in a previous professional context. They might also ask if you have ever made a decision that was either unpopular or, ultimately, ineffective: this is another excellent opportunity to reveal that you are adept at adapting, regrouping, and overcoming obstacles. Remember that it is always best, to be honest and that revealing a negative experience can actually reveal some of your best qualities, should you frame the response in the right way. An unpopular decision might ultimately have led to a greater good (think about parenting in this context: what is "popular" to the kids might not be what is actually good for them, but in the long run, they understand it was for the best). A decision that proved a mistake is another way for you to show that you can learn from past behavior and modify your responses to be a better, more effective, and more well-rounded employee. Nobody is immune from making mistakes, and decision-making skills are complex skills honed over time; past behavior is both predictive of future results and of flexibility, the ability to learn from stumbles. Good decision-making skills indicate that a candidate is knowledgeable and authoritative.

Behavior questions will also ask you to reveal how you prioritize your work and organize your tasks. Your ability to prioritize says a lot about how valuable you can be as an employee, as well as exposes a lot about your decision-making skills (or, alas, the lack thereof). For example, imagine that you are a lawyer working on a number of cases at one time: how do you prioritize which case demands the most of your time? You could consider the relative fees that the law firm stands to make in each individual case, focusing your time on those cases which will generate the most revenue. Or, you could determine that the cases with the strongest chance of achieving the desired results (a win, a dismissal, a deal, whatever the desired outcome might be) deserve the largest portion of your time. Or, you could decide that the cases that are most deserving of social or financial justice should take up most of your workday, even if they aren't necessarily financially lucrative or boons to the firm's reputation. Or, you could determine that each case deserves an equal amount of time and prioritize each uniformly. None of these approaches is necessarily wrong or right: they simply reveal a mindset and a work style that you will undoubtedly reveal in your answer to your potential employee. As with any answer to any question in an interview, you will want to be honest with yourself and your future employer, but you must understand that if your methods are not compatible with the company culture, then you are probably not the best candidate for the job. Thus, it is worth your while both to do research on the company— is it concerned with statistics and rankings, or is it concerned with outcomes and client satisfaction—and to frame your answers with that in mind? Priorities are strong indicators of employee behavior in both positive and negative ways. Even if you have the best of intentions in mind, if your priorities do not connect with that of your supervisor or the company, then you are clearly not a good fit for the position. Likewise, if you have a difficult time prioritizing, seeing everything as equal, then you are sometimes unable to discern what is most important in terms of productivity or general results. If an employee feels that interpersonal interactions at work are coequal with time spent on projects, then a company might rightly conclude that their ability to prioritize is not in reasonable proportion. However, if an employee is able to manage a number of tasks with success and on deadline, then it reveals a superior ability to prioritize.

Most interviews will employ a number of opinions and behavioral questions, in addition to the basic credential and experience questions. Be prepared with some stories, as outlined in Chapter 4, but also read on for some specific ways in which you can prepare particular answers to specific types of questions.

Chapter 9: During the Interview: Answering Techniques Part 1

There are many different ways in which you can answer interview questions, but one technique, in particular, has been utilized successfully in job interviews for many years: the STAR technique gives you specific guidelines for how to respond to the most common types of interview questions, by giving you the basic outline for how to put together the most concrete, detailed but concise answer that you can. STAR stands for situation, task, action(s), and the result(s); each element should be addressed within your answer. Using the STAR technique to outline particular answers to potential questions is one of the most effective ways in which you can prepare yourself for a job interview.

Situation

With regard to the interview itself, the STAR method indicates a path by which you construct your answers to any variety of questions, and the first thing you should do—besides taking a moment to ponder the question—is to lay out the **situation** in your answer. In general, the STAR technique is primarily focused on the kinds of answers that you would give to behavioral questions (though most questions posed in an interview could readily be behavioral questions). As such, when you are asked a question about past experiences or actions, the first thing to do is to illustrate the situation: essentially, you are describing the situation in which the relevant event was taking place. This context could be anything from working on a team project to dealing with a difficult colleague. **Situation** lays down the groundwork from which you build the edifice of your answer, one story at a time. Beware of providing too much background and instead focus on the most relevant parts of the situation: you want to underscore the complexity or depth of the situation so that your resolution seems that much stronger, but you don't want to dwell on details that have nothing to do with your part in the process (an interviewer doesn't need to know that the client had been with the company for three years, for example, just that a client in good standing had an issue that you were able to resolve). Two or three sentences to set up the **situation** is really all that is needed. Remember, there will be plenty more questions to come. Think back to the "five Ws," as your high school English teacher might have said: what, who, where, when, and why.

Still, even if an interview question isn't a clear behavioral question, the STAR method can be applied. Character questions (what are your strengths/weaknesses?), experience questions (what were your previous job responsibilities?), and opinion questions (what do you value in a co-worker?) can all be more effectively answered with a story set up in STAR format. It will give you specific details and concrete actions that more precisely reveal your hard and soft skills.

Task

The **task** portion of your answer details the specific responsibilities you were given in the situation described. These are the tasks that you review before you decide on your course of action, which will be detailed in the following chapter. Tasks allow you to identify concrete details of objectives that will reveal your attendant skill set. You have already relayed the background in the situation part of your answer; now, show what particular tasks were your responsibilities in dealing with the situation. As with the situation, a listing task should be brief, but it is crucially important that the tasks be concrete and familiar to the interviewer. If you are discussing tasks that a personnel manager might not understand, then you aren't really illuminating your skillset. Be aware of your audience before you determine what kind of tasks would best suit an interview question. An interviewer who has deep knowledge of your technical expertise would be better able to relate to highly specialized tasks.

In preparing for an interview, it is an excellent idea to compile a list of skills to which you can refer. These skills should be both soft skills—attitude, communication, conflict resolution, teamwork, flexibility, leadership, problem-solving—and hard skills, the technical expertise, or educational qualifications that you possess. When preparing a STAR answer, refer to your list of skills and be sure that you can relate a particular skill or (better yet) several skills to the tasks you relay in your answer. Being able to show the connection between task designated and skill used to respond is a key component in a strong interview.

Action(s)

When answering behavioral questions during the interview, the **action** is where you detail the specific steps you took to reach a goal or solve a problem. This part of your answer is the place to showcase the wide range and depth of your skills, and it requires attention to detail and a concrete sense of how you determined a course of action that led to positive results. The more specifically, you can convey exactly what actions you took indicate to the interviewer that you possess higher-level soft skills as well as the hard skills to execute results. You should also consider preparing several examples of specific actions you have taken in a variety of different professional experiences; be sure to use examples that showcase different strengths, rather than repeating the same one or two. Show that your skillset has breadth as well as depth.

Now that you have a written list of skills (see the tip in the above section), you should start to think of specific examples using concrete detail that show how you have put these skills into action. It is not enough to suggest that you have "effective communication skills"—anyone can claim that—you must come up with actual examples that reveal how your actions put your effective communication skills to work, producing real, desirable results.

Result(s)

The last part of your answer during an interview should focus on the **results** that your previous actions brought about; you want to emphasize the positive aspects of those results, of course, in addition to any innovative impacts that your actions might have had. Certainly, no interview story should end with, "because my ideas were so radical, I was ultimately let go." This is not a story to be told at an interview. You want to highlight the successes you've had in past work experience (or educational, though most employers want to see something directly related to work, even if it's volunteer or internship work). Even if you are talking about a past experience that might have been negative—a time you failed, for example, or a challenge that seemed insurmountable—you should always endeavor to end on the most positive note you can. This might lead to **results** that reveal how much you learned and changed after a negative experience or how you developed professionally in the face of difficult circumstances. Don't fall into the trap of telling a story that ends flatly, with no positive trajectory out of the negative experience.

Other questions will inherently emphasize the positive, so you should have no trouble iterating **results** that matter: an interviewer doesn't just want to hear about what your responsibilities were or which actions were taken; they want to hear about why those decisions and actions ultimately *mattered*. If these results are measurable, all the better: if your results are quantifiable—sales numbers grew by X percentage, or productivity rose by a factor of X, or customer interest soared by X-fold—then you demonstrate the concrete nature of how you produce positive results out of decisive and skilled actions.

Also note that, oftentimes, when an interviewer asks a behavioral question, he or she will not necessarily ask you to recount what the results were. However, this is implicit in the question itself, so be sure to go beyond just recounting the situation encountered and the actions are taken; an interviewer will want to know what the results, ultimately, were.

Emphasize Employer Expectations

You should already have a thorough grounding in what the job requires and how the company operates, but you should also have a clear understanding of the kinds of skills that employers are generally looking for. These can be grouped into hard skills and soft skills, in addition to some knowledge about overall expectations. When preparing your STAR answers, think about focusing on these particular skills that most employers expect—and want!

- **Hard skills** are the technical and professional skills that are gained through specific education and training. This is the expertise you have gained through formal education and hands-on experience, specific to each particular field or job. This includes not only formal education and technical training, but also apprenticeships, internships, continuing education, certification or licensing programs, and on-the-job experience. Hard skills are easily evaluated through objective definition and measurement.

- **Soft Skills** are the character attributes and personal qualities that a candidate brings with them to the position. These personality traits and behavioral standards are what allow an employee who has standard hard skills to gain an advantage over other candidates. Managers look for soft skills because no matter how good you are at executing tasks or effectively producing if your interpersonal or communication skills are lacking, then you are likely not the best person for the job. Soft skills are also transferrable skills, appropriate in any workplace scenario, meaning that an employee with excellent soft skills is flexible and useful in almost any position. These skills are gained not through formal training, by and large, but via personal experience and self-awareness; because they are gained over time, the employee with solid soft skills adds value to a company beyond their basic functions. Soft skills demonstrate diversity and broadness of experience, as well as attention to detail and openness to others.

- o **Some soft skills to emphasize** include adaptability, attitude (positive!), communication skills (oral and written), conflict resolution, creative thinking, critical thinking, decision making, flexibility, interpersonal, leadership, motivation, organization, problem-solving, teamwork, time management, and overall work ethic.

- Next, consider the position itself: what managers will expect depends largely on the nature of the job and the experience and skill set needed to fulfill that job. Thus, if you are looking at an entry-level position, then the expectations for lengthy job experience or leadership roles will be lower. In this case, it is likely that you are just embarking on your career, and so other parts of your resume will be more significant, such as educational accomplishments and other extracurricular achievements. If you are looking for a job in management or a highly technical or specialized field, then you can expect that interviewers will be looking for specific details on your abilities and accomplishments within that particular field. The position for which you are interviewing plays some role itself in understanding the expectations that hiring managers will have of you.

- Following on the above, however, employers looking to hire new workers will be much more interested in how they have demonstrated effectiveness in past work experience, rather than in educational achievements—unless you are seeking a truly entry-level position. So, emphasizing your experience, especially with regard to some of the top skills that employers are looking for (see the following chapter for more on that), will be the most significant way to impress upon them that you will be a smart choice.

- Also, remember that you are likely competing with several other candidates for the job: think about what in your past work experience makes you stand out. You'll want to be sure to prepare at least a couple of answers that demonstrate your unique abilities and how they are applicable to the current position being offered. Basically, you need to sell yourself as the best applicant for the job.

- Always conduct yourself with honesty and integrity. The conundrum of how honest to be during the application and interview process is a fraught one: some advice out there suggests that you be honest . . . but not *too* honest, that it's acceptable to bend the truth a bit in the service of your ideal job search. Other advice suggests that managers and employers are truly seeking the most honest and forthcoming individuals for their positions. So, which advice is best? Certainly, the old canard "honesty is the best policy" applies to just about everything you do in life; the consequences of getting caught up in falsehoods could do more damage than even the "harmless" fib you peddled in the first place might. It reveals volumes about a person's integrity when lies are exposed, even if they are minor ones—sometimes *especially* if they are minor ones ("why would she lie about something so minor? What's wrong with her?"). Thus, it is always best to err on the side of truthfulness than not. However, that doesn't always indicate that you have to reveal every single thing about your work history or experience: everyone

127

makes mistakes, and if you have learned from them, it might be an advantage to bring such issues to light in an interview (indeed, many interviewers will ask outright to talk about past mistakes and how you dealt with them). But, everyone also deserves to be defined by aspects of their life besides their mistakes: a particularly damaging or difficult time need not be put on the table unless it becomes highly significant to the conversation or position. Know the difference between revealing that you were fired for a mistake that you've since rectified and remaining quiet over an incident with office politics that might be misinterpreted outside the culture of your former company.

- Nevertheless, it is never appropriate to list a certification, license, or other accomplishment that has subsequently been revoked for some reason. Even if the accomplishment in question isn't relevant for the position to which you applied, it is still unwise to elide the full truth. It is likely that the most casual search will reveal your "lie of omission," which will almost certainly knock you out of the running for the job. Additionally, claiming licensure for certain positions that you no longer have is considered a criminal act in many cases.

Chapter 10: During the Interview: Answering Techniques Part 2

Finally, always remember, interviewers like to ask tough questions—indeed, it is their job to do so—in order to give you the opportunity to reveal the best parts of yourself. Don't think of these tough questions as deliberate attempts to trip you up, as obstacles; rather, think of them as clear examples of your opportunity to show how professional and poised you are, how logical and/or creative your thought process is, and how you handle pressure at the moment. Take the view that the interview is, truly and ultimately, in *your* control: with proper preparation, you should be ready to tackle even the toughest questions with clear and ready answers. In addition to the STAR technique, there are some very basic interview techniques to keep in mind, especially right before you embark on the interview itself.

- **Give yourself a moment**: pause before answering, and be sure that you have fully understood the question.
- **Always avoid impulsive responses**: remember, you have spent time and energy preparing your

answers for a reason; take a deep breath and recall the details of your various stories. If a question is asked, that doesn't directly deal with what you have prepared, try to think of a way to bring it back to something that you know and are comfortable with.

- **Be unique**: your answers should always contain enough specific examples and concrete details to be purely and solely *your* answers. The unexpected, as previously mentioned, is an excellent way to make your answers stand out.

- **Don't forget to listen**: certainly, you want to appear attentive to the interviewer in terms of basic professionalism, of course, but you also want to listen carefully to what the interviewer is asking and how they are responding. Listening will give you cues and clues for how to answer follow up questions.

Some other tough types of questions can present potential pitfalls. These kinds of questions might take some extra preparation and careful thought. Be sure to spend some time thinking about some of these difficult inquiries.

- Common to most interviews, the question about weakness will inevitably be asked, in some form or another. "What critical feedback do you receive most often?" is just another version of the same kind of question. This kind of question poses a pitfall because it asks you to reveal something negative about yourself, which certainly leaves us feeling vulnerable, especially in an interview situation. It also poses a pitfall in that you might either avoid the question or forget to steer into positive territory. In the first instance, a candidate might respond by suggesting that the critical feedback he's ever received has been inconsequential; this comes across as arrogant and/or lacking in self-awareness. In the second instance, you reveal a flaw without indicating that you are working on it. The best answer acknowledges that you have a weakness—this indicates self-awareness and humility—and reveals specific and concrete actions that you have been taking to improve—focusing and ending on the positive.

- In a similar vein, potential employers will also often ask about an obstacle that you have overcome in the past. This, again, invites the uncomfortable proposition that you reveal something difficult and/or negative from your past. Nevertheless, if you are prepared with a STAR ready answer, providing details about the situation, tasks, actions, and results that show how you ultimately overcame a said obstacle, then you are actually telling an inspiring story about both your professional abilities and your personal attributes. Telling a story that combines the use of your hard skills and soft skills are the strongest ways to approach this kind of question.

- Because stress is a component of every professional experience, employers will often want to test your facility for handling it, so you should expect a question about how you deal with stress or pressure. Again, don't make the mistake of suggesting that you never get stressed out or that you deal with stress just fine. This is clearly skirting the truth, and the employer knows it. Rather, construct a specific example wherein you acknowledge that you felt enormous pressure (of deadline, on your skillset, or other) but took steps to deal with that stress to overcome it. Make sure that you reveal the results (STAR method, again) of your process: showing that even though you almost buckled under stress but ended up figuring out a way to deal with it and overcome it—to positive ends—is a satisfying and inspiring story.

- Another potential pitfall comes in the form of questions that ask you to comment on your personal experience with management or colleagues. An interviewer might ask what your worst experience was or to describe a conflict that happened in your previous experience. Certainly, you should approach the question with honesty—but also with a healthy dose of tact. An employer wants to know what kind of person and/or management style you work best with, of course, but he or she doesn't really want to know that about past squabbles or the personal foibles of others. Avoid any personal references, names, or other information that might tip the interviewer off to a particular person about whom you might be discussing. Indeed, it is best not to discuss others when answering the question, in general. Instead, come up with a specific example wherein a negative experience—a clash of personalities, or a conflict of interests—created a temporarily difficult working situation, emphasis on the *temporary*. You want to end the story with how it was resolved in as positive a manner as possible.

- If you are currently employed by another company within the industry, then you will most likely be asked about why you are leaving your current job. This question proffers a possible landmine of inappropriate responses, just as with the above question. This is not the time to get personal or to use the interview as a chance to complain about another company, boss, or colleague. Instead, it is the opportunity for you to offer your potential employer an honest assessment of what wasn't working for you in your current position that encouraged you to seek a job elsewhere. Tactful honesty is the best policy here, as well. Try to frame your response in the most positive terms available: "I have thoroughly enjoyed my work with X Company, but at this time, professional growth opportunities are few. I wanted to begin thinking about career advancement at this moment in my professional life, so this job offered me the chance to best use my many skills."

- You will also often be asked a question about either why you wish to work for this employer or why this employer should feel compelled to hire you. These are similar questions, and they are tough questions because you don't know who your competition is or what, exactly, management is looking for. In the first instance, the best preparation you can do for your answer is to conduct adequate research into the company overall; the more you know about what the company does and how its culture functions, the better able you are to make a pitch about your enthusiasm and fittingness for the job. In the second instance, you are essentially being asked how your particular skill set matches the position, review the original job description, and apply your knowledge gained from researching the company as a whole. Review your list of skills and make a clear link between each skill and a component of the job qualifications or expectations. You might also prepare a specific example, with concrete details, about how a particular experience makes you uniquely suited for the job—this is a way of setting yourself apart from the other candidates.

- Another difficult question you might get is to talk about your greatest regrets and/or your greatest achievements: as with questions about weaknesses and strengths, be sure you have a ready answer prepared that doesn't swing too hard to the negative or dwell too much on the arrogance. Showing an ability to learn from regrets is the best approach in that scenario, while relaying one specific achievement in the context of your professional life is the best way to show success without arrogance. Stick to one example that is specific to one past experience.

In general, all interview questions can feel like tough questions, and the best way in which you can handle them is through preparation and practice. Answering questions with specific examples, using concrete details, rather than employing vague generalities, will enable you to tackle any tough question with aplomb. Landing your ideal job is well within your reach if you follow these bits of advice—as well as learning how to avoid mistakes, as detailed more in-depth in the following chapter.

Chapter 11: The Interview: Mistakes to Avoid

If your job search has led you to an interview, then you have probably already avoided some of the common mistakes that will be detailed below: keep up the good work. If you are just now embarking on a job search, then all of these tips will be helpful for your future success. As with any enterprise that we undertake in our professional lives, there are some potential pitfalls, and proverbial bumps in the road; as helpful as amassing the guidelines for positive preparation can be, it can also be just as worthwhile to review these minor mistakes that you can easily avoid, if well informed.

- We often forget how **ubiquitous our internet presence is**; if you fail to consider your online footprint when you apply for professional positions or go to interviews, then you may be ignoring the one barrier between you and your ideal job. It is a good idea not only to maintain a polite and non-controversial social media presence (Facebook and Twitter are now regularly reviewed by human resources departments) but also to avoid participating in forums or other internet outlets wherein you openly discuss your political, social, religious, sexual, or other potentially controversial views—especially avoid doing so when using your own name. When employers view these things, they can—rightly or wrongly—have an oversized impact on whether or not you are hired. If you are comfortable compromising your employment opportunities because you possess strong opinions and views that you feel you must express, then certainly, it is your prerogative to do so. Just be aware that there are likely consequences.

- Another common misstep for young interviewees is **not to understand when the interview begins**: the interview begins long before you actually sit down across from a manager or committee. It begins when you turn in a resume and cover letter, when you are called for the interview, and when you arrive at the building (or pick up the phone) itself. That is, you are being assessed based on every bit of information—including behavior—that you present. Thus, *always* be polite to anyone who you encounter in the lead up to the interview: receptionists, secretaries, guards, even people in the hallways or elevators. You don't have any idea who is actually involved in the decision-making process—that person you snub in the elevator might just be a colleague or a supervisor. Conduct yourself as if you are in the interview itself at all times.

- **Talking too much** is another potential pitfall about which you should be aware. When asked about yourself, keep the answer short and sweet and, ideally, focused on the position itself. Frame your answer so that it reflects what parts of your personality, skill set, and/or experience are well suited to the job at stake.

- **Don't forget why you are there**: no matter how casual the interviewer may seem or how personal the questions might get, don't make the mistake of thinking that the situation is anything other than a highly professional scenario. Becoming overly comfortable or familiar can ultimately hurt your chances.
- **Always be prepared**: this is why you are reading this guide in the first place. Also, check out my other book, *Job Interview Q&A* for more in-depth advice on every type of interview question with sample answers

to   the   toughest   questions.

- **Listening should be nearly as important as speaking** because you will find out from what the interviewer says and asks what they want and how they wish to proceed. Because listening is often underestimated in the job interview process, it would be a good idea to remind yourself of the importance of   careful   listening:

  - Be sure to use your listening skills to perceive **information that may be somewhat implicit rather than explicit**. If an interviewer consistently asks about your ability to handle stressful situations, then you might rightly deduce that this is a high-pressure workplace. If an interviewer seems interested in your future professional development plans, this might signal that you are a candidate for a higher-level position. In any case, the interviewer will consciously or incidentally reveal a lot about the company. Listening to what is said will give you ample opportunity and ammunition to ask pertinent questions and make   smart   decisions.

- o There are specific ways in which you can **hone your listening skills**. Let's face facts: many of us, particularly when faced with being put on the spot in a stressful situation such as a job interview, will tune out what is going on around us. Diligent observation and listening skills take some   practice.

- o **Practice listening** with a friend or family member. Ask them to tell you an unfamiliar story, then try to relay the details back to them a few hours later. Or, simply let your support group know that, in preparation for the interview, you'd like to be made aware of when you are accidentally zoning out. As long as you leave personal feelings aside, you'll likely learn a lot about how carefully you listen—or not.

- o **Prepare for the interview thoroughly**, both in terms of practical preparation and in terms of psychological preparation. Have everything ready to go the night before (outfit, materials, travel plans), as well as conduct stress-relieving

146

activities the day before and get a good night's sleep. The more prepared you are, the better able you are to relax enough to be a good listener.

- Your **body language** will indicate to the interviewer how well you are listening. Show engagement by leaning toward the interviewer when he or she is speaking, nod when appropriate, and avoid interruption. All of these silent signals reveal that you are a good listener—a boon to you during the interview process itself, and a boon to any employer who wishes to hire an employee with excellent communication skills.

- **Repeat back to the interviewer** what he or she is saying in order to be certain that you have the most important details clear. This is a method by which you clearly indicate that you have been respectfully listening.

- Don't worry if you have to **ask the interviewer to repeat a question** or explain something more thoroughly. Nobody is a perfect listener, and that kind of diligence can prevent

147

misunderstanding.

- **Forgetting or ignoring professional etiquette** can also be an impediment to getting the job, as was discussed in Chapter 5. Some quick reminders on how to conduct yourself with the highest professionalism follows:

  o Consider your **first impression**; you must not only look the part but also act the part. A first impression can never be retracted, so it is important not to begin an interview on the wrong foot. Be enthusiastic and look happy— rather than apprehensive—to be there. Make eye contact and introduce yourself politely when appropriate, extending a handshake in most cases. When entering the interview space, be sure to accept instructions politely and strike and open—rather than defensive—posture.

  o Be sure that the **outfit you've chosen to wear** for the interview is appropriate and professional, but also be aware of how it will appear when you are seated. You want to avoid the proverbial wardrobe malfunction (gaping

148

blouse, popped button, overly hiked pants). Typically, you will be seated for most of the interview, so that's how you should test the comforts and utility of your chosen attire.

o Always **remember to smile** and appear interested in what the interviewer is saying. A smile (or, conversely, a frown) can speak volumes. If you appear smiling and approachable, then you are perceived as a team player with valuable character attributes as well as professional skills to bring to the company. A frown, on the other hand, can fluster or annoy the interviewer; it is difficult to know how to interpret the facial expression. Are you angry, annoyed, bored, frustrated, or otherwise unimpressed? This is not the impression you want to convey. Remind yourself that this experience, while somewhat nerve-racking, should be an amicable way in which to showcase your considerable talents and value. This would bring a smile to anyone's face.

o **Body language**, in general, reveals a lot about a person's feelings and character. Crossing your arms against your chest looks defensive, even hostile, while a lazy slump indicates a lack of interest or disrespect. Keeping your hands folded in your lap throughout the interview can have the effect of implying childlike anxiety. "Man-spreading" can look aggressive or arrogant. Again, maintain eye contact when answering questions and avoid sweeping hand gestures. You can hold a pen or pencil in your hand if it helps to center you, and this can come in handy should you wish to jot anything down. Basically, your body language should indicate that you are engaged and open, enthusiastic, and   polite.

o When **greeting others**, be sure that you have a solid handshake, somewhere between limp and crushing. A firm handshake reveals self-confidence and a courteous understanding of overall business etiquette. When meeting someone for the first time, it is considered polite to use an honorific, such as Dr. or Ms. or Mr. If the company for which you are interviewed is owned or operated by foreign nationals, then it would behoove you to do some research into the basic etiquette of the other country. Personal space is defined differently in different cultures, in addition to attitudes about how men and women behave.

- **Addressing someone** by their name is also a powerful piece of business etiquette that you can employ to curry respect. Everyone likes to be noticed and remembered, so try your best to remember and repeat the names of people that you meet. Should you be called in for a further interview, this considerate formality will inevitably be noticed.

- As you are seated for your interview—which you should be invited to do, rather than simply plopping down—place your personal items beside or underneath your chair. For everyone's sanity and to preserve your dignity, **turn off your cell phone** and any other device you may have carried with you. Have your resume and cover letter, along with a notepad or folder for notes, at the ready.

151

o If, for some disastrous reason, your phone should ring during an interview, you will be called upon to do some swift damage control. **_Do not dare look at the phone to check_** (unless you truly have a life-and-death situation on your hands); simply turn it off and apologize to the interviewer. You would have to be an excellent candidate to overcome this most egregious of etiquette breaches. It's better not to take your phone in with you if you have a habit of forgetting to switch it off. And off means *off*, not silent.

o When leaving the interview, be sure to **restate your interest** in the job and your pleasure at having met everyone. Shake hands again and repeat names, when appropriate. Be sure to thank the receptionist who showed you in, if relevant. Basically, just show proper manners on your way out the door.

o After the interview, it is customary to write **a "thank you" note** of some sort to the interviewer or interviewers to acknowledge their time and your opportunity. This will be reviewed further in the following chapter.

 If you are able to avoid these common mistakes and follow professional protocol, then your ideal job is well within reach. You have prepared an excellent resume and cover letter that have led to an interview, for which you have also prepared, reviewing questions and creating potential answers using STAR guidelines and other tips: you are ready to conduct the best interview of your career. Look to the following chapter for what to do once that interview is complete.

154

Chapter 12: Post-Interview Follow Up and Etiquette

While it may appear that the process of applying for and securing your dream job is complete when the interview is over, there is still one more important step up: you should follow up appropriately. When you follow up in appropriate ways, it can have the added benefit of reminding the potential employer of why you are a strong candidate in the first place; it shows respect and attention to detail, as well as allowing you to pursue answers of your own. Here are some details about how to conduct a proper follow-up protocol.

- **Before you leave the interview**, try to find out what the hiring manager's timeline is for making a decision; this can avoid awkward moments in the future. You don't want to call incessantly or otherwise bother your interviewer with questions about hiring: if they say they will have a decision within the month, wait until the end of that time period before you check back with them (though do, of course, write a thank you   response;   see   below).

- **When should you follow up?** There are two distinct answers to this: the first is that you should follow up immediately with some kind of thank you note (more on that below); the second is that you should allow an appropriate amount of time to pass before nudging the interviewer to give you some specific results. At the end of the interview itself, find an opportunity to ask when you might hear back from the company if you haven't already been told. If you don't hear back from them in the allotted time period, wait two or three more days before you send a polite email or place a polite phone call. If you aren't sure when you'll hear back, wait at least a week before checking back in.   As with listening skills, a polite and professional follow up note can remind a potential employer of your qualifications, abilities, and attributes.

- **How should you follow up?** This, of course, will depend upon the nature of the interview and job position. It is rare, however, that you should ever follow up in person. The most common ways to follow up are with an email or a phone call, and which you choose depends on your level of confidence in speaking extemporaneously or needing to script a response. A follow-up email gives you the opportunity to compose your (concise!) thoughts before sending, though it doesn't always provide the kind of immediate gratification that you may want or need. If you decide to call the interviewer or hiring manager, be sure to jot down what you'd like to say beforehand. In either case, be sure that your tone is friendly and that you keep your remarks concise. You can also ask if they require any further materials from you in your follow up—this might be especially relevant if you are concerned that the interview did not go as well as you would have hoped or if you remembered some important information that you weren't able to convey at the time of the original interview.

- Regardless of whether you eventually need to follow up further, **you should *always* write a quick note of thanks after the interview**. While some might suggest that this is rather old-fashioned, it is still very much the case that this practice is routinely followed and clearly appreciated. The more thoughtful the note, the more successful the results. Here are some things to consider when writing that crucial thank you note:

- o Be sure to write and send a thank-you note **within 24 hours** of the interview—any longer, and it becomes a moot point. Today, most thank you notes are sent via email, but one sent via mail can garner special attention; just be sure that it is sent promptly so that you aren't forgotten in the interim. Typically, an email is a better choice because of the short time-lapse, but if you are physically close enough to stop by with a handwritten note, then that might be the best choice.

- o **Address the thank you to everyone** who played a role in your application process, from all the interviewers to the recruiter, when applicable. In some cases, it may be applicable to send a quick note to another employee who participated in some form, as well. In many cases, you will be directing your thank you to one specific interviewer. In other cases, if you are interviewed by a few people, then you might want to send a quick note to all involved, especially if their capacities or responsibilities in the interview differed. If you are interviewed by a full panel of people, then you might consider writing one overarching note to the person in charge, and Cc-ing everyone else.

o   A thank you note should contain **a friendly and respectful greeting**, using the person's name and honorific (Dr., Ms., Director, etc.), with a short paragraph expressing your appreciation for their time and effort, closing with a professional "sincerely" and your name. If you can think of a **specific detail from the interview** that was especially striking, then you might briefly mention it in your paragraph in order to remind them of you. You also might throw in a compliment if it is sincere.

o   Essentially, **your tone should be professional yet personable**. Avoid emojis of any kind, and don't pepper the note with exclamation points or overly excitable adjectives and adverbs. There are numerous templates available online should you wish to review   some.

- Finally, **know when to move on**: if you have sent a thank you note and have made two attempts at follow up without response, then it is time to start preparing for your next interview. Be patient, however, and space out your follow up over the course of a couple of weeks: thank you note immediately, follow up within a few days of when a response was anticipated, and one final follow up a week or so after that. If there is no response within a month, then your time and energy is best spent moving on.

Also, be aware that interviews do not always lead to successful job offers, and it may not always be that the candidate is turned down: you may find yourself in a position wherein you have multiple offers (lucky you!) so you have to decide which of them to take. Or, you may be in a position to take only the job that is right for you (you are financially secure enough to wait until you find the perfect fit). In these cases, be sure to look for some warning signs to indicate that this particular job may not be the one for you. If you have the luxury to be choosy about which position you take, then paying attention to some of the red flags thrown up by interviewers will give you the necessary information to make your final decision.

- If your interviewer **doesn't seem to be perfectly clear** on what the position entails or what your responsibilities might be, then this is a clear sign that there is some miscommunication or disorganization within the company itself.

- If your research prior to the interview reveals a rosy public image with satisfied employees and customers, but **your experience at the company** and during the interview seems at odds with that, then perhaps you should reconsider. The public image of a company might not always live up to its actual culture; this is a time for you to use your best judgment about what's in your best interests.

- If your **interviewer doesn't seem engaged** with your answers or asks only a repetitive set of generic questions, then it is likely the case that either the company has already determined who they will hire (hint: it's not you) or the position is a redundant one, mostly unimportant to the workings of the company. This might indicate that prospects for advancement are low or non-existent.

- If the research you conduct on the company indicates that **leadership is in flux**, is floundering, or has a high rate of turnover, then this is a clear red flag that something is wrong at the core of the company itself. You don't want to chain yourself to a sinking ship, as it   were.

- The same consideration applies to your understanding of the company's mission statement. If their **mission seems unclear or contradictory**, then that's an indication that the company is in trouble or in a rut.

- If your **interviewer seems unprepared**, then you should reconsider, as well. Again, this reveals a lack of organization and clarity within the company; or, if the interviewer will be your direct supervisor, it reveals an indication of their habitual work practices—and that might be frustrating for you in the end.

- Finally, **if the process of interviewing feels too drawn out**—it's taken months to get from resume to interview to follow-up interview—then it's another red flag that indicates disorganization, indecision, or other core problem.

Armed with all of the above information, you should be well-prepared and confident to tackle any part of the interview process, from pre-interview to post-interview to job offer itself.

Chapter 13: Overview and Checklist

At last, you have submitted resumes and cover letters and have been asked to an interview, and you have read through this entire guide, following the steps toward securing and successfully navigating a high stakes job interview. This final chapter will give you a quick overview and checklist to follow once you have absorbed the details that have been proffered throughout the book. Use this to literally mark off each step in the process as you go, and note that you can utilize for each and every application and interview you secure.

1. Personalize your resume and cover letter for each and every job to which you apply. Keep a master list of applications sent, including names of the company, names of directors or hiring managers, job descriptions, dates application sent, and interview scheduled. This provides you with a long-term template toward tracking your success—or lack thereof—and changing your approach as necessary.

2. Review the methods proposed by others: there are innumerable resources to assist with resumes, cover letters, and other pre-interview preparation materials. Familiarize yourself with the basic culture and customs of your chosen field, especially if you are new to the professional workforce or are changing careers. This will boost your confidence and help you secure better opportunities.

3. As soon as you find out that you have gotten an interview, begin your research and preparation. Study like you might have once studied for a final exam. Do diligent research on the company, as detailed in Chapter 3, and brush up on your own resume and cover letter prior to the interview. You might also want to study up on specific skills that are outlined in the job description, especially if you haven't utilized these particular skills for a while or are applying for something that is a bit outside your previous job experience. While you cannot expect to master a new skill within a few days, you can certainly wind up with a more thorough understanding of what you might be asked to do.

4. Remember to prepare for potential interview questions and rehearse potential answers, as detailed in Chapters 7 through 10, and prepare your own set of questions that you would like answered in the course of the interview itself. Outline a couple of stories, as discussed in Chapter 4, so that you are ready to respond to personal and professional questions in a cohesive and coherent manner. Reach out to other employees at the company, if appropriate, or to others working in the industry for some deeper insight into company culture and managerial expectations. You can also utilize databases that compile real-life interview experiences, such as Glassdoor.

5. Remember to review the job description before going to the interview, as well: note specific keywords that you might use when outlining your story or practicing your potential answers. Do practice out loud, as it will help both memory and confidence.

6. If you discover a gap in your skillset, be sure to be prepared to provide a satisfactory answer as to why and/or how you can remedy such a gap. Remember to be honest and authentic when pitching your

experience and attributes in a resume, cover letter, and   interview.

7. Be sure to practice stress relief, especially the night before the interview, and schedule your time wisely so that you get enough rest. Eat a healthy dinner the night before and a decent breakfast the morning of the interview.   Spend some time with positive visualization or meditation before you leave for the interview; see tips and techniques in Chapter 6. The goal in the 24 hours leading up to the interview is to be   as   prepared   but   relaxed   as   possible.

8. Remember to dress professionally but comfortably; follow the tips provided in Chapter 5 for a full complement of what to consider when preparing your interview look. Brush up on professional etiquette, as well, so that your behavior matches your polished and professional   appearance.

9. Give yourself a pep talk before the interview: remind yourself that you were skilled enough to get the interview and worthy of the job offer. Don't forget to make eye contact and to practice a firm handshake. Walk   into   the   building   with   confidence   and

enthusiasm.

10.   Check that you have everything you need before you leave for the interview. Copies of your resume and cover letter, writing utensils, and a pad of paper or other such items for taking notes. Make sure your bag is uncluttered and organized and (as has been repeated throughout this guide) *turn off your cell phone*.

11.   Throughout the process, it might be worth your while to keep a journal of your preparations and experience. Each interview provides an opportunity to learn something new and valuable to take with you into the job itself or onto the next interview. Be sure to debrief yourself directly after the interview, taking down notes as to what you thought was particularly successful, and what you felt could be improved upon. This might prove to be the most beneficial use of your interview preparation time in the long run.

12.   Be sure to follow up, as detailed in Chapter 12: write a concise and professional thank you note within 24 hours of the interview and check-in about results in a patient and polite manner. Even if you did not

get the job, you might indicate that you would be willing to listen to suggestions for how you might be a better candidate in the future. Always avoid burning bridges: you never know when another, more fitting opportunity might arise. You should always be prepared and professional for any chance to shine.

173

Conclusion

Embarking on a satisfying professional career is one of the highlights of our adult lives. We spend countless hours on the job, so the more rewarding and engaging the job is, the better our lives will inevitably be. For these reasons, securing your ideal job is an admirable—if challenging—goal. This guide should assist you in that search, preparing you for the interview of a lifetime, quite literally. All of your experience, all of your knowledge, and all of your extensive preparation will allow you access to the best and most satisfying job for which you can hope.

From understanding the process of how job searches and interviews work to preparing for the experience itself, this guide will get you from your starting point to the finish line. Preparing a thorough but concise resume is the first step, followed by writing an engaging and thoughtful cover letter: these acts will enable you to secure the interview itself. Once you have the interview, you should research the company for which you desire to work, understanding expectations and company culture as well as you can prior to the interview. You should also prepare for the various questions that will likely be posted at an interview, practicing possible answers, and detailing your professional and educational story. Following professional standards and etiquette will also help you shine during an interview, and reviewing potential pitfalls only makes you that much more confident. A proper follow-up and checklist will keep you on track throughout this ultimately rewarding process.

A job interview is a complex enterprise, with numerous moving parts with which one has to keep track. While it may seem like a performance at a job interview is an intuitive exercise—after all, you know yourself and what you have experienced professionally and educationally in the past—it is rarely that simple. Even the most accomplished and confident candidates will benefit from some review and practice.

Maintaining your poise and answering even the toughest interview questions is well within your reach after reading this guide: after all the years of hard work and dedication to education, training, volunteering, interning, and gaining professional experience of all kinds, you now have the chance to get the job of your dreams. Thorough preparation and careful consideration will enable you to perform to the best of your ability. Landing your dream job is the first step toward securing professional, financial, and personal success and happiness.

Job Interview Questions and Answers

A Practical Guide for Most Common Interview Questions and Winning Answering Techniques to the Toughest Interview Questions

unless express consent of the Publisher is provided beforehand. Any additional rights reserved.

Furthermore, the information that can be found within the pages described forthwith shall be considered both accurate and truthful when it comes to the recounting of facts. As such, any use, correct or incorrect, of the provided information will render the Publisher free of responsibility as to the actions taken outside of their direct purview. Regardless, there are zero scenarios where the original author or the Publisher can be deemed liable in any fashion for any damages or hardships that may result from any of the information discussed herein.

Additionally, the information in the following pages is intended only for informational purposes and should thus be thought of as universal. As befitting its nature, it is presented without assurance regarding its prolonged validity or interim quality. Trademarks that are mentioned are done without written consent and can in no way be considered an endorsement from the trademark holder.

Introduction

Preparing for a job interview may be one of the most significant activities you may do in your professional life. Successfully securing your dream job is not only a path toward financial stability but also toward personal satisfaction and happiness. We spend inordinate amounts of our time at work, crafting our careers, and building our skills; we should invest that time wisely in the most fulfilling job that we can possibly find.

One of the most important parts of the job search is the interview itself. This book guides you through the process of preparing for the best job interview of your career. From understanding the variety of questions, you might get to learning how to prepare smart answers, you will learn how to navigate the intricate process of successful job seeking. You will also acquire some techniques following the STAR method: responding according to situation, task, action, and result. At the end of the book, you will find a representative set of tough questions and appropriate answers to help you prepare.

After you are finished reading this guide, you should have everything you need to prepare for the interview of a lifetime. Decide today to quit languishing in an unfulfilling and unrewarding job and start building a successful career for your future happiness and well-being. Preparing for a job interview is like embarking on any other significant project: it takes knowledge, practice, and perseverance to navigate. Here you will find a full road map of how to get from where you are to where you want to be.

Chapter 1: The Typical Interview: An Introduction

While there is no truly typical job interview—the experience encompasses too many variables (candidate, employer, field, and so on) to be wholly predictable—there are some common elements that occur in most interview situations. Understanding the basics of interviewer's categories of questions, as well as honing your ability to answer clearly and cleverly, can give you a significant advantage in the interview process. The importance of a job interview really cannot be overstated: this simple act is the culmination of your years of hard work, focus, and energy. You may have paid tens of thousands of dollars for a higher education or special training just to get to this point; you may have spent your entire life dreaming of this particular job in this particular field; you may have an inkling that this job might be able to propel you to success and security in ways you have only dreamed of. The job interview is one way in which to gain entry into whatever elite group you've always wanted to be a part of.

Job interviews are complex enterprises, as well. You are selling yourself, of course—your set of skills, your personality, your professionalism—but you are also hoping to present your ability to be part of a larger team or company. Indeed, part of the process of interviewing requires understanding subtle and psychological cues; you are not the only person involved, of course, and you need to be able to "read the room," as it were. While there are no specific set of rules for any given situation, as each situation will be markedly different, there are some general ideas about how you can prepare yourself for any eventuality that you might happen upon in an interview. This is what this guide is for, to help you review the heart of the interview process, the kinds of questions you will likely be asked, along with how you might best answer them using particularly tested techniques.

Attending a job interview is a potentially life-changing event, so it should be approached with great deliberation and care—as well as the knowledge that the interview is far more important to you than it is to the interviewer. Having been made aware of that, however, it also behooves you to know something about the interviewer—when possible—and certainly to do research on the company itself. Armed with more information always makes you appear to be a better candidate, well-informed and eager to join this new group.

Thinking about what kinds of questions the interviewer may ask, and preparing some possible answers to potential questions is some of the most valuable research you can conduct. Certainly, you cannot predict every question the interviewer will ask, but you can anticipate some basic ones, based on the job requirements, your own resume, and the knowledge of standard questions frequently asked.

Be sure to review your resume and cover letter before the interview (and, by all means, do bring these with you for reference, of course). It is likely that the interviewer will ask you specific questions related to one or more of your past experiences. The better you know your own resume, the stronger a candidate you will seem. Also think about specific experiences in past working relationships that you might mention or highlight in the interview; the resume lists your experience and your accomplishments, but it doesn't give a clear sense of how you interact with superiors or colleagues in a working situation, and it would be prudent of you to have some stories prepared detailing some of those experiences.

You should also be very clear on what the duties and expectations of the position that you are applying for are: what specifically does the job require, and how best will you be able to fulfill those expectations? A job advertisement will sometimes give you just a few lines of explanation; at other times, it will have a lengthy description. Either way, make it your responsibility, prior to the interview, to find out all you can about the position itself so that you can directly address how your past experiences and present skills can best be suited for said position.

Beyond the position itself, it is always important to understand the broader working culture of the company as a whole. This ensures that you can demonstrate that you are a good fit not only for the specific job, but for the company in general. This includes understanding whether the work environment is collaborative or highly individualized; this difference alone will determine how you will respond to questions asked by the interviewer, as well as whether you are, ultimately, a good fit. Obviously, when you study the company, look into its working practices and traditions. Notice, as well, when you submit your resume or attend your interview, how employees appear to interact and work. This kind of observation can give you a sense of job satisfaction and collegiality in any workplace.

In addition to knowing yourself, your interviewer, the job requirements and company culture, you should also be prepared to ask or ascertain the potential for growth that is inherent to the position. That is, understanding what is required of the specific position is crucial, but knowing what opportunities might exist beyond it is also a way to impress your interviewer that you have even more to offer. In addition, this information is crucial to your personal decision-making process: depending on your age at the time of the interview, it may be very important that you move beyond whatever position you are applying for at the current time. Indicating that you are prepared to learn more or to take on more at the very beginning gives the impression that you are eager to integrate into the company from the start.

Certainly, it is also the case that you should be prepared to ask about salary and benefits, if such things were not made abundantly clear before the interview. This kind of information is obviously important for your own decision-making process, but it is also crucial that you make clear your expectations from the start, as well. When asking about salary and benefits, already have prepared what you will be satisfied to take; that is, don't ask the question without having your own answer ready, as many interviewers will respond by asking you what your expectations are.

Finally, the importance of attitude cannot be overstated: in the end, if you are enthusiastic, prepared, and knowledgeable, this will go a long way towards presenting yourself as an ideal employee. Throughout this guide, you will gain tips on what to do before the interview—building a resume, creating a cover letter, researching the company, outlining your story, and reducing stress—as well as how to develop particular interview skills that will give you that winning approach to interviews for success every time.

Chapter 2: Interview Questions: Credential Verification and Qualifications

Among the simplest kinds of questions you may be asked at a job interview, credential verification questions ask you to verify the details provided on your resume and/or within your cover letter. If you are a recent graduate, these kinds of questions might ask you to discuss your course work, intern opportunities, and extracurricular endeavors, as well as specific grade point averages or other measurable markers of accomplishment. If you have work experience, the questions might focus instead on your tenure at a particular company or your specific positions held, promotions gained, and projects completed. Whatever direction these questions take, they require you to be prepared and well-versed in the details of your educational experience and/or work history. Essentially, you are being asked to vouch for your qualifications objectively and honestly.

Credential verification questions can do a couple of things in the course of an interview: first, they can allow for a breaking of the ice at the beginning, in order to allow both interviewer and candidate to warm up to the process;

second, they can serve as a jumping-off point to elaborate on particular achievements in your educational or work history that will illustrate your fittingness for the job; third, they can give you the opportunity to explain away any gaps or unconventional issues with your resume.

First, credential questions can be a way to ease into the interview, allowing for everybody to settle in and relax a bit. Because these kinds of questions essentially ask you to review and verify your resume, be sure that you have a copy quick at hand in case you need to quickly look at something. Otherwise, you should be able to readily answer these kinds of questions without hesitation. The interviewer may ask a series of verification questions or just one or two that he or she is interested in; partly, this depends on how detailed your resume is in the first place. If certain credentials are of greater interest to your potential employer, then this serves as a way into broader issues, as follows.

Second, certain credentials might encourage interviewers to ask some follow up questions: for example, they might be interested in knowing why you stayed for so long (or so short) at a particular place of employment; or, they might be interested in knowing how certain kinds of coursework were relevant to your overall educational achievement. They might also use credential questions to prompt you to show a link between various activities and interests you've engaged with in the past: that is, you might be encouraged to show how seemingly disparate parts of your overall credential portfolio actually link together. Say you've been working as a graphic designer and you also list that you volunteered at a food pantry: these credentials don't necessarily seem to have anything to do with one another. You should be prepared to show how you have learned skills from each that complement the other. Additionally, credential verification questions could lead to the interviewer following up on how these past credentials might serve the current position for which you are applying. That is, you might be asked not only how your credentials have reinforced your growing skillset through past experience but also how these credentials link to the requirements being asked of you for the current job.

Third, when an interviewer asks credential verification questions, he or she might be giving you the opportunity to explain or justify particular gaps in your resume. For example, if there is a gap in employment, then the interviewer might ask you what you were doing during that time and why the gap exists in the first place. In this case, be very prepared to answer honestly and thoroughly. For another example, the gap in your resume might be related to a particular set of skills. An interviewer can use a credential verification question to prompt you to expand on the kind of soft skills—leadership, effective communication, conflict resolution—needed to fulfill the requirements of a particular position. It can also be a prompt for you to expand upon a specific promotion or project. Finally, when reviewing your resume, an interviewer might candidly ask why certain skills seem to be missing. Be prepared to explain this, as well, and demonstrate how you intend to develop this skill or fill in your resume's gaps.

Beyond those opportunities, credential verification questions are also closely related to qualification questions. In this case, you are being asked to expand upon how your credentials and experience make you qualified for the position at hand. Your credentials reveal your qualifications in a concise and concrete way; however, the qualifications you possess represent more than mere credentials but also general work and life experience, in addition to the possession of a variety of soft skills that will assist you with any position you might want to tackle.

For example, if it isn't abundantly clear from your resume and cover letter why are qualified for the position, then you need to be prepared to show how your experience—while seemingly tangential—does actually apply. This is relevant when you are just starting out your career or when you are trying to make a shift in careers. This is also one of the reasons why relaying your soft skills is so important: soft skills carry over to whatever job you might be wanting, from adaptability and flexibility to dependability and attitude. For example, if you have worked in a non-profit environment and you are switching to a corporate position, then you need to be able to elaborate on how the skills at a non-profit might translate. This could be as concrete as suggesting that developing strong accounting skills is necessary at a non-profit, where budgets can be tight, will assist you in helping generate more profitability in a corporate setting. Or, it could be as abstract as revealing that your communication skills in your work at the non-profit will easily transfer to the corporate world; writing a newsletter to potential donors requires the same skill set as composing coherent and concise interdepartmental memos.

On the other hand, you might be asked to explain why you are applying for a job that you appear to be overqualified for: say you have a master's degree, yet you are applying for an entry-level position. Many factors would determine your answer, but do prepared to explain. It might be that you are shifting careers or industries, as in the example above, or it might be that you are interested in a greater balance between life and work, so you are scaling back your responsibilities. It might be that you are simply passionate about the opportunity afforded by this particular position and are willing to accept a lower-level position in order to get a foot in the door. These kinds of questions might also apply if you have been in management-level positions but are currently seeking a non-managerial job.

Qualification questions might also ask you to go into detail about certain abilities that you list or infer on your resume or cover letter. Why is it that you feel you have a particular facility for XXX? Or, what do you think are your greatest strengths (concomitantly, weaknesses)? This might also take the form of asking you why you are the best candidate for the position: that is, what is about your credentials and your broader qualifications makes you better than any other candidate who will interview? Be sure to prepare some sort of answer for this question beforehand, choosing something from your past educational, work, or life experience that is truly unique to you—or, be able to show how, in the aggregate, the skills and experiences you have are greater than the sum of their parts. Some specific ideas of how to deal with qualification questions will be addressed later in this guide.

These are just a few of the kind of qualification questions you might be asked to relay during an interview: others might address what you consider to be challenging (again, this speaks to potential gaps in credentials or skills) or press you to justify how your experience and qualifications will impact the company's productivity and bottom line. Many qualification questions veer into experience verification questions, which are discussed in the following chapter.

Chapter 3: Interview Questions:
Experience Verification

These kinds of questions serve to give you the opportunity to evaluate your experience in an objective manner. That is, you aren't being asked, necessarily, to describe the kind of soft skills that you have acquired in your educational or professional experience, but rather you are being asked to elaborate on the concrete tasks you executed in the service of a particular position or experience. This type of question will also give you the opportunity to relay what was most significant and most relevant about your previous experience, as well as potentially leading to an opportunity for you to describe your work style and preferences.

Some experience verification questions will simply ask you what particular, concrete tasks did you perform during your past workplace situation. This might be something like "on your resume, you mention that you participated in Project X. What were you responsible for contributing?" This is an example of why it is so important for you to review your resume and have a clear sense of how you might explain each individual job position, task, or other event on it. These questions give you the opportunity to demonstrate that the variety of skills necessary to work on concrete tasks is valuable skills to any position to which you might be applying.

Experience verification questions also give you the opportunity to talk about past accomplishments, whether they be in the form of increased production and/or revenue, promotions, awards, or unique opportunities that you were able to take advantage of because of your exceptional previous performance. Oftentimes, an interviewer will simply ask you what your greatest accomplishments at a particular job or other experience might be. One effective way to prepare for an interview, in general, would be to keep a copy of your resume, wherein you take notes about particular talking points for each element of the resume: you may not necessarily have the space to list every accomplishment from every position, of course, but if you jot down notes about interesting accomplishments, the interview gives you the space during which to talk about a wider variety of successes than your resume can reveal. For example, if you worked on a particular project that received a significant amount of external attention and you were asked to speak to the media about it, this is an accomplishment that may not merit being listed on your resume but is certainly legitimate and strong enough to discuss in an interview. It reveals not only your expertise and dedication to a particular project, but also your effective communication skills and flexibility to perform duties beyond the specific tasks required for production.

Another kind of experience verification question will ask how you handle difficult situations, in particular how you previously handled conflict resolution issues. Conflict resolution is one of those crucial soft skills that employers are looking for, especially in industries that prize teamwork and cross-departmental cooperation. Demonstrating that you have the ability to work with a diverse group of people, with varied skillsets and personality attributes, reveals that you are a valuable asset beyond the actual hard skills that you have been educated or trained to perform. Conflict resolution questions ask that you show a variety of attributes that allow you to resolve issues as they arise, including mediation, empathy, facilitation, creative problem-solving, and accountability. There are even entire positions within organizations that are dedicated to conflict resolution capabilities, but this is a valuable skill for any employee. Be sure to identify, prior to the interview, a particular instance at a specific job wherein you were called upon—or, better yet, simply took up the responsibility without being expressly asked—to resolve conflicts between staff members or between co-workers and management.

Showing that you can handle conflict with poise and thoughtfulness reveals a lot about your worth as an employee overall. It also reflects your ability to understand and navigate a complex situation without creating more conflict. Be especially careful not to assign blame to others or to otherwise project negativity; focus on the attributes that you have, as well as the concrete actions you undertook, in order to resolve a difficult matter during a previous work experience.

Experience verification questions also ask you to expand upon and extrapolate about skills gained from particular experience(s) that occur while on the job. That is, while we are all educated or trained to produce particular results with a set of hard skills (technical expertise, mathematical application, standards for analysis, industry norms), we often acquire additional skills via the various experiences that we undergo on the job itself. These kinds of questions ask you to demonstrate that you are a continuous learner, open to new ways of thinking and approaching performance. These kinds of questions might ask about expectations— both the expectations that you had of what your previous position entailed and the expectations that were asked of you and how you fulfilled them (or did not). Basically, this gives you the opportunity either to show how well you handle on-the-job stress and change or to explain why you were only employed for a short time at a particular company (a resume gap). In the first instance, you might tell a story about how you were hired to complete this specific function, say review and update accounting procedures, but as you began to familiarize yourself with the company books, you realized that there were deeper issues that needed to be re-visited. Thus, you became instrumental in a basic restructuring of how disparate teams worked together to meet productivity goals: this shows the interviewer that your experience allowed you to pick up new skills; you should be comfortable sharing that you weren't previously confident in your ability to perform large scale analyses, yet your experience in that particular position imbued you with greater confidence. In the second instance, you might explain how the expectations of a previous position didn't match with the realities of daily experience. For example, you were hired to perform a particular task, such as job training, but ultimately you were asked to intervene in interdepartmental arguments regarding who was responsible for what task; thus, you were thrown into an uncomfortable scenario wherein you had no particular expertise to solve and, therefore, exited the company more quickly than you intended. The expectations that were outlined by the company were violated by actual issues within the company. Either way, these questions reveal that you are quick to learn from experience, as well as resolved to understand your strengths and weaknesses. These kinds of questions veer into the realm of behavioral questions, which will be addressed at greater length in Chapter 5.

Experience verification questions might also be posed in order to help the interviewer see how your past experience links to the current position for which you are interviewing. If you can demonstrate that your skillset and past experience are aligned with the expectations that an employer has for the position, then you are indeed a valuable asset. One way to get at this issue is to discuss past job responsibilities with a keen eye toward how they might translate into the current position. Study your resume for the most appropriate past experience that would be relevant to what you are interviewing for currently, then prepare a clear answer based on a specific set of responsibilities. This will also require you to review the job description carefully, to see how you can connect the dots, as it were. When preparing, think about several different aspects of your previous responsibility: first, understand what you know overall about performing this particular function—what does it require in technical expertise, hard skills, and soft skills—then describe how you specifically applied them to a concrete situation. Second, analyze how effectively you were able to use your skillset to perform tasks that met expectations and demonstrated your ability to handle all job responsibilities. Think about specific skills that were used, then try to make connections between what your past job responsibilities required and how those are suitable for the position at hand. Making those links clear to the interviewer demonstrate clearly how you are the most effective person for the position at hand. Certainly, interviewers will often make these connections for themselves (indeed, there may be aspects of the position that you are not necessarily aware of prior to assuming it), but if you are able to do this yourself, it shows a high level of analytical ability and problem-solving.

Experience verification questions will also likely bring up your experiences with previous management styles and your various responses to them. These kinds of questions are both excellent opportunities for you to demonstrate flexibility and teamwork and potential pitfalls for you to avoid. Some potential examples of these kinds of questions are as follows: "what do you expect from a manager?"; "how are you well suited to company culture?"; and/or "have you ever had difficulty working with a manager/describe a conflict with a supervisor/who was the best boss and who was the worst boss you worked for?" Let's take these one at a time to see what kinds of opportunities and potential pitfalls they present.

If you are asked to describe what you expect from a manager, then this requires that you recall past experiences with managers—the more specific and concrete the better— and how those experiences have shaped your current expectations. Before the interview, be sure to single out at least one previous work experience wherein you can talk about how your experience with a manager, or management in general, has impacted how you think about your role as an employee. On one hand, you can talk about how you learned a great deal about effective communication, delegation of responsibilities, the importance of teamwork, and other such examples of how a strong management style leads to a productive workplace environment. On the other hand, you may have had negative experiences that taught you to be distrustful of management. In the latter case, you must be careful to avoid the temptation to speak negatively of managers and management, in general. Instead, you might relate how you learned that certain styles of management can lead to dysfunction in the workplace so that you now value a style of management that encourages open communication and values each team member.

Basically, as with almost any interview question that you are asked to answer, framing or reframing it in a positive manner is almost always the path to take. The interview shouldn't be a space wherein you air previous grievances or relay bad experiences—this leaves the impression that you might be difficult to work with or, worse, a person with a generally negative attitude overall.

The second question—"how are you well suited to company culture?"—strikes a slightly different note. In this instance, you are essentially being asked to evaluate the company for which you are being interviewed to work as a whole: how are your values and ideas commensurate with those of the company? This question also provides opportunities and poses pitfalls. On the one hand, you can easily talk about how passionate you are about the company mission and how it falls in line with what you've always wanted to accomplish in your career; or how, during your research, you discovered that the management style here values the particular skill set you have to offer; or, how your past experience has led you to value a different kind of company culture that is clearly on display within this current company. You have the opportunity to emphasize particular skills and experience in order to show how you are a good fit for the company. On the other hand, be careful to avoid the pitfalls of overgeneralizing about company culture—don't talk about what you don't know enough about—or to offer critiques about corporate culture in general. Interview questions are designed to reveal something about yourself and your work style and ethic, not to proffer opportunities to expound on your fundamental philosophical beliefs. Answer the question with specific examples of how your abilities and experiences match up to what you have seen of company culture thus far.

The third question invites you to discuss previous experiences with management that may not have been overwhelmingly positive. Conflicts with management (and/or colleagues) are not unusual in the workplace, so you shouldn't feel apprehensive or work to avoid the question altogether; however, as mentioned above, try to reframe the answer to showcase the positive outcomes of such an experience. For example, if you have an experience wherein you had an actual conflict with management but it was resolved in a positive manner, then, by all means, share this specific tale. If you have had an exceptionally bad experience with a particular manager or company culture, then work to reframe the answer: "I've learned from each and every supervisor I've had; from some of them, I've learned how to conduct myself with professionalism and enthusiasm, while from others, I've learned what doesn't work well in professional settings." Essentially, you're revealing that you might have had a negative experience, but that, ultimately, you took away a valuable lesson from it—this is a much more appealing way to explain a previously difficult working relationship with a manager.

As with most interview questions, experience verification questions provide you with ample opportunity to display your best attributes and talents—as long as you carefully consider the links to the current position and avoid the pitfalls of emphasizing the negative.

LEARNING
KNOWLEDGE
EXPERIENCE
SKILLS
ABILITY
COMPETENCE
GROWTH
TRAINING

Chapter 4: Interview Questions:
Opinion Questions

Beyond questions that require you to answer with concrete and verifiable examples, there will be interview questions that allow you to explore and reveal who you are as a person as well as how you behave as an employee. In the following chapter, we will explore how behavior questions work, while in this chapter, we will explore opinion questions. These open-ended questions present some of the greatest opportunities for you to showcase how well you are suited for the position, how ideally you meld with the company culture, and how your soft skills make you a versatile and valuable employee, no matter what the position. These questions have the additional advantage in that they aren't necessarily the kinds of questions for which you have to prepare thoroughly—most of us already know how to express our views on particular topics or how to talk about ourselves—but they do bear considering in that they can sometimes lead either to rambling, unfocused answers or unintentionally unflattering ones.

Some of the most common kinds of opinion questions will ask you to reveal opinions about yourself. In particular, interviewers will often ask candidates to discuss what they think are strengths and what they think are weaknesses in their character attributes or job performance. When this kind of question is asked, first be certain as to what the interviewer is asking you to discuss: are they asking about strengths and/or weaknesses of character, such as empathy or impatience, or are they asking about strengths and/or weaknesses with regard to performance, such as leadership or disorganization? You should review your resume and flag experiences that reveal strengths, as well as those that reveal weaknesses, and be sure to indicate what kind of strength or weakness it is (character or performance). It doesn't always matter what kind of strength or weakness it is, but it is good to have concrete examples of various types prepared.

Also remember that both questions offer you the opportunity to reveal something positive about yourself, in addition to the obstacle of inadvertently showcasing something negative about yourself. If you are asked about your strengths, then you should obviously address particular skills, either hard or soft, that you have demonstrated in specific and concrete ways in the past. It is not enough to say that you have "very effective communication skills"; you need to be able to reveal how you have specifically used those skills in past positions: "I think that one of my greatest strengths is my effective communication skills, which I demonstrated in writing the annual report and providing press releases to the media." Or, "My effective communication skills led to a role within the team as mediator in solving problems and conflicts." With regard to a hard skill, you might show how your facility with programming led to a specific promotion or a coveted position on a high-level team; in this case, describe the specific project and your role in it. Still, displaying one's strengths takes some humility and finesse: if you come across as a braggart—"I was the best salesperson the company had ever seen"—then you are effectively undermining your candidacy.

With regard to the question about personal weaknesses, it offers the same dual potential. If you are asked about your weaknesses, you should be honest and forthright—if you get the position, those weaknesses will be revealed soon enough—but also emphasize how you are working on those weaknesses. Many employers like employees who are honest about their shortcomings—we all have them, after all—because it reveals someone who is both humble and self-aware. Revealing a weakness need not be an exercise is self-immolation, but rather one of a clear-eyed exercise in identifying areas where you are still working to improve.

The caution here is either to downplay the weakness to the point of futility—"I don't have great communication skills, but since I work with numbers in accounting, it doesn't come up very often"—or to end up suggesting that your weaknesses are really the problems of others: "My previous manager didn't understand me very well, so she thought I had poor communication skills." Own up to your weakness, showing that you understand how it can impact your work or productivity, and suggest how you are working to improve it: "I realize that my communication skills haven't been as effective as I would like, because most of my experience has been in working with numbers rather than people, but I have been studying some TED talks online about how important interpersonal skills are." Showing an awareness of your weakness, as well as a willingness to work on it makes you a stronger candidate.

A similar kind of opinion question will ask how you handle success or, conversely, how you handle failure. Again, these kinds of questions ask you to reveal your personal opinion of yourself, and they are similar to the strengths and weaknesses questions in how you might handle them. If you are asked how you handle success, be honest but humble; if you are asked how you handle failure, also be honest but measured. As with the previous example of strengths and weaknesses, you should be armed with specific examples and concrete details to illustrate your opinion: "When I am successful, I often find myself motivated to find new challenges to tackle. After completing X project, I immediately volunteered to work on X innovation." Or, with regard to failure (as with weakness), you want to emphasize the learning aspect of the event: "I was demoted from the position due to my lack of communication with other team members; I realized that I needed more than technical expertise to be successful, so when recruited to work on X project, I began listening more than talking, keeping careful notes and discussing each part of implementation with team members." Any employer wants to see that a candidate is capable of seeing themselves clearly and learning how to grow when necessary.

You might also be asked your opinion on how you handle stress or pressure on the job. This is an opportunity for you to tell a specific story about a particular project or role you experienced in a previous position. What the interviewer ultimately wants to know is if you will be a good fit for the position and how dependable and reliable you are. If the position to which you are applying is a management position or one with multiple responsibilities and a multitude of tasks, then the interviewer will want to know if you can keep up with this without crumbling under the pressure. Provide specific examples of time-sensitive assignments wherein you were able to apply strong organizational skills and additional work effort to meet deadlines, for example, or of projects that required you to learn new skills in order to successfully complete them. It is also appropriate to suggest—if true—how you are able to use additional pressure to work more effectively: stress can be a strong motivator for some people. Remember to review the job description, looking for subtle cues as to what kinds and how many responsibilities you will be expected to take on; this will give you a clue as to how fitting your candidacy is for a particular position.

Another kind of opinion question asks you to evaluate how well you work in teams and/or how self-motivated you are to get things done in a professional and timely manner. As with the above examples, these questions are two sides of the same coin. On the one side, you want to showcase how well you are able to work with others, emphasizing important soft skills such as communication, empathy, and mediation. On the other side, you want to display your ability to get things done without being asked or under constant supervision. Again, make sure that understand the job description and which of these is most important to the employer—they are both important, to be sure, but typically speaking, a position might require more finesse in one than the other. Working in a team environment requires the ability to balance a number of moving parts, both with regard to delegating hard skills and navigating soft skills. If the job to which you are applying requires lots of teamwork, then you likely already have experience in working well with others; find a specific example to relate, as with all questions. Likewise, if you are self-motivated, then find a specific example of how you've applied that skill to your experience; this might be an excellent opportunity for you to talk about your volunteer work or other unpaid experience. Discussing experiences you have had that weren't required or financially rewarded reveals your desire to be productive and/or contribute to your larger community. With regard to specific work experience, you might have an example of how you functioned in a largely unsupervised role: for example, working as teachers or trainers are largely unsupervised on a daily basis, but results can be quantified based on graduation or success rates. This shows that you have strong personal organization skills, as well as a clear ability to meet performance expectations without direct guidance.

Many opinion questions will also lead to a discussion of what you "like" or "dislike" about working styles or job preferences. These open-ended questions can be disconcertingly vague, so be sure that you have prepared a couple of specific examples of experiences in your past positions that were exceptionally positive and fulfilling, as well as examples of what didn't work as well for you. Again, remember to avoid the pitfalls of pointing accusatory fingers at others or dismissing particular ways of working as negative. You are here to present yourself in a positive light, so stay focused—even when asked what you might "dislike." Reflect on how you work best and run with that. Various areas in which you might focus are as follows: you might mention that you work quickly or efficiently with little error; this shows your style emphasizes speed and accuracy. You might talk about how your structure your day, which reveals that you like organization and routine, or that you tackle tough projects first rather than last. You might discuss how much you prefer collaborative projects because you value a diversity of opinion and skill to create innovation. You might talk about how you work best if given a specific goal and deadline, then left to complete it on your own, which reveals strong organizational skills and self-direction. You might discuss that you prefer electronic communication to phone conversation because of its efficiency and precision; you can think through and answer more carefully in a written response than in verbal communication. All of these examples reveal something about your working style and, thus, how well you might fit into this company's culture. As with previous examples, always try to come up with specific examples and concrete descriptions to illuminate how your preferences affect your working style.

Finally, one of the most common—and potentially most dreaded—opinion questions is the alarmingly open-ended "tell me about yourself." This prompt encourages you to reveal something of your personality as well as professional strengths, often used as an icebreaker to allow both interviewer and candidate to settle into the interview. It is also a way in which the interviewer can gauge how quickly you think in a spontaneous atmosphere and allow you to show how comfortable you are in interpersonal communications. While it may not seem that you need to prepare for this question—after all, you know exactly who you are—it is important to anticipate the question and have some sort of prepared response. If you are thrown off by the question and have no particular idea of where you might focus, then you will inevitably get caught up in a rambling and/or irrelevant response that sets a wobbly tone for the rest of the interview. Instead, think about this question beforehand in light of the position to which you are applying, your relevant past experience and personality traits, and the company culture that you have researched. One simple way to prepare this kind of answer is to give a concise sketch of where you are now, personally and professionally, how you got there, and what you hope to accomplish in the future.

Chapter 5: Interview Questions: Behavior Questions

The old saying that past behavior is a predictor of future results applies to job interviews, as well. When an interviewer asks a candidate about how they handled particular situations in the past, it is because they are trying to get a sense of how a candidate will behave in the current job position in the future. Past behavioral responses reveal a lot about how a candidate will respond when on the job in the future. These questions offer a measurable way to determine whether the candidate's attributes are suitable for the job at hand. Like experience and qualification verification questions, these questions call for specific and observable or measurable detail to be most effective in an interview setting.

Oftentimes, behavioral questions will ask for a straightforward example of a time in which you did X. Not only do these kinds of questions give you a chance to highlight the kinds of hard skills you gained from educational or training experiences, but they offer a chance for you to emphasize the kinds of adaptable soft skills that you have used—and, presumably, will continue to use in the future—to handle various professional situations and personal challenges.

Behavioral questions will often be focused on problem-solving skills. Detailing a story in which you successfully confronted and eventually resolved a problem reveals a host of abilities that are applicable in virtually all workplace scenarios. Problem-solving includes a variety of soft skills that are necessary to professional success: the ability to analyze a situation showcases your ability to utilize logic and unbiased observation to generate possible responses to a specific issue. It also reveals your ability to evaluate which response will be most effective before implementing a coherent plan and assessing final results. When asked about how you solved a problem, use this formula to create a story regarding one specific instance at a previous workplace wherein you had to apply these important skills. Outline each element and formulate a concise and coherent answer, from identifying and analyzing the problem to generating and evaluating various responses. No matter what the position, problem-solving skills touch on virtually all of the most logical and significant of the so-called soft skills. This can allow you to prove that you are quick to respond and intelligent in your reaction.

Another kind of behavioral question that you might be asked to answer deals with goals: how do you show that you are goal-oriented; how do you specifically go about reaching goals. In the first case, your past behavior demonstrates that you are interested in and adept at striving towards productivity and success. In the second case, your story should outline specific and concrete steps that you undertook in order to reach the goals. These kinds of questions can take many forms: "give an example of a goal you set and how you achieved it"; "give an example of a goal that you failed to meet and why"; "why are goals important to your ability to perform?" These are just a few examples of how you might be asked to explain behavior that leads to achieving success and cultivating motivation. Prepare at least two examples of goals that you once had and met to varying degrees: you can showcase how you overcame obstacles or adversity to achieve your goals, for one example, or you can detail how you implement plans in a specific way to pave the way for your accomplishments. In any case, be sure to identify a specific goal that led to a concrete result, focusing on the kinds of skills that you needed in order to reach the goal. This might mean hard skills—you had to learn a new computer skill in order to reach the goal you set—or soft skills—you had to learn greater flexibility in order to overcome the obstacles presented before you can reach your goal. Ideally, you will able to detail both kinds of skills in showing that you are motivated by goals and—most importantly—able to demonstrate behavior that allows you to meet them.

Behavioral questions will also often involve a description of how you make decisions. Decision making is a key component of critical thinking overall and reveals an independent, well-informed, and decisive employee. For example, an interviewer might ask you simply how you make decisions in the workplace, and sometimes they will give you a particular scenario to work through. This requires preparation in terms of reviewing the concrete details of how you came to an important decision in a previous professional context. They might also ask if you have ever made a decision that was either unpopular or, ultimately, ineffective: this is another excellent opportunity to reveal that you are adept at adapting, regrouping, and overcoming obstacles. Remember that it is always best to be honest and that revealing a negative experience can actually reveal some of your best qualities, should you frame the response in the right way. An unpopular decision might ultimately have led to a greater good (think about parenting in this context: what is "popular" to the kids might not be what is actually good for them, but in the long run, they understand it was for the best). A decision that proved a mistake is another way for you to show that you can learn from past behavior and modify your responses to be a better, more effective, and more well-rounded employee. Nobody is immune from making mistakes, and decision-making skills are complex skills honed over time; past behavior is both predictive of future results and of flexibility, the ability to learn from stumbles. Good decision-making skills indicate that a candidate is knowledgeable and authoritative.

Behavior questions will also ask you to reveal how you prioritize your work and organize your tasks. Your ability to prioritize says a lot about how valuable you can be as an employee, as well as exposes a lot about your decision-making skills (or, alas, the lack thereof). For example, imagine that you are a lawyer working on a number of cases at one time: how do you prioritize which case demands the most of your time? You could consider the relative fees that the law firm stands to make in each individual case, focusing your time on those cases which will generate the most revenue. Or, you could determine that the cases with the strongest chance of achieving the desired results (a win, a dismissal, a deal, whatever the desired outcome might be) deserve the largest portion of your time. Or, you could decide that the cases that are most deserving of social or financial justice should take up most of your workday, even if they aren't necessarily financially lucrative or boons to the firm's reputation. Or, you could determine that each case deserves an equal amount of time and prioritize each uniformly. None of these approaches is necessarily wrong or right: they simply reveal a mindset and a work style that you will undoubtedly reveal in your answer to your potential employee. As with any answer to any question in an interview, you will want to be honest with yourself and your future employer, but you must understand that if your methods are not compatible with the company culture, then you are probably not the best candidate for the job. Thus, it is worth your while both to do research on the company—is it concerned with statistics and rankings, or is it concerned with outcomes and client satisfaction—and to frame your answers with that in mind. Priorities are strong indicators of employee behavior, in both positive and negative ways. Even if you have the best of intentions in mind, if your priorities do not connect with that of your supervisor or the company, then you are clearly not a good fit for the position. Likewise, if you have a difficult time prioritizing, seeing everything as equal, then you are sometimes unable to discern what is most important in terms of productivity or general results. If an employee feels that interpersonal interactions at work are coequal with time spent on projects, then a company might rightly conclude that their ability to prioritize is not in reasonable proportion. However, if an employee is able to manage a number of tasks with success and on deadline, then it reveals a superior ability to prioritize.

Part of being able to prioritize effectively is in employing effective organizational skills, of course. Thus, behavior questions will often ask you to describe how you structure your day, implement a project, or delegate responsibility. There are some simple ways to respond to questions regarding your organizational skills, such as relaying how you keep track of your work week: using planners, color-coded calendars, reminder alerts, as well as describing your ability to achieve work-life balance are all straightforward if non-specific ways to reveal your organizational abilities. Outlining a story about how some or all of these techniques—or others unique to you—assisted you in completing a project or meeting a deadline is more effective because it shows how your methods influence your behavior. Another way in which an interviewer might get at your style of organization is to ask how you deal with interruptions: your answer will not only show how you effectively organize but it will also demonstrate your flexibility in the demands of a dynamic workplace.

Another behavioral question will deal with how you handle disagreements, whether it be with or among colleagues, supervisors, and/or customers—each scenario requires its own set of skills. Resolving a disagreement with a colleague requires effective communication skills—including listening!—as well as an openness to others' points of view. If you are overly rigid or rule-oriented, then you might not be the best fit for a company that emphasizes teamwork and innovation. If you have been successful at overcoming disagreements with colleagues, then you should tell a story about what led to the disagreement and what skills you employed to resolve it. Remember, though, to keep the story about your positive behavior rather than a colleague's negative behavior—this can unintentionally make you seem like a difficult or imperious employee who demands to get their way. After all, you can't ever know exactly what was in your colleague's heart and mind that initiated the disagreement in the first place; you can only show how you dealt with the situation in a positive light.

Dealing with disagreements with supervisors or other managerial figures requires another set of skills—not entirely distinct from those used to deal with colleagues but certainly more refined. Speaking frankly to supervisors about disagreements is both necessary and risky; most employers value honest opinions from their employees, within reason, and great employers will openly listen to employee concerns. However, there is a significant difference between voicing a disagreement and demanding a concession. That is, dealing with a disagreement with a superior might mean that you speak your mind and, ultimately, accept that your opinion—no matter how right you deem it, or how far-sighted it is—is not taken into consideration. Telling a story like this emphasizes your ability to work with a team, accept authority, and move on without holding a grudge. This is valuable behavior in any employee.

Learning how to deal with disagreements you may have with customers demonstrates yet another set of skills to an interviewer. If you are applying to work in any kind of service job, then you must be prepared to answer a question about how you handle customers—and, oftentimes, that question will ask you to demonstrate how your past behavior was able to resolve that disagreement for the good of the company. Tact and deference are often necessary in these kinds of interactions: the customer may not always be right, as the canard goes, but the company is dependent on the customer and a good employee knows how to resolve disagreements to the satisfaction of all involved. Strong mediation skills and effective communication skills (especially listening!), as well as a flexible and positive attitude, are requirements for any customer service position.

Chapter 6: Interview Questions: Competency and Case Studies

Competency questions follow on behavior questions by asking you to show how your past behavior aligns with your current level of competency for the job. Essentially, competency questions will ask you to provide examples that demonstrate your competency in both hard skills and soft skills; these kinds of questions require specific examples and concrete details—all answers benefit from specificity, but competency questions demand it. Case studies, on the other hand, can constitute a different kind of interview than most of what we've been discussing previously. Most job interviews take the simple form of question and answer between a single candidate and an interviewer or panel of interviewers. However, in an interview devoted to case studies, oftentimes the candidate is given a task to analyze and resolve, or a work to critique, with some additional time to prepare. The purpose of the case study is to showcase the candidate's problem-solving skills in specific and applied ways. Even if you're not participating in a full-blown case study interview, it is helpful to know how these kinds of questions work, as they can still be used within the context of a traditional interview. Both competency and case study questions are concerned with how a candidate applies his or her skills to demonstrate intellectual engagement and analytical problem-solving.

Competency questions, as separate from qualification or behavioral questions, are designed to get at underlying levels of ability: it's not just that you've trained in the past or have educational qualifications for the job; it's that you are able to demonstrate that you have the intellectual competence to perform specific tasks and learn new ones. Thus, competency questions are difficult, both to pose and to answer. For the interviewer, competency questions require that they know a great deal about the position to be filled in addition to what the candidate has to offer; competency questions are asked mostly of high-level applicants. For the candidate, competency questions probe your fundamental intelligence and abilities independent of past successes or achievements.

One of the best ways to think about competency questions is to understand what the core competencies of the position are, what core factors are necessary for any applicant to be able to satisfy the requirements of the job. Another way that some business leaders might put it is to consider the "critical success factors" for the job, or CSF for short. Depending on the position, these CSFs could be baseline intelligence, risk-taking, analytical abilities, strategic planning, tactical skills, overall drive, creativity, ambition, and life balance. The best way to think about competency questions is to think about how to prove—with specific evidence and example—that you have one or more of the aforementioned competencies. For example, if intelligence is a key competency for the job, then you could produce standardized test scores or IQ results. This is an uncommon request, but it is found in jobs that require high levels of education or specialization (think of college professors: they must produce not only proof of degrees—credential verification—but also have passed particular tests and met higher standards for professional inclusion). Sometimes, a competency interview will require you to perform certain tasks to demonstrate competency (to use the professor example again, an applicant may be asked to critique a paper that has been published in their field as a requirement of their hiring). If you are asked to participate in a full competency interview, then there are some specific ways in which you can prepare.

Think about your competencies and write out a summary of what you think they are and how you have been able to demonstrate that you have them. This is a worthwhile exercise even if you have not been called upon to do a full competency interview, as this kind of process will lead to an understanding of your underlying abilities to compete in your filed for any position; these kinds of answers can also be used when responding to behavioral questions, so it is not a waste of time or energy to think about this. You can also consider the ten core critical success factors that most employers are seeking: positive attitude; proficiency in field; oral and written communication skills; basic interpersonal skills; self-confidence and motivation; critical thinking; problem-solving; flexibility; leadership; and teamwork. If you can come up with an example of how you have specifically demonstrated at least half of these, then you are coming into an interview with an advantage over other candidates.

There are some basic pros and cons to competency interviews: on the one hand, they are often considered to be highly objective with a set of scoring standards that rank candidates, thus providing a level playing field. All interviewees are asked the same questions, typically speaking. Competency interviews also ask that candidates expound upon their abilities and their previous achievements at length, which some people find comfortable and advantageous. On the other hand, they can be long and rather grueling, with a standard set of questions often encouraging rote answers. As well, some people freeze up when put on the spot about how to demonstrate competency in a particular area—hence why preparation is so important.

With regard to case study questions and interviews, they are intended to reveal a candidate's basic problem-solving ability within general and particular parameters. These questions will require you to have a breadth and depth of knowledge with regard to your field and, like competency questions, are required in highly specialized, high-level fields and positions. Case questions can ask you to analyze and provide information that allows you to function in your field, from the general (how many power plants run on coal in Europe?) to the specific (estimate the global market for textbooks). As mentioned before, in full-blown case study interviews, you are often given the chance to review materials and prepare further before the interview itself. Depending on the industry and the company, case study interviews may be presented in written format, as well as verbal, and cover a number of topics within the field. The questions, for the most part, will ask you to identify the most important issues in a scenario, employ sound and logical analysis in order to develop an action plan for addressing the problem(s) and then making recommendations.

Oftentimes, an interviewer will deliberately leave out key information from a scenario, effectively testing the candidate's ability to infer whatever other issues may be at stake in the analysis. This allows the candidate to reveal creative thinking and innovative problem solving which may stand out from the other applicants. Potential employers are essentially looking for intelligent candidates with sound logical and analytical abilities who are able to apply abstract ideas to concrete problems.

In fact, it is often the case that case study interviews are less interested in a candidate who derives a "correct" answer (indeed, there may not even be one correct answer) than in a candidate who shows the most potential problem-solving ability in their process. Whatever scenario you are given, the task is to identify the parameters of the problem and the key factors contributing to that problem; once you have accomplished this, then you can drive the narrative of the interview with your own analysis of those parameters and factors and attendant suggestions for solutions.

For example, say you are asked to address declining profits at a particular company. The first task would be to identify the parameters; in this case, let's assume that it's a simple matter of the imbalance between total revenue and total costs—thus, revenue and costs are your defining parameters. Then, you must determine what the key factors are in driving both costs and revenue; for example, the average cost of product sold versus the average volume of product sold, in addition to understanding fixed costs, variable costs, and total costs. Once you've identified these core parameters and factors, then you can provide an analysis of how the interactions between these four—total revenue, total costs, average cost, and average volume—are leading to declining profits. It might be that variable costs are rising or fluctuating without a clear analysis of why; it might be that the average volume of goods sold has fallen due to new competition within the field; it might be that fixed costs of production have risen in contrast to pricing which has remained static. Whatever the case may be, this is your chance to show how you analyze problems and come up with feasible solutions.

Some other examples of case study questions are as follows:

- How would you introduce a new product or service into a foreign market? This would require you to analyze how the product or service performs in the domestic market, as well as the factors that create differences among foreign markets (cultural, financial).

- Company X is struggling to stay viable. Should it be restructured? If so, how? Identify three or four key areas that need to be addressed and provide recommendations that will potentially rescue the failing company. This also assumes that you provide reasonable explanations for your recommendations.

- Develop a new marketing strategy for Company Z, whose products have been falling behind the competition for the past two holiday seasons. Remember to think about pricing, product packaging and placement, as well as other factors that drive sales.

- Case study questions can also deal with how you might restructure a training program or educational curriculum; how you might expand or franchise a successful local business; how you might market a new service in a particular market, and so on.

The best ways to answer case study questions are to remember the following:

- Pay attention to all information gathered before you determine how to respond.

- Be sure to identify key issues and prioritize in a logical fashion before you start proposing solutions.
- Be decisive and concise in your decision making, while being able to expand if necessary.
- If you are presented with a case study to review on the spot, manage your time as efficiently as possible and provide the most appropriate analysis that you can: this is designed to see how you perform under pressure.
- Also be aware that you should identify resource constraints, as well; this shows that you understand the real-time implications of your abstract solutions. It is perfectly fine to suggest an increase in production, but it is even better to note that this would clearly require more personnel and drive up initial costs in additional wages. This shows that you are analyzing multiple factors when implementing strategic plans.
- In many cases, these scenarios will involve a customer base: be sure to include some understanding of customer needs when providing your analysis; again, this is one of those additional factors that will impact the ultimate solution.
- This is an opportunity for you to show that you are a creative thinker and an innovative problem solver:

don't be hesitant to implement novel plans and original ways of thinking or approaching a problem. Do your research on the company to determine how much originality they seem to want and follow that lead.

Competency and case study interviews are among the most complex kind of interview that you can undergo; they are designed to vet the highest level employees who will be instrumental in the development of their field. This is a quick overview of how any candidate for any job can demonstrate the highest competencies and greatest problem-solving skills while competing for a position. Even if you aren't participating in this kind of interview, this guide can help you prepare for any interview in a highly sophisticated way.

team
concept
strategy
quality
reliability
service
performance
experience
ability
goal
professionalism
knowledge
competence
creativity
dynamics
responsibility
flexibility

Chapter 7: Interview Questions: Brainteasers and Other Non-Sequiturs

While the previous chapters dealt with the main types of interview questions common across industries and positions, this chapter deals with the numerous kinds of seemingly random questions you might be asked in an interview. This category of "other" questions represent questions that intend to reveal whether you are quick on your feet, to unearth something interesting about your character, or to probe an aspect otherwise relevant to what a particular employer might be looking for. Some of these kinds of questions are tangentially related to the ones explored in previous chapters. This is a quick overview of the other kinds of questions that often crop up in interview situations.

Brainteaser questions are generally reserved for the last round of interviews, designed to see how quickly you can think and how acute your mental capacities are. There is no real way to prepare for these kinds of questions, other than knowing that they might come up and being sure to get enough rest before the interview so your mind is sharp. Most brainteasers are mathematical or logical puzzles that test your acuity in solving them quickly and accurately.

Some examples of the kinds of brainteasers you may encounter are as follows:

- A common question in a brainteaser scenario is "How many [things or items] are in [designated location]?" These questions might ask you such random facts as how many cattle are located in North America, or how many gas stations are there in Europe. The trick isn't necessarily to get the exact correct answer but to have some idea of the scope of potentially relevant items.

- "How many [things] can fit into [a particular container]?" This kind of question requires spatial ability and might ask anything from how many trees might fit in Yosemite National Park to how many ping pong-sized balls would fit in a jet airliner.

- Brainteasers often pose quick mathematical questions, as well, such as what is the sum of the numbers one through 50, or if I roll two dice, what is the probability that the sum will equal nine.

- A more logically oriented brainteaser might ask you to connect cause and effect, as in the question "Why is [common object] [the way it is]?" For example, you might be asked something like why is a tennis ball fuzzy on the outside, or why are manholes round in shape.

- There are also logic questions that test your flair for detail and description, such as "explain [a concept] to [someone who'd have difficulty understanding concept] for [a particular reason]." For example, you might be asked to explain the color red to a blind person, or describe the internet to someone who'd been in a coma the past thirty years.

- Occasionally, interviews might confront you with a word problem, phrased like a mystery you are supposed to solve. There are several examples of these on the internet, but again, as with most brainteasers, there is no real way to prepare for what it might be.

- Finally, you might be asked to reveal your creative thinking and problem-solving skills in fairly ridiculous scenarios, such as "how would you fight a bear?" or "how would you catch a fly?"

Remember that brainteaser questions aren't common in all interviews; they are reserved, typically speaking, for high level technical or analytical positions, and they are usually not posed until the final round of interviewing. Also understand that the questions are designed to reveal something about how you think, not necessarily testing you on how accurate your answers are. Responding to brainteaser questions is more about knowing what the interviewer wants—what skill or intellectual competency is he trying to elicit from you—and taking your time to construct an answer that shows logical capacities.

In addition to the randomness of brainteaser questions, there are occasions in which interviewers might ask other nonsensical questions—again, the purpose is so that the interviewer can assess some innate skills or character traits, rather than elicit a "correct" answer. And, sometimes, let's face it, interviewers can ask questions that might seem relevant to them but not so much to you, and at times an interviewer can ask random questions just out of personal curiosity. Nonsense questions fall into one of three categories: funny or ridiculous questions that are designed to get you to reveal something about your character; negative questions that can turn into pitfalls quickly without some preparation; and random or personal questions that may or may not be appropriate or relevant to the interview—yet you still should have some plan for how to deal with them. Some examples of questions in each category follow.

- One of the most common nonsense questions posed at interviews is "what kind of animal [or a cartoon character, or superhero, or type of tree] would you most like to be?" Your answer essentially gives you the room to talk about character traits that you do or would like to possess. For example, when asked what cartoon character a candidate was most like, the response was "Thumper from Bambi, because he's always saying stuff he shouldn't. I have a tendency to speak before thinking, which is something I'm aware of and working on." A safer example to a different version of the question might say "I'd be an oak tree, because I am dependable and durable."

- Another nonsense question that is designed to reveal something innate about you is "how would solve X problem if you were from Mars?" This kind of question is trying to get you to think creatively and look at issues from an entirely different point of view—a valuable asset in positions that are looking for innovation.

- A final question that is designed to showcase something of your personality and core traits is "are you a hunter or a gatherer?" While this most likely doesn't have any relevance to the position at hand (unless you happen to be interviewing for an anthropology position), it can actually reveal what kind of employee you might be: a hunter might be a good fit for a competitive job that requires lots of self-direction, or for a job that relies on physical action; a gatherer might be a good fit for a job in data collection, or a job that relies on teamwork and the delegation of responsibilities. Only the interviewer will know for sure what your answer reveals: the best advice here is simply to be honest and to give reasons for your particular response.

- A question in the negative pitfall category might ask you what you dreaded about your previous job: the trick here is that you should almost *never* suggest that you dreaded anything about your job, especially if the position to which you are applying is similar at all. Try to deal with negative questions by putting a positive spin on them: "I don't get terribly excited about the weekly X meeting, because it can grow long and it cuts into time for the work I need to accomplish that day. However, I've learned that listening to my managers and colleagues can often give me valuable insight that I hadn't thought of before." Or, "Because I don't like how long the meetings drag on, I've learned to keep my presentations concise and quick. Now, others are doing the same."

- Another negative question might ask you about a rough patch in your career or a bad experience you've had in another position. Again, use this as an opportunity to talk about your capacity to learn from seemingly negative events: "When the company brought in this new software, I had a difficult time adjusting. However, I learned a lot about how to track down resources and ask for help when necessary." Or, "This job wasn't a good fit for me at that time in my career. I needed further experience to understand how that particular work environment could actually be advantageous."

- A seemingly irrelevant or distracting question that is occasionally asked is "what historical figure would you most like to have dinner with?" This is the kind of question that is reprinted in interviews with famous people all the time as a way of making us feel like we know them better—which is exactly what the question is trying to do. The best way to handle this is to try to think of someone who is famous within your field; this way you can control the narrative, keeping it on track for what you want to talk about.

- Finally, you might get some personal questions that most interviewers would find irrelevant or off limits— but some interviewers ask for reasons of their own. For example, you might be asked such things as "who was your first love?"; "do you plan to get married (or remarried)?"; or "do you want to have children?" All of these questions could reasonably considered biased, and they can all pose pitfalls for how you answer—this is especially true of women (still yet, in some professions, marriage and children will derail the prospects for young females). Always try to answer as generally as possible, or reframe the response to again take charge of the direction of the interview: for example, when describing a first love, describe it as you falling in love with your profession or some particular aspect of your career. When asked about marriage, suggest that if the right person at the right time came along, then potentially you would—vague is best. When asked about children—wholly inappropriate yet it still happens—simply say "I'm not thinking about it at this time." If you are asked about children and you already have them, frame your response in such a way that emphasizes childcare and familial support.

In the grab bag of "other" interview questions that commonly crop up in interviews, perhaps the most frequently asked are questions about the future: "where do you see yourself in five years?" is a standard one, and it poses another possible trap. Because you cannot know what the interviewer is actually wanting to know (it could be they want to groom you for promotion; it could be that they're checking to see if you'll be worth training, if you'll stick around) and you don't know who else might be vying for the job, the safest answer is to suggest that this current position offers everything that you're interested in and you'd be very happy in it. Other questions about your future include "what are your plans for professional development?" and "if you aren't hired here, then what's your next step?" In the first case, beware of revealing too many weaknesses while still being honest and open about further learning. A good idea is to talk about trends within your industry and how you might try to learn more about these; you could also use this as an opportunity to remind the interviewer of your technological savvy and suggest that you hope to become even more proficient in X technology. It doesn't hurt to have a handful of goals ready to discuss, as well. In the second case, this kind of question is more common to internal interviews, wherein you are competing with colleagues for a promotion or a new opening in the department. You should handle the question with care, both emphasizing that you would genuinely love to have this position for these specific reasons and acknowledging that you would support whoever got the position as much as you can. You could also say that, if you didn't get the position, it would offer you the chance to explore educational training or professional development opportunities that would make you a better candidate in the future.

As with all interview questions, remember to think about the interview as your moment to shine: work to control the narrative in how you answer and always try to think in the positive.

Chapter 8: STAR Interview Answers: Situation

Now that we have covered all of the various types of interview questions, we will turn our attention to the most effective ways of answering those questions, along with some general guidelines on interview interactions. One of the most common techniques used in interviewing is the STAR technique, which is an acronym representing Situation, Task, Action, and Result. By analyzing each of these categories in turn, any candidate should be prepared to face nearly any interview scenario and any question asked. In this chapter, we will focus on the **situation**—the fundamentals of the scenario, as well as the details that illuminate your example.

The examples utilized in the following chapters are some of the most basic and most common to interviews of all types. Specify these examples with the concrete details of your own experience.

Behind the Scenes

In order to effectively employ the STAR technique—really, in order to be effective in an interview situation—you must spend some time preparing prior to the interview itself. Now that you've secured the interview and have reviewed your professional etiquette, start thinking about the specific logistics of the interview itself. There are numerous practical and psychological issues that you should anticipate before attending the interview and getting started. First, not only should you arrive on time and looking professional, but you should also anticipate practical preparations. Second, you should review your willingness to take on the job, as well as what that role entails. Third, before you show up for your interview, spend some time thinking about potential questions and practicing your proficient answers. For more detailed information about the best possible planning, see my book *Job Interview Preparation*.

Also be aware that understanding and identifying **situation** applies not only to the answer that you are about to give to an interviewer's specific question, but it also applies to the situation in which you are interviewing. That is, while most of the STAR technique outlines how you can effectively set up answers to particular (mostly behavioral-based) questions, it is also a smart idea to consider the interview situation itself, as the ways in which you answer depend in large part on what your current situation is:

- Is this your first interview for the position, or a second or a third? Each round of interviewing demands its own preparation and protocol. A first interview should review all the basics as outlined in this guide, while a second or third round interview might require more in-depth research on the company and/or position, as well as a more thorough review of your own professional expertise. Be prepared to pass litmus tests—or actual tests—at that stage in the process.

- Are you being interviewed by a personnel manager, your potential direct supervisor, or a departmental committee? Again, considering the situation in which the interview will take place has an impact on how you prepare and what you plan to do during the interview itself. If you are being interviewed by a personnel manager, then you should be prepared to talk a lot about your soft skills, such as effective communication, teamwork, and/or leadership qualities (these are just a few: brush up on all of them, as outlined in my book *Job Interview Preparation*). A personnel manager will be focused on hiring someone who is a good fit for the company and won't necessarily have deep insight into the specific skills or tasks that will be necessary for the job itself. If you are being interviewed by your potential boss, then you should be prepared to answer more questions regarding your experience, qualifications, and competency: a direct supervisor will want to know what specific hard skills you bring to the job and will have more experience in knowing what those skills should be and how valuable your skills are to a larger team. If you are being interviewed by a departmental committee, then you should be prepared for a wide variety of questions, as well as understanding that the more specific and concise your answers are, the better you will position yourself as a candidate; when there are lots of voices in a room wanting to be heard, it takes away the time you have to shine, so make your answers short and powerful.

- Situation, in this context, also applies to your understanding of the practical business of the company for which you're interviewing, as well as the culture it presents. Knowing something about the daily conduct and corporate culture of the company gives you an immeasurable advantage in the interview itself.

- Prior to the interview, you absolutely *must* have some particular stories about past work experience (or volunteer or educational) that will illuminate particular qualities that you bring to the table outside of your technical training or educational qualification. Employers will be looking for some of the following: problem-solving skills, analytical capacity, teamwork orientation, self-direction, leadership, creative thinking, effective communication (written and oral), interpersonal skills, perseverance, organizational and prioritization skills, among others. When reviewing your past history and outlining a story you might tell in the context of a particular question, think of at least one of these qualities to emphasize—you must make the connections between your behavior and one of these soft skills clear.

During the Interview

With regard to the interview itself, the STAR method indicates a path by which you construct your answers to any variety of questions, and the first thing you should do—besides taking a moment to ponder the question—is to lay out the **situation** in your answer. As mentioned above, the STAR technique is primarily focused on the kinds of answers that you would give to behavioral questions (though most questions posed in an interview could readily be behavioral questions). As such, when you are asked a question about past experiences or actions, the first thing to do is to illustrate the situation: essentially, you are describing the situation in which the relevant event was taking place. This context could be anything from working on a team project to dealing with a difficult colleague. **Situation** lays down the groundwork from which you build the edifice of your answer, one story at a time. Beware of providing too much background and instead focus on the most relevant parts of the situation: you want to underscore the complexity or depth of the situation so that your resolution seems that much stronger, but you don't want to dwell on details that have nothing to do with your part in the process (an interviewer doesn't need to know that the client had been with the company for three years, for example, just that a client in good standing had an issue that you were able to resolve). Two or three sentences to set up the **situation** is really all that is needed. Remember, there will be plenty more questions to come. Think back to the "five Ws," as your high school English teacher might have said: what, who, where, when, and why.

Tip to remember: even if an interview question isn't a clear behavioral question, the STAR method can be applied. Character questions (what are your strengths/weaknesses?), experience questions (what were your previous job responsibilities?), and opinion questions (what do you value in a co-worker?) can all be more effectively answered with a story set up in STAR format. It will give you specific details and concrete actions that more precisely reveal your hard and soft skills.

Example 1

Question: How do you handle deadlines? Describe for me a time when you had to work under pressure.

Answer: Typically speaking, I work under deadlines very well. In one particular instance, a member of my team had a family emergency and was unable to be at work during the last crucial phase of implementation (**situation**). As team lead, I immediately reviewed the plan, assigned additional tasks to each person equally, and kept a spreadsheet that everyone could review in real-time to see what was being accomplished on a daily basis. We were able to get the project done in time, as well as assure our colleague that his necessary time away was manageable.

Explication: In the above answer, the candidate is able to describe a specific situation (although it should be even more exact in your example: actual project name/description) and demonstrate qualities of leadership, organization, delegation, and empathy.

Example 2

Question: Tell me about a goal you once considered out of reach. How did you finally accomplish it?

Answer: When I was working as a marketing professional at my previous company, there was a decision to focus all marketing efforts on an aggressive email campaign (**situation**). I was tasked with increasing our email list by at least 50 percent within one quarter—a daunting prospect. So, I began by looking back through our previous blog lists, adding some extra content that incentivized viewers to create email subscriptions. In addition, I worked to create and implement an industry-wide webinar that required an email registration, which led to a large number of interested viewers to grow our email list. Ultimately, I was able to grow our list from 25,000 subscribers to 40,000, which was beyond the original request.

Explication: In the above answer, the candidate uses a specific scenario to reveal excellent creative thinking skills, self-directed initiative, effective communication, as well as demonstrating the hard skills necessary to create content for blogs and webinars.

Example 3

Question: How do you respond when a member of your team isn't really pulling their weight?

Answer: Effective communication is always crucially important in teamwork, and I find that, when employed routinely and thoroughly, situations such as the one you describe are usually avoided. For example, when working on X project as team lead, I was aware that two of the team members also assigned to the project had unresolved issues from past work experiences; their personalities were very different, and while both very skilled, they were often at odds with one another (**situation**). So, I arranged a full team meeting before beginning the project to openly discuss the assignments and allowing members to voice concerns about who worked on what and on what deadline. This both gave everyone an equal voice so everyone felt invested, as well as allowed the two team members to allocate tasks in a way that kept them feeling equally validated—thus, it prevented the past bad feelings from ever coming up.

Explication: In the above answer, the candidate was able to draw on past experience and effective communication skills to reveal a strong sense of foresight and proactive behavior, as well as a sophisticated understanding of team dynamics and a strong work ethic.

275

Chapter 9: STAR Interview Answers: Task

The second part of the STAR interview method is to elaborate on the **task**. After you have described your situation, then you must outline the specific task or tasks that you were either assigned or self-directed to take on. Don't confuse this with the action part of your response: the **task** or tasks are the specific list of responsibilities that you are handed *before* you delve into acting on them. Task is the objective accounting of what you were asked to accomplish; action reveals the ways in which you behaved in resolving each task at hand. Tasks should be identified precisely and concisely when constructing your answers.

Behind the Scenes

As with situation, **task** offers us an opportunity to review the tasks one might undertake prior to the interview, as well as applying the term to your answers during the interview itself. Since tasks specifically refer to practical, objective things that you can do to prepare for any number of events, think about them in terms of interview preparation. The following suggestions are practical tasks you can undertake before you embark upon your interview. For a more detailed overview of how you can best prepare for your interview, see my book *Job Interview Preparation*.

- **Bring your resume and cover letter** with you to the interview. You will want to have a copy for yourself, as well as additional copies for the interviewer or interviewers. This is just in case you need to reference something in the course of the interview, or if additional interviewers end up coming to the session unbeknownst to you. This can also assist in future interviews, so that others who might end up being involved in your hiring have copies of your credentials. Of course, the company can make additional copies, but it looks professional and organized if you happen to have a few extra copies on hand. Also be sure to have a pen or pencil with you, examples of any materials that might be relevant to the position (portfolios, for example), and copies of a printed **list of references** with names, titles, company and contact information. Most often, you don't need to provide this information with your resume, but if you get the interview, make sure to have this ready. Also, as mentioned before, *turn off your cell phone* before you go into the interview. Don't just silence it, turn it completely off.

- **Review your resume, cover letter, and job description** before the interview. While you will have a copy of at least two of those things on hand, you should be prepared enough not to have to reference them frequently or at all. If you're not absolutely clear on your employment history and duties that you have listed on your resume, then it comes across as inept (or even potentially inflated or false). Your cover letter should have included at least one or two more personal statements about your employment history, business ethics, or mission statement: be prepared to elaborate on anything that you have discussed there. As well, review the original job description that you used to respond so that you are clearly able to anticipate how to answer questions that match your experience and skill set to what the company originally advertised.

- **Clean out your purse and/or bag** before you go to the interview. You don't want to waste time or to seem disorganized rooting around through your bag in order to locate any items you may need. Also, think about anything that you might need in the course of an interview for practical use—tissues, hand sanitizer, breath mints, eye drops, or other emergency toiletries—before or during the interview. It is always better to be prepared than not.

- **Use the product or otherwise familiarize yourself with what the company does/makes** prior to the interview. Get as much practical, hands-on experience as you can with what the company does overall, in addition to what you yourself have applied to do specifically. Understanding the product will allow you to be able to take the first steps toward learning how your role can enhance that product's viability or marketability. An interview isn't time for a critique, of course, but it is a time to show that you are aware of the product value and how your skills can contribute.

During the Interview

The **task** portion of your answer details the specific responsibilities you were given in the situation described. These are the tasks that you review before you decide on your course of action, which will be detailed in the following chapter. Tasks allow you to identify concrete details of objectives that will reveal your attendant skill set. You have already relayed the background in the situation part of your answer; now show what particular tasks were your responsibilities in dealing with the situation. As with the situation, listing task should be brief, but it is crucially important that the tasks be concrete and familiar to the interviewer. If you are discussing tasks that a personnel manager might not understand (see previous chapter for advice on how to prepare for different kinds of interviewers), then you aren't really illuminating your skillset. Be aware of your audience before you determine what kind of tasks would best suit an interview question. An interviewer who has deep knowledge of your technical expertise would be better able to relate to highly specialized tasks.

Tip to remember: in preparing for an interview, it is an excellent idea to compile a list of skills to which you can refer. These skills should be both soft skills—attitude, communication, conflict resolution, teamwork, flexibility, leadership, problem-solving—and hard skills, the technical expertise or educational qualifications that you possess. When preparing a STAR answer, refer to your list of skills and be sure that you can relate a particular skill or (better yet) several skills to the tasks you relay in your answer. Being able to show the connection between task designated and skill used to respond is a key component in a strong interview.

Example 1

Question: Give me an example when you faced a complex problem at your previous place of employment. How did you come up with a specific solution?

Answer: I was working in retail as an assistant manager during the holiday season. One of our customers had gone online to purchase a particularly "hot," in-demand item for that season to ensure she had it in time to send it to her nephew in another state. When it was delivered to the store, one of the associates mistakenly put it directly out on the shelf; she knew it was in high demand, and sure enough, it was immediately purchased by someone who walked into the store that afternoon. Of course, as management, my responsibility is to respond to customer needs quickly and with a high level of service (**task**). Once I discovered what happened, I immediately called our other two locations and our main warehouse to see if anyone had another one of these in stock. The warehouse was getting in a new shipment within the week, so I had them directly express mail it to her address with a short apology. She was so impressed that the problem was handled before it was even discovered that she gave our store a five-star review.

Explication: In the above answer, the candidate not only gave a specific and concrete answer to a general question, but was also able to reveal a clear understanding of job responsibilities—reprimanding the employee would not serve her employer's interests as much as resolving a customer concern—and a level of detail that shows self-direction and leadership.

Example 2

Question: Tell me about a time that you had to utilize written communication skills in a work situation. How effectively were you able to get your ideas across to the team?

Answer: While I am an effective communicator in person, I feel that my written communication skills are sometimes lacking, but I have been challenged to overcome that shortfall in my recent past. I was working as a graphic designer in a freelance capacity and was hired to rebuild a web site for a local company (**task**). This local company was a non-profit entity that was governed by a diverse set of entrepreneurs who served on the board. They all had varying ideas of what the site should look like and what content should be preserved or revised. There would have been no possible way for me to please everyone without a clear and agreed-upon plan. So, I drew up a detailed spreadsheet that outlined each page of the site, with synopses of the content for each, and an overview of design elements and other visuals. Because my plan was thorough and easily readable, there was very little dissent to the ideas therein, and the site was completely ahead of schedule to everyone's satisfaction.

Explication: In the above answer, the candidate is able to show how a seeming weakness can be transformed into a strength: perhaps the candidate isn't the most skilled at long forms of written communication, but in breaking it down into manageable parts with a spreadsheet—surely a handy tool for any visual thinker—and effectively communicate her vision to the client. It also shows an understanding of how to work well with others and handle diversity of opinion and style.

Example 3

Question: How do you go about meeting goals that you set for yourself?

Answer: That is an excellent question, and I can give any number of responses. In a general sense, you have to set goals that motivate you in order to have any chance of reaching them. Second, I follow the SMART goal formula, an acronym for Specific, Measurable, Achievable, Relevant, and Time-Bound. As a specific example, I wanted to increase my productivity goals for our new line of merchandise, but a goal to simply "work more" isn't enough. Setting a specific goal to increase output by 25 percent, which has the built-in attribute of being measurable, is a specific and achievable goal (**task**). But for a goal to be truly motivating, you must be able to answer the "whys": why am I doing this? First, because I want to challenge myself to become a better employee; second, I am interested, ultimately, in a promotion—which I finally got. Last, I made sure that the time frame was reasonable, because goals can sometimes become overwhelming if you set unreasonable demands on yourself. So I set myself a target to meet the goal within six months and made an action plan for how to do it. When you set motivating goals with clear outcomes, measurable results, and maintain a strong organizational focus, you are almost always successful.

Explication: In the above answer, the candidate demonstrates a number of attributes: first, she indicates that goal setting—while an abstract concept—should be tied to specific and measurable outcomes, also noting her familiarity with a key concept in business and life success models, the SMART method. In addition, not only did the answer reveal logical thinking and both short-term and long-term analysis, but it demonstrated that the candidate is self-motivated and organized, with a strong work ethic and positive attitude toward providing a more valuable contribution to the company.

Chapter 10: STAR Interview Answers: Action

Now that you've set up the situation in which you had responsibility for certain tasks, you need to explicate the actions that you took in order to achieve results (which will be discussed in the following chapter). This is the ideal moment at which you get to reveal some of the fundamental qualities, as well as particular skill sets, you possess. Revealing what actions you took in a given situation shows what kind of thinker you are, how well you solve problems, as well as demonstrating that you are a creative thinker and, in some cases, a dedicated employee and/or team player. The actions that we take in professional situations depend, in large part, on the soft skills that we have learned—it is quite rare for any problem to be solved or goal to be reached wherein hard skills (technical expertise or educational qualification) were the sole variety of skills used. Even if you are an adept programmer or a qualified, licensed attorney, you are likely not going to be professionally successful without some core values and character traits to guide you. Knowing what action to take (decision making) and assessing results (analysis), sometimes regrouping (flexibility, creativity), are inherently a part of any action that you take.

Behind the Scenes

Action in a pre-interview context reminds you that showing up for the interview requires a great deal of active preparation. This kind of action doesn't necessarily relate to the answer you'll construct for an interview, but it also reveals something about your attributes overall. Aside from the practical considerations of what to bring and what to ask before the interview, you will also need to prepare some information that will undoubtedly come up during the interview—your actions prior to the interview will inevitably impact the relative success of the interview itself. Being ready with these answers helps you to feel calm, confident, and fully prepared even before any questions are asked; past actions pave the way for present and future success.

- **Know the job inside and out** before you arrive. That is, you should understand as fully as possible what the job requirements are for the position. If you have only a short description from the original advertisement, see if you can find out more detailed information from the company web site, social media, or a contact within the company. The more you understand what the ins and outs of the job entails, the better able you are to think about how to match your skillset to those requirements. Also think about why it is that you *want* the job; that is, think about why you are best for the position, of course, but it is advantageous to display some enthusiasm about why it is that you are truly excited about the prospect of working in this particular capacity for this particular company. A little bit of genuine enthusiasm goes a long way.

- **Know your audience** before you come to the interview, if at all possible. Find out who will be interviewing you and do some specific research on them, if available. The more you know about your interviewer(s), the better equipped you will be to anticipate what kinds of questions they will ask and what kind of expertise they are looking for. This information should give your confidence a boost, knowing (at least to a degree) what you are walking into.

- **Ask about the interview**, as different companies will employ different kinds of interviews: it could be a one-on-one interview with a boss or a human resources manager—knowing which it will be should help you know how to prepare. A direct supervisor will likely want to know more specific details on your specific skill set, while a human resources interviewer will likely ask more general questions about your fitness for the company culture and team structure. Other companies will employ committees or teams to interview you, which means that you should be prepared to answer a wide range of questions. Finally, it is completely fair to ask what kinds of questions might be addressed at the interview (see more on that below), so that you can be prepared with some potential answers in advance.

- **Review your skills** and be sure that you know how to elaborate on their applicability to the particular position. Be sure that you can adequately explain how a particular skill—effective communication, for example, or past leadership experience—connects with a specific job requirement. As with resumes and cover letters, throwing out these timeworn phrases is ultimately meaningless if you don't have any idea how they will connect with the real-time, practical demands of the job. For example, you might suggest that your effective communication skills will serve you in leading a team via clear, concise and consistent email threads or will assist you in creating newsletters or memos for the department or will be crucial to your ability to generate efficient reports for management. Each skill that you listed on your resume should be applicable to a particular facet of the position for which you are interviewing. Those practical connections show that your skills have concrete value and make you a more memorable candidate.

During the Interview

When answering behavioral questions during the interview, **action** is where you detail the specific steps you took to reach a goal or solve a problem. This part of your answer is the place to showcase the wide range and depth of your skills, and it requires attention to detail and a concrete sense of how you determined a course of action that led to positive results. The more specifically you can convey exactly what actions you took indicate to the interviewer that you possess higher-level soft skills as well as the hard skills to execute results. You should also consider preparing several examples of specific actions you have taken in a variety of different professional experiences; be sure to use examples that showcase different strengths, rather than repeating the same one or two. Show that your skillset has breadth as well as depth.

Tip to remember: now that you have a written list of skills (see tip in previous chapter), you should start to think of specific examples using concrete detail that show how you have put these skills into action. It is not enough to suggest that you have "effective communication skills"—anyone can claim that—you must come up with actual examples that reveal how your actions put your effective communication skills to work, producing real, desirable results.

Example 1

This first example illuminates the difference between a general answer and a specific STAR answer. You decide which is most effective.

Question: How well do you handle stress on the job? What specific methods do you employ when you are pressured to produce?

Answer 1: We all undergo stressful situations, and I admit that I am not always the best at it. However, because I am aware of this shortcoming, I try to prevent situations from getting stressful at work: I try to organize thoroughly and manage my time with great precision. In addition, I like to keep open communication with everyone else working on a project, so that nothing is left by the wayside or comes up at the final hour to disrupt the smooth process of production and meeting deadlines (**actions**). When stressful situations do arise among team members, I remind myself to listen attentively so I can address concerns immediately.

Answer 2: While I don't always handle stress or pressure very well, I do try to organize my professional life in such a way that I can circumvent most potentially stressful situations. For example, I was working in the training division of the human resources department for some years and was told that the old manual was to be thoroughly revised by the end of fiscal year, about four months away. Knowing that each member of the team had expertise in a couple of different areas, I drew up a chart that assigned everyone to an equal amount of sections they felt comfortable revising. I also devised a clear schedule that was broken down into monthly goals, weekly goals, and even daily tasks to be completed—building in a couple of cushion days in case other responsibilities intruded (**actions**). Therefore, what at first looked to be a high pressure, stress-generating assignment began to look wholly manageable. As the old saying goes, "how do you eat an elephant? One bite at a time." Breaking down tasks into smaller, manageable pieces prevents a big job from becoming a high stakes pressure keg.

Example 2

Question: Tell me about an example of when you failed in your professional life. How did you handle it, and what did you begin to do differently to prevent that in the future?

Answer: Everyone experiences some kind of setback in their careers, though it's always hard to confront this directly. My experience was one that opened my eyes to my true strengths, in the end. I was working a customer service position for a non-profit entity; it had an educational mission attached to its fundraising activities and I was hired to oversee that program. I had worked for non-profits previously and thought that my skills would readily transfer. Indeed, I had no problem with designating a particular curriculum, contacting local schools to see what the kids would be learning at particular times during the school so we had a variety of programs to dovetail with local schools. I was also able to create interactive presentations and activities to go along with this program that I was quite pleased with (**actions**). I was told I could take on an assistant but felt that I could most effectively present the material I had developed. However, whenever it came time for me to lead the groups, to teach the material I had gathered and designed, I was truly terrible! I had never taught before, and I didn't have effective presentation skills—especially for children—and I realized quickly that the organizational and time management skills I had developed in other aspects of my career didn't apply to the realities of presenting and the pressures of thinking on your feet (**secondary actions**). It was clear to my supervisor that, while I was good at planning and designing programs, I wasn't really good at the delivery. An assistant was hired and trained to do this on a part-time basis, so that I could concentrate on the other aspects. It taught me that cultivating effective communication skills requires different talents in different aspects; it also taught me that there is ultimately no shame in asking for help. I was a better team player after that experience.

Explication: In the above answer, the candidate reveals strengths amid her weaknesses—always a smart idea when asking to talk about something negative. She also shows a sense of self-awareness and humility, all the while discussing her motivation and work ethic, as well as highlighting organizational skills and written communication skills. The weakness of presenting is offset by the knowledge that cultivating certain skills doesn't always translate across tasks. Last, the ability to delegate and become more of a team member is crucial to her overcoming that failure.

Example 3

Question: why should we hire you rather than another candidate? What do you have to offer that is different or unique?

Answer: I am certain that all the candidates for this position are highly skilled and qualified, as am I. I believe, though, that I have two attributes to offer that are unique and present me as the best candidate. First, I am extremely passionate about the field of marketing, in which I have extensive experience; however, this would be my first chance to employ those skills in the service of marketing organic products, which I am tremendously excited about. My family and I have been dedicated to environmental causes for years, and the organic aspect of the company appeals to me. As a volunteer for my local farmers market, I assisted farmers and others in spreading the word about their products, monetizing what I felt was a truly valuable product (**actions**). Our market grew by about a third over the five years I spent volunteering to help with advertising and started to draw thousands more customers. I worked to design flyers and posters, fix up a web site, and helped to generate an email newsletter. It was one of my proudest accomplishments.

Explication: the temptation with this kind of question is to simply emphasize what skills you have already demonstrated through your resume, cover letter, or other answers. It often leads to a vague answer about your superior XXX skills, rather than something concrete that the interviewer can verify. In the above answer, however, the candidate speaks to a specific experience that helped him to develop a superior—and ineffable—quality of interpersonal connection. Linking this to a volunteer experience sets the speaker apart even more. It is a concrete, specific, and measurable example of the hard and soft skills that this candidate has to offer.

300

Chapter 11: STAR Interview Answers: Results

The final part of the equation in successfully answering interview questions using the STAR method is to talk about results: now you have the opportunity to show that, no matter the situation and objective set of tasks, you have the ability to take the appropriate actions that directly lead to desirable **results**. This part of your answer—where you can show that your decision-making skills in combination with your training or expertise (hard skills) along with other attributes (soft skills)—is your chance to shine. What you are revealing to the interviewer is that whatever the situation, you will be a valuable employee, an asset to any team or company, and that you are the right choice for this particular position. Thus, you should always think about how the results part of your answer(s) line up with the specific requirements of the job; your actions and the results that you produce from those actions should be relevant to the position for which you are interviewing. If you can, make those links clear and concrete.

Behind the Scenes

When considering **results** as a part of the interview preparation process, you obviously want the best possible outcome—getting offered the job that you want. Part of generating good results is inherent in the process of managing expectations. The more you understand what is being expected, the better able you are to prepare yourself to provide the desired results. Thus, prior to an interview, you should take some time to consider the various expectations that might be harbored on all sides. Then, you can work on preparing specific interview questions that showcase your ability to take appropriate actions in particular scenarios to get the best possible results.

- First of all, **consider the position itself**: what managers will expect depends largely on the nature of the job and the experience and skill set needed to fulfill that job. Thus, if you are looking at an entry-level position, then the expectations for lengthy job experience or leadership roles will be lower. In this case, it is likely that you are just embarking on your career, and so other parts of your resume will be more significant, such as educational accomplishments and other extracurricular achievements. If you are looking for a job in management or a highly technical or specialized field, then you can expect that interviewers will be looking for specific details on your abilities and accomplishments within that particular field. The position for which you are interviewing plays some role itself in understanding the expectations that hiring managers will have of you.

- Following on the above, however, employers looking to hire new workers will be much more interested in how they have **demonstrated effectiveness in past work experience**, rather than in educational achievements—unless you are seeking a truly entry-level position. So, emphasizing your experience, especially with regard to some of the top skills that employers are looking for (see the following chapter for more on that), will be the most significant way to impress upon them that you will be a smart choice.

- Also, remember that you are likely competing with several other candidates for the job: think about **what in your past work experience makes you stand out**. You'll want to be sure to prepare at least a couple of answers that demonstrate your unique abilities and how they are applicable to the current position being offered. Basically, you need to sell yourself as the best applicant for the job.

- Within that set of unique skills that you are presenting, you want to emphasize what managers might call "hard" skills: these are the particular technical skills that are required for the job, whether it be in teaching or tech development. "Soft" skills, such as effective communication and a team-building attitude, should be on display during the interview, as well, of course. But what might set you apart from the other candidates is a surplus of expertise in a particular arena (for a teacher, say, you might have published case studies in your field; for a graphic designer, say, you may have developed new software that enables easier manipulation of features).

During the Interview

The last part of your answer during an interview should focus on the **results** that your previous actions brought about; you want to emphasize the positive aspects of those results, of course, in addition to any innovative impacts that your actions might have had. Certainly, no interview story should end with, "because my ideas were so radical, I was ultimately let go." This is not a story to be told at an interview. You want to highlight the successes you've had in past work experience (or educational, though most employers want to see something directly related to work, even if it's volunteer or internship work). Even if you are talking about a past experience that might have been negative—a time you failed, for example, or a challenge that seemed insurmountable—you should always endeavor to end on the most positive note you can. This might lead to **results** that reveal how much you learned and changed after a negative experience, or how you developed professionally in the face of difficult circumstances. Don't fall into the trap of telling a story that ends flatly, with no positive trajectory out of the negative experience.

Other questions will inherently emphasize the positive, so you should have no trouble iterating **results** that matter: an interviewer doesn't just want to hear about what your responsibilities were or which actions were taken; they want to hear about why those decisions and actions ultimately *mattered*. If these results are measurable, all the better: if your results are quantifiable—sales numbers grew by X percentage, or productivity rose by a factor of X, or customer interest soared by X-fold—then you demonstrate the concrete nature of how you produce positive results out of decisive and skilled actions.

Tip to remember: oftentimes, when an interviewer asks a behavioral question, he or she will not necessarily ask you to recount what the results were. However, this is implicit in the question itself, so be sure to go beyond just recounting the situation encountered and the actions taken; an interviewer will want to know what the results, ultimately, were.

Example 1

Question: describe for me a time when you had to make a difficult decision. How did you decide what to do?

Answer: I have always felt like decisions that you have to make within a team are the hardest decisions to make; this is because there are several competing personalities and sometimes different agendas that make it hard for a consensus to be reached. However, I also feel that, once a team comes to a particular decision, it tends to be an even better decision than if made by an individual, because it contains elements from everyone's expertise. For example, when I was working on Project X, our team had very little in the way of budgetary resources, and our initial meetings quickly devolved into petty squabbling for dribs and drabs of the budget. Realizing that this wasn't going anywhere positive any time soon, I drew up a quick balance sheet, showing how different parts of the budget might create more revenue streams later down the line, thus making the argument to allot resources to this part of the project early which would generate more for the later marketing campaign. The group discussed it and agreed. Project X ended up being completed ahead of schedule and under budget by about 15 percent, once the additional revenue was factored in. Not only was the project a success, but I learned a lot about the dynamics of working in a team (**results**).

Explication: in the above answer, the candidate not only provided a broad overview of decision-making skills needed in particular scenarios, but also gave a specific and concrete example—with quantifiable results—of how he was able to generate thoughtful decisions and work in tandem with a disparate group of people. The candidate showed that he was thinking not only about making decisions that would encourage the group to work toward a common goal, but also about making decisions that positively impact the company's bottom line.

Example 2

Question: How well do you find you fit into company culture? How do you get acclimated to a new environment?

Answer: in my career, I have worked in a variety of companies with a variety of cultures, and this experience has taught me that there are a multitude of paths to success. Having to develop a broad range of skills to fit diverse situations has equipped me with solid strategies for success and made me very adaptable. For example, early in my career I worked for an educational institution wherein the students were the main customers, but the company culture very much favored the role of the educators as arbiters of where the company's time and resources were spent; even though the company required student retention for financial solvency, the culture was dominated by the viewpoint of the educators. This required negotiating very charged relationships between students who felt they weren't getting the best equipment or other resources against educators who felt they were most important to the equation regardless of student wants. I learned how to speak to these two different groups of people and to work with administration on budgetary constraints, which often involved teacher pay versus equipment purchasing, to come to a compromise on how the resources were allotted (**results**). This experience taught me a lot about how to adapt to a culture wherein you are dealing with competing groups with very different points of view. Now, I would say that I am able to carefully consider everybody's perspective before responding.

Explication: in the above answer, the candidate relays not only the general sense of what skills she employs to assimilate, but also gives specifics in terms of an example that led to positive results, *even though the question itself didn't actually ask for the latter information*. Think about how effective the above answer would be if it stopped after the general overview; certainly, it wouldn't make the candidate stand out until the specific example is relayed.

Example 3

Question: Tell me about a time in your previous experience where you were expected to make a strong impression on a potential client. What did you do, and how did it go?

Answer: I had just been promoted to accounts manager for the marketing division of the company, and my boss thought it would be a good challenge for me to start working on a notoriously difficult account—the client wanted to micro-manage every step of every campaign. I was incredibly nervous at taking on this challenge, but I reasoned that I had earned this promotion for my good work in the past, so I went into the initial meeting with that for confidence. I also had reviewed the past notes from other managers about working with the client and decided I would take a slightly different approach: instead of presenting a pitch to him, I would put the ball in his court immediately and listen. When I simply asked him, what are your ideas for this campaign? He looked taken aback and, after a pause, mused that he was actually interested in hearing my ideas. I learned that the client's argumentative style was the result of needing to feel in charge without necessarily being in charge. We quickly outlined a plan for the new campaign with only minor suggestions from him; it was the fastest we were able to put a plan in place for this client, and the sales projections increased by threefold from previous campaigns (**results**).

Explication: in the above answer, the candidate reveals that making an impression could be as simple as approaching a situation from a different point of view. Doing research is always an excellent way to ground yourself in a particular situation before deciding how to approach. The answer also contains verifiable and quantifiable results.

Chapter 12: Job and Interview Preparation: Mistakes to Avoid

If this is your first time preparing for a professional job or undertaking a broad search, then there are some potential pitfalls that you would be wise to avoid. Likewise, if you have been searching for your dream job for a while now and have yet to be successful, you may accidentally be committing some of these potential pitfalls. It is always a smart idea to review some of the "don'ts" when job seeking; these can ultimately be as important as the "dos." Additionally, interviewers themselves make mistakes that can pose red flags for candidates; this will help you to make the best decision you can in seeking out the best fit for you.

- We often forget how **ubiquitous our internet presence is**; if you fail to consider your online footprint when you apply for professional positions or go to interviews, then you may be ignoring the one barrier between you and your ideal job. It is a good idea not only to maintain a polite and non-controversial social media presence (Facebook and Twitter are now regularly reviewed by human resources departments), but also to avoid participating in forums or other internet outlets wherein you openly discuss your political, social, religious, sexual, or other potentially controversial views—especially avoid doing so when using your own name. When employers view these things, they can—rightly or wrongly—have an oversized impact on whether or not you are hired. If you are comfortable compromising your employment opportunities because you possess strong opinions and views that you feel you must express, then certainly it is your prerogative to do so. Just be aware that there are likely consequences.

- Another common misstep for young interviewees is **not to understand when the interview begins**: the interview begins long before you actually sit down across from a manager or committee. It begins when you turn in a resume and cover letter, when you are called for the interview, and when you arrive at the building (or pick up the phone) itself. That is, you are being assessed based on every bit of information—including behavior—that you present. Thus, *always* be polite to anyone who you encounter in the lead up to the interview: receptionists, secretaries, guards, even people in the hallways or elevators. You don't have any idea who is actually involved in the decision-making process—that person you snub in the elevator might just be a colleague or a supervisor. Conduct yourself as if you are in the interview itself at all times.

- **Talking too much** is another potential pitfall about which you should be aware. When asked about yourself, keep the answer short and sweet and, ideally, focused on the position itself. Frame your answer so that it reflects what parts of your personality, skill set, and/or experience are well suited to the job at stake.

- **Don't forget why you are there**: no matter how casual the interviewer may seem or how personal the questions might get, don't make the mistake of thinking that the situation is anything other than a highly professional scenario. Becoming overly comfortable or familiar can ultimately hurt your chances.

- **Always be prepared**: this is why you are reading this guide in the first place. Also check out my other book, *Job Interview Preparation* for more in-depth advice on everything from resumes and cover letters to reducing stress and creating a professional persona.

- **Forgetting or ignoring professional etiquette** can also be an impediment to getting the job. Some advice on how to conduct yourself with the highest professionalism follows:

- Consider your **first impression**; you must not only look the part but also act the part. A first impression can never be retracted, so it is important not to begin an interview on the wrong foot. Be enthusiastic and look happy—rather than apprehensive—to be there. Make eye contact and introduce yourself politely when appropriate, extending a handshake in most cases. When entering the interview space, be sure to accept instructions politely and strike an open—rather than defensive—posture.

- Be sure that the **outfit you've chosen to wear** for the interview is appropriate and professional, but also be aware of how it will appear when you are seated. You want to avoid the proverbial wardrobe malfunction (gaping blouse, popped button, overly hiked pants). Typically, you will be seated for most of the interview, so that's how you should test the comforts and utility of your chosen attire.

- Always **remember to smile** and appear interested in what the interviewer is saying. A smile (or, conversely, a frown) can speak

317

volumes. If you appear smiling and approachable, then you are perceived as a team player with valuable character attributes as well as professional skills to bring to the company. A frown, on the other hand, can fluster or annoy the interviewer; it is difficult to know how to interpret the facial expression. Are you angry, annoyed, bored, frustrated, or otherwise unimpressed? This is not the impression you want to convey. Remind yourself that this experience, while somewhat nerve-racking, should be an amicable way in which to showcase your considerable talents and value. This would bring a smile to anyone's face.

o **Body language**, in general, reveals a lot about a person's feelings and character. Crossing your arms against your chest looks defensive, even hostile, while a lazy slump indicates a lack of interest or disrespect. Keeping your hands folded in your lap throughout the interview can have the effect of implying childlike anxiety. "Man-spreading" can look aggressive or arrogant. Again, maintain eye contact when answering questions, and avoid sweeping hand gestures. You can hold a pen or pencil in your hand if it helps to center you, and this can come in handy should you wish to jot anything down. Basically, your body language should indicate that you are engaged and open, enthusiastic and polite.

- When **greeting others**, be sure that you have a solid handshake, somewhere between limp and crushing. A firm handshake reveals self-confidence and a courteous understanding of overall business etiquette. When meeting someone for the first time, it is considered polite to use an honorific, such as Dr. or Ms. or Mr. If the company for which you are interviewed is owned or operated by foreign nationals, then it would behoove you to do some research into the basic etiquette of the other country. Personal space is defined differently in different cultures, in addition to attitudes about how men and women behave.

- **Addressing someone** by their name is also a powerful piece of business etiquette that you can employ to curry respect. Everyone likes to be noticed and remembered, so try your best to remember and repeat the names of people that you meet. Should you be called in for a further interview, this considerate formality will inevitably be noticed.

o As you are seated for your interview—which you should be invited to do, rather than simply plopping down—place your personal items beside or underneath your chair. For everyone's sanity and to preserve your dignity, **turn off your cell phone** and any other device you may have carried with you. Have your resume and cover letter, along with a notepad or folder for notes, at the ready.

o If for some disastrous reason, your phone should ring during an interview, you will be called upon to do some swift damage control. ***Do not dare look at the phone to check*** (unless you truly have a life-and-death situation on your hands); simply turn it off and apologize to the interviewer. You would have to be an excellent candidate to overcome this most egregious of etiquette breaches. It's better not to take your phone in with you if you have a habit of forgetting to switch it off. And off means *off*, not silent.

o When leaving the interview, be sure to **restate your interest** in the job and your pleasure at having met everyone. Shake hands again and repeat names, when appropriate. Be sure to thank the receptionist who showed you in, if relevant. Basically, just show proper manners on your way out the door.

o After the interview, it is customary to write **a "thank you" note** of some sort to the interviewer or interviewers to acknowledge their time and your opportunity.

Besides your own performance at a job interview, there may be times when the interview itself presents some red flags for a candidate. If you are uncertain about the job prior to the interview, or if you have several choices between jobs that you might take, then the ball is in your court, so to speak. If you have the luxury to be choosy about which position you take, then paying attention to some of the red flags thrown up by interviewers will give you the necessary information to make your final decision.

- If your interviewer doesn't seem to be perfectly clear on what the position entails or what your responsibilities might be, then this is a clear sign that there is some miscommunication or disorganization within the company itself.

- If your research prior to the interview reveals a rosy public image with satisfied employees and customers, but your experience at the company and during the interview seems at odds with that, then perhaps you should reconsider. The public image of a company might not always live up to its actual culture; this is a time for you to use your best judgment about what's in your best interests.

- If your interviewer doesn't seem engaged with your answers or asks only a repetitive set of generic questions, then it is likely the case that either the company has already determined who they will hire (hint: it's not you) or the position is a redundant one, mostly unimportant to the workings of the company. This might indicate that prospects for advancement are low or non-existent.

- If the research you conduct on the company indicates that leadership is in flux, is floundering, or has a high rate of turnover, then this is a clear red flag that something is wrong at the core of the company itself. You don't want to chain yourself to a sinking ship, as it were.

- The same consideration applies to your understanding of the company's mission statement. If their mission seems unclear or contradictory, then that's an indication that the company is in trouble or in a rut.

- If your interviewer seems unprepared, then you should reconsider, as well. Again, this reveals a lack of organization and clarity within the company; or, if the interviewer will be your direct supervisor, it reveals an indication of their habitual work practices—and that might be frustrating for you in the end.

- Finally, if the process of interviewing feels too drawn out—it's taken months to get from resume to interview to follow-up interview—then it's another red flag that indicates disorganization, indecision, or other core problem.

Chapter 13: Sample Q&A: Some Tough Questions and Ready Answers

Throughout this guide, we have reviewed the various types of interview questions, techniques for answering, and looked at various examples of questions and answers. In this final chapter, we will look at what most experts consider to be the toughest interview questions—either because they steer a candidate into negative territory or they run the risk of producing a rambling, pointless answer. We will also take a quick look at some interview questions that cross the line: you should be aware of what you are allowed *not* to answer during an interview, legally and ethically speaking.

Remember, interviewers like to ask tough questions—indeed, it is their job to do so—in order to give you the opportunity to reveal the best parts of yourself. Don't think of these tough questions as deliberate attempts to trip you up, as obstacles; rather, think of them as clear examples of your opportunity to show how professional and poised you are, how logical and/or creative your thought process is, and how you handle pressure in the moment. Take the view that the interview is, truly and ultimately, in *your* control: with proper preparation, you should be ready to tackle even the toughest questions with clear and ready answers.

- Common to most interviews, the question about weakness will inevitably be asked, in some form or another. "What critical feedback do you receive most often?" is just another version of the same kind of question. This kind of question poses a pitfall because it asks you to reveal something negative about yourself, which certainly leaves us feeling vulnerable, especially in an interview situation. It also poses a pitfall in that you might either avoid the question or forget to steer into positive territory. In the first instance, a candidate might respond by suggesting that the critical feedback he's ever received has been inconsequential; this comes across as arrogant and/or lacking in self-awareness. In the second instance, you reveal a flaw without indicating that you are working on it. The best answer acknowledges that you have a weakness—this indicates self-awareness and humility—and reveals specific and concrete actions that you have been taking to improve—focusing and ending on the positive.
- In a similar vein, potential employers will also often ask about an obstacle that you have overcome in the past. This, again, invites the uncomfortable proposition that you reveal something difficult and/or negative from your past. Nevertheless, if you are

prepared with a STAR ready answer, providing details about the situation, tasks, actions, and results that shows how you ultimately overcame said obstacle, then you are actually telling an inspiring story about both your professional abilities and your personal attributes. Telling a story that combines the use of your hard skills and soft skills is the strongest way to approach this kind of question.

- Because stress is a component of every professional experience, employers will often want to test your facility for handling it, so you should expect a question about how you deal with stress or pressure. Again, don't make the mistake of suggesting that you never get stressed out or that you deal with stress just fine. This is clearly skirting the truth, and the employer knows it. Rather, construct a specific example wherein you acknowledge that you felt enormous pressure (of deadline, on your skillset, or other) but took steps to deal with that stress to overcome it. Make sure that you reveal the results (STAR method, again) of your process: showing that even though you almost buckled under stress but ended up figuring out a way to deal with it and overcome it—to positive ends—is a satisfying and inspiring story.

- Another potential pitfalls are questions that ask you to comment about your personal experience with management or colleagues. An interviewer might ask what your worst experience was or to describe a conflict that happened in your previous experience. Certainly, you should approach the question with honesty—but also with a healthy dose of tact. An employer wants to know what kind of person and/or management style you work best with, of course, but he or she doesn't really want to know that about past squabbles or the personal foibles of others. Avoid any personal references, names, or other information that might tip the interviewer off to a particular person about whom you might be discussing. Indeed, it is best not to discuss others when answering the question, in general. Instead, come up with a specific example wherein a negative experience—a clash of personalities, or a conflict of interests—created a temporarily difficult working situation, emphasis on the *temporary*. You want to end the story with how it was resolved in as positive a manner as possible.
- If you are currently employed by another company within the industry, then you will most likely be asked about why you are leaving your current job. This question proffers a possible landmine of inappropriate

responses, just as with the above question. This is not the time to get personal or to use the interview as a chance to complain about another company, boss, or colleague. Instead, it is the opportunity for you to offer your potential employer an honest assessment of what wasn't working for you in your current position that encouraged you to seek a job elsewhere. Tactful honesty is the best policy here, as well. Try to frame your response in the most positive terms available: "I have thoroughly enjoyed my work with X Company, but at this time, professional growth opportunities are few. I wanted to begin thinking about career advancement at this moment in my professional life, so this job offered me the chance to best use my many skills."

- You will also often be asked a question about either why you wish to work for this employer or why this employer should feel compelled to hire you. These are similar questions, and they are tough questions because you don't know who your competition is or what, exactly, management is looking for. In the first instance, the best preparation you can do for your answer is to conduct adequate research into the company overall; the more you know about what the company does and how its culture functions, the better able you are to make a pitch about your enthusiasm and fittingness for the job. In the second instance, you are essentially being asked how your particular skill set matches the position; review the original job description and apply your knowledge gained from researching the company as a whole. Review your list of skills and make a clear link between each skill and a component of the job qualifications or expectations. You might also prepare a specific example, with concrete details, about how a particular experience makes you uniquely suited for the job—this is a way of setting yourself apart from the other candidates.

- Another difficult question you might get is to talk about your greatest regrets and/or your greatest achievements: as with questions about weaknesses and strengths, be sure you have a ready answer prepared that doesn't swing too hard to the negative or dwell too much on the arrogance. Showing an ability to learn from regrets is the best approach in that scenario, while relaying one specific achievement in the context of your professional life is the best way to show success without arrogance. Stick to one example that is specific to one past experience.

- Finally, beware of some questions that skirt the line between what is allowable in an interview scenario:
  - An employer is allowed to ask your address but not whether you rent or own, nor are they allowed to ask with whom you live.
  - An employer is allowed to ask about age only in the context of requirements for the job (such as working as a bartender). Otherwise, they are not allowed to ask what year you were born or when you graduated high school.
  - Beware of probing questions regarding availability, as well: while not always illegal, these kinds of questions can be used to screen for religious affiliation (can you work weekends?) or to discriminate against parents (do you have evening childcare?).
  - Citizenship questions can be asked in certain scenarios, but only in the context of "are you legally permitted to work in the United States?" An employer cannot ask citizenship status, legally speaking.
  - Questions about credit and finances are also not permitted, such as "do you have a bank or savings account?"

- o If asked about a disability, only answer if it is relevant to the position to which you are applying.
- o Basically, know your rights before you enter the interview space to best protect your privacy and candidacy.
- In general, all interview questions can feel like tough questions, and the best way in which you can handle them is through preparation and practice. Answering questions with specific examples, using concrete details, rather than employing vague generalities will enable you to tackle any tough question with aplomb. Your dream job is just a few questions and answers away!

Conclusion

Learning how to anticipate interview questions and formulate strong answers is a particularly important professional skill—perhaps one of the most important in terms of reaching your ultimate goals. A job interview is potentially a life-altering event: you have been searching for your ideal job, amassing skills and experience along the way to help you secure what you need for professional success and personal satisfaction. While an excellent resume and cover letter will enable you to secure a foot in the door, the interview itself also requires a particular set of skills and some significant amount of practice for it to be as successful as possible. Employers often consider the interview a litmus test not only for how an employee will be productive and valuable at specific work-related tasks but also for how an employee will fit in with corporate culture and be a productive team member beyond the technical skills they bring.

As such, you should treat the job interview as a process much like an educational or training opportunity: it requires research and knowledge, experiential training and practice to be good at job interviews. This guide has provided you with a plethora of tools you can utilize in order to become the most attractive candidate out of many. Not only have you reviewed the most common types of interview questions, but you have also learned how to answer these with specificity of detail and confidence of form. From looking and acting professionally to being thoroughly prepared for any style of interview, any kind of question, you know now how to demonstrate that you have both the hard and soft skills that will make you a valuable employee to any industry or company.

Ultimately, the importance of a job interview really cannot be overstated: this simple act is the culmination of your years of hard work, focus, and energy. You may have paid tens of thousands of dollars for a higher education or special training just to get to this point; you may have spent your entire life dreaming of this particular job in this particular field; you may have an inkling that this job might be able to propel you to success and security in ways you have heretofore only dreamed of. The job interview is the gateway to embark on the path to success and satisfaction: now you have the knowledge and ability to make it swing wide open.

Job Interview Preparation

Practical Strategies Guide for What to Do Before the Interview to Get Any Job You Want.

How to Have a Winning Approach to Interview

Introduction

Preparing for a job interview may be one of the most significant activities you may do in your professional life. Successfully securing your dream job is not only a path toward financial stability but also toward personal satisfaction and happiness. We spend inordinate amounts of our time at work, crafting our careers, and building our skills; we should invest that time wisely in the most fulfilling job that we can possibly find.

Getting that dream job takes time, effort, and some specific expertise. This book guides you through the process of preparing for the best job interview of your career: from resumes and cover letters to researching companies and practicing stories, you will learn how to navigate the intricate process of successful job seeking. You will also acquire some techniques to help you reduce stress, look and act professional, demonstrate your top skills, and follow up at the end of the process. At the end of the book, you will find a checklist to guide you through the process from start to finish.

After you are finished reading this guide, you should have everything you need to prepare for the interview of a lifetime. Decide today to quit languishing in an unfulfilling and unrewarding job and start building a successful career for your future happiness and well-being. Preparing for a job interview is like embarking on any other significant project: it takes knowledge, practice, and perseverance to navigate. Here you will find a full road map of how to get from where you are to where you want to be. Embark on your journey without delay!

Chapter 1: The Importance of the Job Interview: An Introduction

The importance of a job interview really cannot be overstated: this simple act is the culmination of your years of hard work, focus, and energy. You may have paid tens of thousands of dollars for higher education or special training just to get to this point; you may have spent your entire life dreaming of this particular job in this particular field; you may have an inkling that this job might be able to propel you to success and security in ways you have only dreamed of. The job interview is one way in which to gain entry into whatever elite group you've always wanted to be a part of.

Job interviews are complex enterprises, as well. You are selling yourself, of course—your set of skills, your personality, your professionalism—but you are also hoping to present your ability to be part of a larger team or company. Indeed, part of the process of interviewing requires understanding subtle and psychological cues. You are not the only person involved, of course, and you need to be able to "read the room," as it were. While there are no specific set of rules for any given situation, as each situation will be markedly different, there are some general ideas about how you can prepare yourself for any eventuality that you might happen upon in an interview.

This is what this guide is for, to help you gain the skills needed to procure the interview, as well as hone the skills necessary to perform at your very best during the interview.

Attending a job interview is a potentially life-changing event, so it should be approached with great deliberation and care—as well as the knowledge that the interview is far more important to you than it is to the interviewer. Having been made aware of that, however, it also behooves you to know something about the interviewer—when possible—and certainly to do research on the company itself. Armed with more information always makes you appear to be a better candidate, well-informed, and eager to join this new group.

Think about what kinds of questions the interviewer may ask and prepare some possible answers to potential questions (for more detailed advice on this kind of preparation, see my book *Job Interview Q&A*). Certainly, you cannot predict every question the interviewer will ask, but you can anticipate some basic ones, based on the job requirements and your own resume.

Be sure to review your resume and cover letter before the interview (and, by all means, do bring these with you for reference, of course). It is likely that the interviewer will ask you specific questions related to one or more of your past experiences. The better you know your own resume, the stronger a candidate you will seem. Also, think about specific experiences in past working relationships that you might mention or highlight in the interview; the resume lists your experience and your accomplishments, but it doesn't give a clear sense of how you interact with superiors or colleagues in a working situation, and it would be prudent of you to have some stories prepared to detail some of those experiences.

You should also be very clear on what the duties and expectations of the position that you are applying for are: what, specifically, does the job require and how best will you be able to fulfill those expectations? A job advertisement will sometimes give you just a few lines of explanation; at other times, it will have a lengthy description. Either way, make it your responsibility, prior to the interview, to find out all you can about the position itself so that you can directly address how your past experiences and present skills can best be suited for said position.

Beyond the position itself, it is always important to understand the broader working culture of the company as a whole. This ensures that you can demonstrate that you are a good fit, not only for the specific job but for the company in general. This includes understanding whether the work environment is collaborative or highly individualized; this difference alone will determine how you will respond to questions asked by the interviewer, as well as whether you are, ultimately, a good fit. Obviously, when you study the company, look into its working practices and traditions. Notice, as well, when you submit your resume or attend your interview, how employees appear to interact and work. This kind of observation can give you a sense of job satisfaction and collegiality in any workplace.

In addition to knowing yourself, your interviewer, the job requirements, and company culture, you should also be prepared to ask or ascertain the potential for growth that is inherent to the position. That is, understanding what is required of the specific position is crucial, but knowing what opportunities might exist beyond it is also a way to impress your interviewer that you have even more to offer. In addition, this information is crucial to your personal decision-making process: depending on your age at the time of the interview, it may be very important that you move beyond whatever position you are applying for at the current time. Indicating that you are prepared to learn more or to take on more at the very beginning gives the impression that you are eager to integrate into the company from the start.

Certainly, it is also the case that you should be prepared to ask about salary and benefits if such things were not made abundantly clear before the interview. This kind of information is obviously important for your own decision-making process, but it is also crucial that you make clear your expectations from the start, as well. When asking about salary and benefits, already have prepared what you will be satisfied to take; that is, don't ask the question without having your own answer ready, as many interviewers will respond by asking you what your expectations are.

Finally, the importance of attitude cannot be overstated. In the end, if you are enthusiastic, prepared, and knowledgeable, this will go a long way towards presenting yourself as an ideal employee. Throughout this guide, you will gain tips on what to do before the interview—building a resume, creating a cover letter, researching the company, outlining your story, and reducing stress—as well as how to develop particular interview skills that will give you that winning approach to interviews for success every time.

Chapter 2: Before the Interview: Building a Resume

Obviously, the first piece of information that you must create before you even attempt getting the job interview is the resume. Building your resume is, really, a two-part process. First, you have to acquire education, experience, and skills that are appropriate to put into a resume; second, you have to understand how to assemble that information in an impressive, professional, and attractive manner. In the first case, think about your experiences and skills in the broadest manner possible. Clearly, educational accomplishments are important, but other activities and experiences can also apply to a variety of job requirements. Especially if you don't have a wide variety of experience yet, think of how even minor things that you have done could be applicable to certain skills attractive to a job market (leadership, independent thinking, and teamwork, for example). In the second case, there are numerous tips and techniques that you can follow in order to build the most impressive, most readable, and most successful resume.

General Resume Tips and Techniques

- First, if the sincerest form of flattery is an imitation, then flatter some successful job seekers out there and review some examples. You need not build your resume completely from scratch; the internet provides a plethora of samples for you to review and to adjust according to your own needs. Be sure to review samples that are relevant to your field, as different fields have different standards. A basic business resume, for example, is typically a short, one-page recitation of education and past experience, along with a skill list, while an academic resume (or curriculum vitae, also known as a CV) can be numerous pages that list publications and/or experiments along with conference participation and administrative roles. Review examples that are the right fit for your chosen field.

- Second, if you are feeling apprehensive about creating your own resume—perhaps this is your very first one—then use a template. Again, the internet is awash with templates (most of them are free) that can help get you started. Do be aware, however, that the template is just the base on which you build:

customize it to fit your specific experience and personal story.

- Third, consider the format of the resume, as well as the field. Resumes can be organized chronologically (this is perhaps most common), listing educational and professional achievements and positions in the order at which they occurred, from most recent on down. However, there are other types of resumes: a functional resume, for instance, lists skills and abilities with relevant examples, rather than a chronological work history; a targeted resume is one that is "targeted" specifically to one particular position so that it lists only skills and work experience relevant to the specific job itself. A combination resume would do some sort of mixture of the aforementioned. The format you choose, ultimately, will be dependent on your experience and skill set. Review various kinds to see what might be best for you—and, again, be sure to customize it.

- Once you begin typing up your resume, consider various practical factors such as font: avoid fancy or funky fonts, as these are both hard to read and annoyingly unprofessional. Choose a basic, clear font such as Times New Roman or Arial that is large enough to read (usually 12-point is standard). Be aware that Times is a serif font—it has the little tail flourishes at the top and bottom of letters—and is sometimes harder to read in electronic formats, while Arial is a sans serif font and maybe more appropriate when uploading materials electronically.

- Still, it is difficult to resist the urge to want to stand out, especially in hotly contested fields. There are ways to do this—and certain fields, such as graphic design or video production, will demand that you add some visuals—but be careful and professional. If you are applying electronically, be aware that anything other than standard fonts and formatting may get lost in translation. But if you are applying with a hard copy, then you can—*with caution*—add a bit of color or iconography to make it stand out.

- Always include contact information, though this no longer means that you need to provide a physical address (with so many workplaces themselves not adhering to one particular physical address and the growth of remote work, this has become moot). Do include a phone number at which you can be reached, of course, as well as an email address—a *professional* address, not butterflykisses22@gmail.com. It's fine to use Gmail, as long as the address is professional; create a new account if you have to. You should also include links to other professional sites at which you are associated, such as LinkedIn or other social media that you utilize for professional purposes.

- Relevant to the above point, you can create your own website for professional purposes: if your resume feels agonizingly short—and most employers prefer shorter resumes—then creating a personal, professional site is one way in which you can tell more of your story before landing the interview itself. Provide a link to this space on your resume, and allow your prospective employer to peruse it at will. This has become ever more important in the "gig" economy.

- Back to the resume itself, be sure to make it as "skimmable" as possible: while we all want to believe that each prospective employer reads our hard-won accomplishments with great care and thoroughness, they probably do not, especially for highly competitive fields. Some ways in which you can make your information easily readable are as follows:
  - use a basic font, as discussed above;
  - don't justify your margins, which creates odd gaps in formatting;
  - keep dates and other numbers aligned to the right;

- use digits when employing numbers (10, rather than ten);
- avoid centering any information;
- use boldface to highlight either the company for whom you worked or your respective roles at previous workplaces, but not both;
- avoid all caps;
- when using bullet points, keep it to two lines or less;
- employ a separate section for skills, so prospective employers can read through quickly;
- and be consistent in formatting throughout your resume, leaving some white space for ease of reading.

- There is no need to include a list of references on your resume itself; if you get the job interview, the interviewer will expect that you have references, and you should be prepared to provide them.
- Finally, if you are truly intimidated by creating a resume yourself, then consult a professional: there are many sites and services available to those just starting out on the job search journey.

Work Experience First

- Always start with the most recent relevant work experience and work your way backward, chronologically. Typically speaking, you should only include the last decade of work experience (up to fifteen years is acceptable) and only work experience that is relevant to the position to which you are currently applying. That said, be sure to use space wisely: you may have done a college internship that is more relevant to the current position under consideration than your previous work experience. Customize thoughtfully.

- If you don't necessarily have a lot—or any!—work experience in the field to which you are applying, you need not give up. This is the occasion to create a functional resume, wherein you list relevant skills and activities you have acquired and experienced that fit with the job. This is also the occasion to write a strong cover letter that will detail why you are, in fact, a good fit for a job in which you have little professional experience (see the following chapter for advice on creating strong cover letters).

- When listing your work experience, you may be tempted to mention every little skill or duty or accomplishment you've accrued, but again be aware of space and relevance. Keep any bullet list of accomplishments to five or less, with only two lines or less per bullet point: you have the interview (and cover letter and personal web site) during which you can elaborate.

- Avoid jargon, even if you are applying for a high-level job in a particular field. Jargon may reveal that you have extensive experience in the industry, but remember that the person who reviews your application may not necessarily be the person who is working in the trenches with you; resumes are often reviewed by managers without direct technical experience or by human resources personnel who are looking for the best general fit.

- While the most effective resumes will showcase your "soft skills"—such as good communication and strong leadership—they will do so in a direct and active manner. That is, don't simply state that you have effective communication skills, formulate a bullet point under a relevant work experience that demonstrates how you employed effective communication skills or strong leadership on the job. Specificity is key, and it allows you to stand out far more than fancy fonts or colorful graphics.

- Also remember that work experience doesn't always have to indicate traditional, paid employment: if you have volunteered for years at a facility or for an organization that has relevance to the job position, then, by all means, consider including this experience in your work history. This is part of what will make you an effective employee and a passionate contributor—in fact, this kind of work often showcases your passion to a greater degree.

- Choose words carefully: first, use keywords effectively; review the job advertisement for "buzzwords" that you might be able to employ, as well as information from the company portfolio that might pique a reviewer's interest. Second, beware of repetition: if each of your bullet points begins with "Responsible for," any reader will quickly grow bored. Third, use words that are specific rather than general: to say you are "detail-oriented" is to say nothing very specific; to say that you initiated a color-coded calendar for a group project that was completed two months ahead of schedule is to reveal something about your work experience that is both meaningful and quantifiable.

Education History Second

- Again, keep the education section of your resume in reverse chronological order, with the most recent

360

first. Also, you should always list your work experience first, unless you have just graduated from college or other educational institution. Work experience will almost always be more relevant to your current job search than your college education.

- While numbers can be important to work experience— showing how long you were employed at a particular job, or revealing a particular salary range—it is less important in an educational experience. When you graduated is not as relevant as the fact that you did graduate, and your GPA is less important than your achievements and honors along the way.

- If you have engaged in any continuing education, whether it be in your field or adjacent to it, then you should include that, as well, as long as it is marginally relevant. It shows not only a broader skillset but also a commitment to lifelong learning and personal growth.

Other Relevant Skills and Awards

- Here is where you can clearly list your particular skills that are relevant to this specific position, such as technical skills and other experiences that have merit. Be sure, when including technical skills, not to list skills that even the most basic employee would be expected to have (like using Microsoft Word or email); this will reveal your technical gaps rather than your savvy.

- In certain cases, you may want to highlight particular skills if you have broader experience with them, such as language skills; this category in itself could include other bullet points, like study abroad or translation work.

- Also consider listing some of your interests here, as well—*if* they are relevant and lacking controversial content. These are where you can show some of your personality but beware of revealing information that could be off-putting to employers.

- Finally, here is where you can show off some of your more impressive accomplishments: list awards of significance and relevance to the position.

Addressing Gaps or Other Red Flags

- In most cases, it is perfectly appropriate to eliminate listing short-term jobs from your resume, though always be honest about whatever questions are asked of you at the interview. Be sure to have a clear response to any questions that may be asked about gaps in employment history.

- If you do have significant gaps in employment history, then there are several ways to handle it, depending on circumstances. First, instead of listing specific start and end dates, simply list years employed (2012-2015, for example). Second, if you have several gaps in your employment history, a succinct explanation for each would be appropriate, such as "company closed" or "relocated for spouse's job" or "laid off because of downsizing." Last, if you have a long gap in your employment history, then this is the time to put a summary at the beginning of your resume, which can serve to explain why you are re-entering the workforce at this particular time.

Finally, be sure to keep a master list of all the jobs for which you have applied, as well as copies of the particular resumes and cover letters that you ultimately send out. Always keep your basic template in place, but save versions of the basic resume that are customized to each particular job search. This is also sound advice for cover letters, as well, which the next chapter addresses specifically.

364

Chapter 3: Before the Interview: Creating a Cover Letter

Along with the resume, the cover letter is the most significant part of the pre-interview process: a cover letter showcases who you are and why you would be the best fit for this particular job. Not every job application requires a cover letter, but most professional level positions do—even if they don't require it, it's often a good idea to prepare one, just in case, as it can often help you organize your thoughts when preparing for an interview. Many people dread writing a cover letter—there are overwhelming numbers of examples online—but it can be both beneficial to you and to your potential employer. In fact, some employers rely on the cover letter more than the resume to decide who to select for the interview process; it is an equally important part of your desire to land that ideal job.

Getting Started: Fundamental Advice

- One of the most fundamental bits of advice that anyone could receive regarding writing cover letters is to craft an individual and specific cover letter for each job application. While this might sound like a lot of work—and it potentially is—it is the only way to ensure that you are perceived as someone who is knowledgeable and passionate about this particular position. Address the cover letter to your interviewer, hiring manager, or potential employer, when possible, and customize the letter to address the requirements requested and the skills you possess that will allow you to thrive in the job. Some research into the company (this is addressed in the following chapter) may also help you in crafting the perfect cover letter for a particular company.

- Having said the above, it is still appropriate to use a template to get started or to recycle a handful of words or phrases for each cover letter. The trick is to avoid sounding generic: like using "To Whom It May Concern" or "I am applying for a position (rather than noting which) at your company"—these are vague and reveal a lack of interest on your part.

- If you don't know the name of the person to whom you should address the letter, then resort to something else more specific than "To Whom It May Concern." For example, you could address the letter to "Department Hiring Manager" or "Executive Search Committee," again specifying which department or position that your search would fall under.

- Remember that first impressions are meaningful, and craft your letter with that in mind. Your opening line should be to the point, of course, but it can also be the place wherein you put a little personality and passion into your desire for the job. Rather than opening your letter with "I am applying for the blank position in this department at your company," try personally stylizing it. For example, "Teaching, for me, resides in the intersection between inspiration and practical application, which is why I was excited to apply for the lead instructor role in your graphic design group." Or, customize it to appeal to the company itself: "I have shopped at the local farmers' market for years, reveling in the products and people, which is why I knew I would be a good fit for a marketing position with your restaurant group." Customize it to the job and your own experience.

Your Cover Letter: Basics and Body

- One of the first mistakes you must avoid when writing a cover letter is rehashing a ground that is already in your resume. The cover letter is the place where you can expand upon the basics of employment position and time period and allow your accomplishments and personality shine. When thinking about how to construct a cover letter that reveals a fuller portrait of you as an employee, ask yourself some pointed questions: choose a particular activity mentioned on your resume, and ask yourself how you approached implementing this task, what skills it called upon; ask yourself what specific details are important to understanding how you accomplished a particular task or landed a specific job; finally, ask yourself what parts of your personality were key in how you landed and handled a specific job and/or task. These kinds of questions not only help you craft a stronger cover letter, but they also prepare you for the interview that will surely come.

- Be sure to focus on the skills and experiences you have that are directly relevant to the position—and to the larger company. Avoid suggesting how wonderful the job would be for *you*—certainly, any hiring manager will be aware of what is at stake for a potential hire—but do mention what you would bring to the company, the department, and/or the group.

- The cover letter is also the place wherein you can make the case that you are the ideal fit for a particular position—even if you don't necessarily have the employment history to back it up. That is, you can really showcase your skillset here, to show your potential employer exactly what it is that you have to offer, even if your resume is either thin or disparate from the exact position you're aiming to get.

- Also be sure to focus your cover letter on what you have done, what skills you do have, rather than apologizing for any gaps you may have. Avoid even the suggestion that this job might seem a far-fetched fit; instead, emphasize what you possess that makes you an ideal fit. Oftentimes, people will start a sentence with "Despite my limited experience . . ." which only highlights the lack rather than emphasizes the qualities you do possess that are in line with what the manager wants. Also, beware of spending too much energy emphasizing educational accomplishments; in most fields, employers are more interested in the work you have done and the skills you have amassed (whether it be through traditional employment or non-traditional activities, such as volunteering) than in how hard you studied.

- When appropriate, utilizing numbers and testimonials can give your cover letter a unique appeal. In the first case, statistics can highlight your efficiency or your tenacity ("I oversaw a 30% increase in sales within the first year on the job"), and in the second case, specific praise from a colleague or manager can be meaningfully applied ("Not only was she equipped to run the department, her organizational skills made her equipped to run a small country," my manager once said).

- Typically, a basic three-to-five paragraph format is what you want to use for your cover letter: an introductory paragraph, a body paragraph or two (this is where the specific details are most usefully applied), and a concise conclusion. However, in doing research on the company or manager, you may find an atmosphere that is more open to innovative styles. Use with caution and finesse, of course, but personal stories, clever anecdotes, stylistic additions can make your letter stand out. The best advice you can follow when writing just about anything: *know your audience*. If you don't know who your audience is— even in a general sense—then you won't be able to employ a tone, style, or detail that is appealing and relevant to him, her or them.

Beyond the Basics: Tone and Style

- In terms of tone, there is a balancing act to strike: on the one hand, you are writing a professional piece for a professional purpose; on the other hand, you are trying to come across as a personable and pleasant person who will fit in with a larger team or company.

Excessive formality makes you seem stiff and distant, while too much conversational personality can appear sloppy or flippant. You want to appear approachable and professional.

- This is also a moment at which the research you've done on the company (see the following chapter for more on that) comes in handy: craft your cover letter using the style and lingo of the company to which you're applying. Read their web site and absorb some of their keywords and phrases—beware of overdoing this, as it can sound sycophantic, but it does show that you would be a good fit.

- Work to sound passionate about the position, but avoid overly enthusiastic screeds. Avoid exclamation points and all caps: these look like you're yelling in print form (you want to come across as a rational and personable team player, not a rabid fanboy or fangirl). Overuse of adverbs can also lead to overkill: "I absolutely couldn't be more excitedly anticipating a call from you."

- Finally, think about the fine line between bragging and celebrating your accomplishments: you should never hold back with false modesty, but you don't want to portray yourself as infallible or arrogant. The more genuine your tone, the better your results.

Final Edits

- Alas, a cover letter should, ultimately, be short and sweet. All of the aforementioned advice should be used to hone a letter that is about 250-300 words, never longer than a page. While employers and managers will want to read your cover letter, they will want to be impressed in three short paragraphs.

- If first impressions are important, last impressions are crucial. You don't want to end your well-crafted cover letter with a banal "I look forward to hearing from you." Instead, "I am truly passionate about your company's mission, and I am excited to bring blank expertise to the job." One pitfall to avoid: never suggest that you yourself will follow up with regard to an interview; it oversteps boundaries of accepted professional behavior.

- Edit carefully, proofread thoroughly: a cover letter with errors is a blatant dead end. Have someone else read it if you fear your writing skills are not quite up to par. Last, this is one of the single most significant pieces of advice that you can get for any piece of writing you are doing: READ IT ALOUD before your final edit and submission. Reading aloud can help you capture the tone (is it too stiff and formal? Too conversational?) and flow (is it too rambling? well organized?), as well as alert you to mistakes (if you're gasping for breath at the end of a sentence, then it probably needs some editing). By the time you are called in for the interview, you should know your cover letter like your own reflection—because, indeed, that's what it is, a reflection of who you are and will be as an ideal employee.

Chapter 4: Before the Interview: Researching the Company

It would seem to go without saying, but many job seekers fail to do diligent research on the company or organization for which they wish to work. This research is crucial, not only in understanding how to present yourself (as well as how to structure your resume and craft your cover letter) but also in gleaning the necessary information about how you might fit into the broader company culture. This kind of research also reveals that you are a passionate candidate who cares about the company to which they are applying, as well as an organized candidate who will take the time to put in the extra effort. Ultimately, though, researching the company provides you with valuable information as to how to approach the job interview and how appropriate a fit you are for this particular company. Start with basic, practical research to find out the basics of the company's purpose and culture, and then move to secondary research to give you a more in-depth understanding of how the business works.

Primary Research

- Obviously, review the company's web site thoroughly. This will reveal many truths about a company, from the most basic information to the mission statement to overarching themes that seem to run throughout the organization. You should know all the basic information about a company, such as its history and size. Be sure to read the "About" page on the web site, as it will give you the bottom line regarding a company, but also pay attention to keywords and phrases that come up throughout the site, which will give you greater insight into the corporate culture and specific goals of this particular organization. In addition, the web site's very structure and organization, as well as the quality of its design and writing, will speak volumes about a company—such as whether clear communication or flashy graphics are more important.

- The same process applies to a company's social media presence: a lot can be inferred about a company based on its presence—or lack thereof—on social media. If there isn't a social media presence, then you can be reasonably confident that the company considers itself traditional or artisanal in some form or fashion. If there is a social media presence, but it is not professionally or consistently run, then you can infer that either the company needs assistance in this area or that its public image is poorly distributed. This is helpful information for you personally, as well as professionally. It would be imprudent to go into an interview with a detailed critique of a company's social media presence, but it might, under cautious circumstances, be a place for you to suggest your worth.

- LinkedIn, of course, is the most prominent social media spot for companies and professionals. Do take a glance at that, as well, and if you know the interviewer's name, also be sure to peruse his or her profile in addition. This can give you valuable insight into their specific role within the company and how you can speak directly to that. It can also help with breaking the ice, as well: perhaps you have something in common with the person (school or colleagues, other activities or interests).

- Glassdoor is another invaluable site, especially with regard to the interview itself. They offer sets of interview questions and responses that you can peruse, as well as providing reviews from former candidates with information about how interviews were conducted or how companies were operated. These reviews may not always be perfectly accurate— disgruntled employees can certainly vent on this site—but it will allow you to form an overall impression of company culture and practices.

- You can also do a quick Google search (Google News is even more pinpointed) to see what is currently going on in the company at large. This is especially valuable if you are applying to a smaller subsidiary or segment of a larger, international company. Basically, you are researching to find out what has been in the news regarding their development and activities in recent months.

- Last, it also makes perfect sense to spend a little time researching the industry as a whole: knowing what the competition is doing and how they operate can offer ideas as to how you might be able to position yourself as the ideal employee with a breadth of industry-wide knowledge. It can also significantly impress an interviewer if you gain some insight into how your company is responding to particular competition and how you see your presence in that initiative.

Secondary Impressions

- Once you've conducted your practical research as suggested above, you can start to spend some time formulating some secondary impressions of the company to give you a sense of how you will fit in and how important this particular job interview is to you. Occasionally, what you might discover in your research will be disconcerting and you may decide to devote more effort to another position or company armed with that knowledge.

- Barring that, be sure that you feel well-informed about the company's strengths. This will be an excellent way to ensure your interviewer that you are enthusiastic about the progress of the company, as well as give you the ability to showcase how your skills dovetail with their strengths.

- Take a minute to discern how financially healthy a company is—especially if you are applying to work at a start-up or other emerging company. This allows you to be a better decision-maker, as well as potentially making you an impressive candidate. Knowing some details about the financial dealings of the company can be an advantage in certain cases.

- Reinvestigate social media sites with a different goal in mind: how does the company interact with the larger community? Updates about goals and progress, welcoming new customers or divisions within the company, reports about upcoming promotions and events: all of these things will give you a stronger sense of how engaged the company is with the local community, with employees, and beyond. This kind of review can also give you insight into how a company responds to complaints or delays or other problems.

- A way to get to know a company in-depth is to seek out someone who works there or once worked there: they will be able to provide direct advice on company culture and goals. Be sure to conduct yourself professionally when undertaking such an attempt—this is for a job interview not for personal gossip—and know who you are talking to. A former employee may not have the most recent, relevant information, and an unhappy employee may not provide the most accurate assessment.

- Do some specific research on the company's history and its top employees, such as the CEO, CFO, and other top management. Name-dropping in an interview can be inappropriate, of course, but you may discover an interesting tidbit that fits perfectly with your own experience. On some occasions, interviewers might expect you to have a working knowledge of a company's founder or historical development. It can't hurt to come prepared.

- At this point in your research, you should have been able to glean some information regarding the company's values and how they align with your own. This becomes important with how you will approach certain topics within the interview or hiring process. For example, the subject of work-life balance is always an important one but a sensitive one that should be handled with care. If you notice that the company's values are skewed toward production and shareholders, then you must be willing and ready to put in a long and devoted work week. If the company is devoted to sustainability, then you should be aware of how you present yourself (plastic straws are probably frowned upon). Basically, when you agree to work at a particular company, you are implicitly agreeing with the company's values; be sure that you feel comfortable with and knowledgeable about these core concerns.

- While you may not be able to bring up everything you discover in an interview, doing company research has the benefit of preparing you for what to expect not only during the interview but also when you are successfully hired. Certainly, be prepared to talk about a company's history, mission, and major players, as well as any major achievements that have recently been made. The more that you can present yourself as an already well-informed employee, the better you demonstrate how well you fit into the company culture and its overarching goals.

385

Chapter 5: Before the Interview: Outlining Your Story

The best interviews are ones that incorporate stories within a clear framework of what you have to offer to the position and to the company. As such, you should always be prepared when an interviewer asks you the simple (but potentially intimidating) question: what did you do when…? Or, how would you approach…? These open-ended questions practically beg you to tell a coherent story, rather than simply drop a set of vague characteristics that you might possess or amorphous hypotheticals that don't reveal anything specific about yourself or your abilities. These open-ended questions will inevitably crop up and being prepared for them requires you to think in advance about how you might present yourself in the story: preparing an outline and underscoring characteristics that reveal your value as an employee is a powerful way to impress an interviewer both with your skills and with your poise.

- These kinds of questions are called behavioral interview questions ("Tell me about a time when you made a mistake"); they are designed to allow you to reveal behavioral characteristics that show strengths and abilities that can be applied to workplace scenarios. (For more on types of interview questions, see my book *Interview Q&A.*) The best way to handle these kinds of questions is to be prepared in advance with at least a couple of stories that you have spent some time outlining. The interviewer wants a specific answer, not a meandering and vague recitation of how your leadership skills helped you out. Additionally, the interviewer is interested in your response to a situation—your behavior, your *actions*—rather than a passive recitation of generalized qualities.

- Your first response should be concise and direct: "One of the most memorable professional mistakes I made was when XXX happened." Thus, you clearly indicate to the interviewer that you understand the question and give them a basis for following your story. Then, fill in the context: briefly indicate the background surrounding the event, what the consequences were, and then give details as to how you specifically handled it—and, ideally, what you learned from it, as well.

- Be sure to explain your role in the process honestly and thoroughly; there is no need to assign or deflect blame. The interviewer is trying to determine how you might respond to a difficult situation, not to assess your perfection or lack thereof. The more honest and genuine you are, the more you reveal the strength of character.

- In addition, be certain that you provide some specific details: what exact steps did you take to remedy the situation, and what particular qualities in you did those actions reveal? The more detailed (though not long-winded) you are about your role, the more you address the specifics of your overall character and qualification for the position.

- Elaborate on the end results and, particularly, be sure to point out what you learned from the particular event. Especially if you are asked to recount a negative event from your professional history, like a mistake, you want to assure the interviewer that, rather than seeing it as a failure, you viewed it as a learning opportunity, one that allowed you to develop certain skills more fully.

- The importance of stories in any setting is that they reveal common ground among people and allow for emotional connection: the more familiar you are with the hero of your story (that would be you) and the motivations for your actions, the more genuine and emotionally personable you come across. For that reason, good storytelling requires some advance preparation and practice.

389

- Before you begin to prepare your story, remember that the most effective stories in an interview setting will have the following qualities: the story should be simple and straightforward; it should be unique to you with an unexpected detail or two; it should be clear and concrete in its details; it should seem credible and genuine (this is *not* the time for fiction!); and it should create some sort of emotional connection.
- Even if you feel skilled at answering questions "off the cuff," as it were, it would benefit you to spend some time with your story before an interview. Create an outline that would serve you for any number of stories:
  - Give your story a name, which serves as an anchor of the overarching topic.
  - Identify the problem or opportunity the story presents.
  - Identify the players within the story. You should be the main character, of course, but clearly note who else was involved and how.
  - Relay the central action of the story: what happened and why.
  - Convey the results of the action: what followed from the central action and what was its impact.

- o Identify what **competencies** this story reveals about its hero (you).
  - o Identify what **characteristics** this story reveals about its hero (you).
  - o Determine what about the story is **unexpected**.

- **Competencies** are skills that you possess that are valuable to the interviewer and employer. The most common competencies identified by prospective employers are that of leadership, problem solving, teamwork, management or organization, communication, and customer-focused. Highlight one or more of these skills within the context of your story.

- **Characteristics** are traits that you possess that are valuable to the interviewer and employer. The most common character traits identified by employers are honesty, passion, confidence, motivation, reliability, and efficiency. Highlight one or more of these skills within the context of your story.

- The **unexpected** may be one of the hardest things to discover within your story, but it important to create some interest in the listener, especially considering that he or she has likely listened to more than one interview during the course of a day or a week; you want to stand out somehow. You can find unexpectedness in several places: the action itself could arise from something that is unusual or unanticipated; the characters involved could be unusual (an outsider is somehow involved, or a quirky colleague); the response to the action could be risky or innovative; the result was surprisingly efficient or positive; or, the original approach was scrapped in favor of something new and daring. Finding the unexpected creates greater interest in your story—a hook, as it were.

- Consider using STAR guidelines to help you outline your story: Situation, Task, Action, and Result. This will keep you on track and focused on the importance of the story as a whole.

- Even with all this preparation, you don't want to sound too rehearsed. First, you cannot anticipate the specific question that an interviewer might ask that would prompt a story, and if you answer with a canned response that doesn't quite fit the question, this is awkward and can seem disingenuous. This is why having two or three various stories that could be used to answer a variety of behavioral questions is most effective. Make sure you know the details and keep your story focused: practice so much that, instead of sounding rote, it rolls off the tongue like a spur-of-the-moment response. Don't write the story itself out and memorize a script; instead, memorize the outline and follow it to tell a naturally evolving story.

- Some particular kinds of stories that are always good to have ready to relay are as follows:
  - Be prepared to "tell a little about yourself." Most people don't bother with spending any time with that, but it often leads to rambling and incoherent responses. Instead, use some of the ideas above to reveal something relevant about yourself in light of this position: the best idea is to keep it a short one-minute synopsis of what makes you the ideal candidate for the job.
  - As in the example above, being asked to tell about the time you made a mistake is a classic interview question and can reveal a lot about you as a candidate. Even a disastrous story wherein you learned a valuable lesson can showcase your tenacity, determination, and flexibility—as well as creative thinking and problem solving.
  - Prepare a story about teamwork: showcasing your ability to work with others in positive and productive ways is key in many, if not most,

work situations. Support and teamwork are just as important, if not more so than leadership and individual initiative.

o Talk about a particular challenge you have faced in your professional life (or personal, if it can be made relevant) and how you confronted it and dealt with it. Overcoming obstacles is one of the core actions that reveal our deepest personality characteristics; additionally, these stories also offer a chance to make a lasting emotional connection with the listener.

o You might also relate a story about a time that you showed impressive leadership skills. Even if you are just now embarking on your career, you should be able to come up with a story wherein you took the lead in creating something meaningful or fixing a problem.

o Problem-solving also gives you an opportunity to reveal your professional and personal qualities. Tell a story about a time you resolved a complex problem and what skills you used in order to do so.

o There is also room in storytelling to reveal something more personal about yourself, especially in today's marketplace and within certain industries. "Tell me what you are passionate about" is a more common prompt than not in interview settings today. Find a way to tell a story about your passions and dearest interests that apply to the position for which you are interviewing.

o Finally, there are occasionally appropriate moments during which you can tell a story about what you do for fun, or for a hobby—things that are important to you personally. The purpose of telling such stories—and of the interviewer asking more personal questions—is to reveal particular traits that highlight who you are. For example, if you enjoy gardening, you could tell a story about the challenges and joys of overcoming weather and pests to harvesting some homegrown food for your family. This kind of story says a lot about perseverance.

Telling stories about our experiences and ourselves is a way to humanize a sometimes sterile interview setting. Storytelling creates emotional connections and reveals more about you than the bullet points on your resume. Make these stories count by thinking them through and organizing them prior to your interview. If they are genuine, unexpected, and thoughtful, they will invariably become some of the most memorable things about you.

397

Chapter 6: Before the Interview: Reducing Stress

We all experience stress in our daily lives, being pulled from one task to the other and trying to balance work with family, what we have to do with what we'd like to do. Add to that the stress of trying to find a new job, and you have some significant issues weighing on your mind and body. Now that you've completed a successful and attractive resume, written a thoughtful and creative cover letter, done your company research and outlined your stories, it's time for the interview. The problem now is: how do you relax and get enough sleep to be fresh and alert for the interview? This chapter focuses on reducing stress, both in a general way— these tips and techniques can be used for any kind of stress you might face (such as starting that new job once you've aced the interview!)—and in a specific way, with advice on how to calm your nerves before and during the interview itself.

General Tips and Techniques for Reducing Stress

- One of the best ways that you can reduce stress in your life in a regular and reliable way is to **exercise**. This is a habit that contributes to your overall health and well-being, as well as having the additional effect of aiding in sleep and boosting confidence. People who exercise regularly experience stress to a lesser degree, because it reduces stress hormones while promoting sleep and a greater sense of self-worth. Any kind of regular exercise, from light, to moderate to vigorous, will help to reduce your overall levels of stress.

- There are also various **supplements** available out there that will assist the mind and body in coping with stress. These natural substances can calm anxiety, increase serotonin levels, and promote relaxation: some to try are lemon balm, valerian, and kava kava which all are said to reduce anxiety and lower stress. Green tea is also a readily available substance that contains healthy antioxidants, as well as providing a serotonin boost.

- Practicing **meditation** is another way in which you can reduce stress. This can take many forms, such as guided meditation (these can be found online and in local classes) or focused meditation. For the particular stress associated with a job interview, you can practice positive visualization, envisioning your successful performance and future at your new job. An offshoot of meditation, the vogue for practicing **mindfulness**—being present in your daily life, rather than being stuck in the pattern of guilt and worry—is another excellent way in which to alleviate stress.

- Another way to relax that has grown in popularity over the last few decades is the practice of **yoga**. Yoga has the benefits of exercise and meditation rolled into it, depending on the style practiced. You are able to connect your mind with your body while learning to breathe in a deliberate, relaxing manner. Yoga is a helpful assistant for any number of ills, as it can be practiced by anyone regardless of their fitness level or age, and it can be particularly good for those who have limited mobility.

- Some ways in which to facilitate meditation are to burn **candles or incense**. There are numerous aromatherapy scents that are specifically designed to create relaxation and/or focus. **Essential oils** are another way to add aromatherapy to your de-stressing routine. Some of the most popular scents for relaxation are lavender and sandalwood.

- In some cases, avoiding certain substances is beneficial for reducing stress, such as caffeinated beverages. **Reducing caffeine intake** can calm nerves and help sleep, especially if you avoid caffeine later in the day or evening. Beware of sugar, as well, as it can cause the same amped-up, jittery feeling.

- Another way to de-stress, especially in a specifically tense situation, is to **keep a journal**. This is a way for you to let go of thoughts and feelings that are interfering with your ability to calm down and relax. Using your journal prior to a stressful job interview is an excellent way to let go of any negative feelings and anxiety that you have, as well as to imagine your way to success: write down all the negatives first—be honest and thorough—and acknowledge them, then write down everything that you plan to do to make the interview a success, as well as how getting this job will improve your life. Mark through the negative and circle the positive, focusing your energy on what you can do to make the interview—and the job—a resounding success.

- For a super quick stress reliever, such as right before you go into the interview, chew a stick of gum or munch on a mint or two. The act of chewing actually releases the tension in your jaw muscles, which helps you to relax all over. It has the added bonus of giving you nice fresh breath.

- Another way in which people can alleviate the stressful times in life is to cultivate a strong **support system**. Spend time with your family and/or your friends; surround yourself with positive people who are supportive of your goals and dreams. Having some positive reinforcement during the stressful process of job seeking is invaluable as a way in which to maintain a healthy attitude and keep your stress levels to a minimum.

- During the quality time that you spend with friends and family, be sure to spend some of it **laughing**. Watch a comedy special, tell jokes or old stories, play fun games: the act of laughing is a natural way to alleviate physical and mental stress. There's nothing quite like a good, deep belly laugh to help your anxieties melt away.

- There is, of course, something infinitely comforting about **being with loved ones**, especially a significant other: cuddling and engaging in physical affection of any type is an extraordinarily effective stress reliever. Even just a big hug can reduce cortisol levels and lessen stress.

- Don't forget about **pets**. Playing with your dog or cat (or turtle or rabbit, and so on) is an excellent way to take your mind off of stressful things. The actual act of petting an animal has shown to release happy brain chemicals and to slow rapid heart rates. Pets are very good for our overall health—usually!

- A crucial lesson to learn, especially during highly stressful times in your life, is how to **say no**. Essentially, there are certain kinds of stress in our lives that we cannot avoid—work, family, external factors that we cannot control—and will always be there. But you can control certain aspects of your life, and learning how not to overextend your commitments to others is one way of regaining your focus and spending your time in some much-needed self-care. Be sure to scale back on social and other commitments before your job interview; don't isolate yourself, of course—you need your support system!—but be sure you give yourself enough time for planning, preparation, exercise, and sleep.

- Whenever our lives get very stressful, we often cope by avoiding unpleasant tasks, but the **habit of procrastination** only makes things worse. Letting the mail pile up or leaving the bills unpaid is ultimately far more stressful down the road. Don't avoid keeping up with your current job while you search for your new one: it's tempting to let things slide at work when you are actively seeking something new and better; however, keep in mind that there are no guarantees that the new job will immediately come your way. It's best not to burn bridges, as they say, either. You might need recommendations in the future.

- **Music** is another method by which we can reduce our stress levels. Soothing, calming, quiet music can allow our mind to let go of its swirling thoughts as we relax into the rhythm. This is also, for some people, an effective sleep aid. In that instance, repetitive sounds (as in a sleep machine or white noise machine) are most helpful.

- Last, **take a deep breath or two**. Deep breathing physically relaxes the body and soothes the mind. You literally slow down your central nervous system in this process, slowing your heart rate and calming your mind. This practice can also help you get to sleep at night. And certainly, taking a few deep breaths before you walk into a job interview will keep you calm and focused.

Specific Skills for Coping with Interview Stress

- It is never easy to put yourself out there for someone else to judge—especially in the context of what could be a life-altering job offer. The stress and anxiety that you feel before a job interview are perfectly natural; to acknowledge your nerves is to give you some control over how you respond. Some people even become so nervous that they are worried they might sabotage their own interview. The first step toward overcoming these kinds of nerves is to acknowledge your anxiety and to remind yourself that it is normal. Remind yourself that being somewhat nervous can also enhance performance, keeping you alert and ready for whatever question comes your way. Accept that a little bit of nervousness is just fine.

- In order to overcome overwhelming feelings of stress before an interview, there are some exercises you can do to relax prior to the interview. For one, instead of just practicing your story or going over your resume, you can actually visualize the interview in your mind: conduct a **mental dress rehearsal** of how it will go, envisioning the most positive and powerful performance that you can give. Practicing this mental model will reassure you that you are capable of confronting anything that might come up. Boost your confidence by imagining the best possible outcome.

- Another way to prepare for an interview is to enlist **motivational tools**. You can create a playlist of motivational music to listen to while getting ready in the morning or working out at the gym. Or, you can find some motivational speakers (TED talks are an excellent resource) who will give you handy tips and tools for handling stress and anxiety. Also remember to look towards your greatest motivators: your support system of friends, family, and others who will motivate you to stay calm and focused.

- Give yourself a nice, long **pep talk**. Remind yourself that you have the skills, the ability, and the determination to get through this interview with grace and success. After all, you already were able to secure the interview; this means that the prospective employer already found lots to value in you, so remind yourself of everything that you bring to the table. The company would be fortunate to have you.

- **Watch** humorous and meaningless videos before the interview to calm and soothe your mind. Laughter releases stress, for one, and letting your mind occupy itself with something random shouldn't hurt at all if you are prepared and ready to go. In fact, it might sharpen your performance to allow your brain to relax a bit before the interview.

- **Exaggerate** your fears then dismiss them. Go over the worst possible scenarios you can think of, then assure yourself that these will likely never even come close to happening. This is an excellent mechanism by which we learn how to confront our greatest fears, and in confronting them, let go of them. It is highly improbable that you will throw up or faint in an interview: imagining that, then laughing at your exaggeration is one way to soothe your greatest (and surely exaggerated) fears.

- A lot of people's greatest fear is that they will **say the wrong thing**. To avoid this pitfall, remind yourself that this is actually quite a simple stressor to overcome. Keep it simple: avoid profanity or offensive language and just be yourself. That's really all the advice you need to conquer that particular fear.

- While in the interview, if you need a moment to **compose yourself**, then take it. Ask the interviewer to repeat a question, or rephrase the question back to him or her to give you a chance to think about it before answering; take a sip of water; check in with the interviewer that you've fully answered a given question. There's nothing wrong with allowing yourself a moment of time to think. It's perfectly acceptable to say, "That is a really good question. Let me think about that for a moment."

- Remember, as well, that the interviewer himself or herself is also in a stressful situation: you are not alone. It is difficult to conduct an interview with a group of people you don't know in order to choose for a competitive position. Recognizing that you aren't the only one in the room who may harbor some anxiety can be something of a relief.

- Remind yourself that, ultimately, **you are in control** to a large degree. The interviewer only has a set of questions, while you are in control of the answers. This is *your* job interview; take ownership of it.

- If you tend to overheat or sweat when you get really nervous, then make sure you prepare for that, as well. Wear the most comfortable professional clothes you can find, and don't worry if your short sleeves seem out of place for the time of year. It's better to be as comfortable as possible. Looking professional is important, but not at the cost of feeling faint.

- Finally, the most important way that you can overcome stress prior to an interview is to **be prepared**. Have your resume and cover letter with you; practice your stories; look professional; be on time; demonstrate your skills; listen and follow up. Executing your best, most successful interview is only a few steps away. Read on for in-depth advice on the most important skills to cultivate for job interview preparation.

410

Chapter 7: Interview Skill 1: Looking Professional

Certainly, any good job interview begins with an idea first impression, and that first impression is informed by how we look, in particular, how we are dressed and groomed prior to the interview. In recent years, the standards for what constitutes "business" dress have been changed and, for the most part, expanded. Still, a job interview is more than likely more formal than typical employee dress standards (especially when considering the proliferation of "casual Fridays" and tech start-ups jeans and t-shirts). Whatever the company for which you are interviewing, you should follow some basic guidelines to ensure that you are looking professional and making a smart first impression.

General Guidelines for Professional Presentation

- In doing your company research, you should have some broader knowledge of company culture, including how employees are supposed to present themselves in the workplace. Use that knowledge to base your understanding of how to present yourself at an interview: as stated above, an interview is likely a more formal affair than an everyday work look, but it gives you a starting point. Be sure to peruse any company photos, especially on social media, to get an idea of how employees dress when they are representing the company.

- While you are trying to look your best—professional and poised—you should also take into consideration your comfort level. That is, don't wear something that is too tight, too bulky, or too warm to an interview. The more comfortable you are in your professional attire, the more confidence you project. Be sure to take the seasons into the occasion, and wear layers if you tend to get warm during an interview; you can take off a jacket should you need to, if you are wearing a nice dress shirt or blouse underneath.

- Avoid wearing anything that is revealing, such as a sundress or low-cut blouse. This guideline doesn't at first appear to relate to men, but a vee-necked shirt or lack of socks might fall along these lines for men. The idea is not to look like you're going out with friends, but you are representing yourself professionally for a company.

- Be certain that your clothes are recently cleaned, especially if you plan to wear a suit or other truly formal attire, and check for stains, tears, or other signs of distress. If you do not have an appropriate outfit for an interview and lack the financial ability to purchase one quickly, there are many resources in communities, like Dress for Success, that will help you find something appropriate at a reasonable price—or for free.

- Lay or set out your clothes the night before the interview. This ensures that you make a good inspection of everything (if you have pets, be sure to give yourself a quick roll before you leave the house) and that you don't have any last-minute delays. One of the worst things you can do is to show up late for an interview: give yourself plenty of time to get ready and to get there on time.

- Finally, don't second guess yourself or overthink it. If you feel reasonably comfortable and have chosen a clean, pressed outfit that seems to meet the standards of the company, then you are probably going to be just fine.

Considerations for Men

- In nearly every case of interviewing for a traditional company, a suit is required, regardless of standards for an everyday dress as an employee. Again, do your research, but always err on the side of being conservative when in doubt.

413

- According to most experts, a dark suit with a light-colored shirt is the most standard suit attire. Be sure that you have a matching tie, coordinated socks, and a nice belt, in addition.

- Again, if you do not own a suit, now is the time to invest in one—one that fits and is comfortable, not something that you have leftover from a cousin's wedding ten years ago. If you need assistance financially with acquiring a suit, check into local organizations that help people find employment.

- Beware of loud colors or overbearing ties; certainly, you want to avoid anything that seems overly whimsical or novelty (this is not the time to wear cartoon- or NFL-patterned ties).

- Of course, you want to appear neat and clean, but also be aware to avoid strong colognes or other scents; you do not want to trigger a reaction in an interviewer. Check your nails, too, as your hands will be noticed during an interview, from your handshake to handing out of documents and such.

- Avoid smoking before the interview if at all possible. You don't want to bring in lingering smells of tobacco or other odors that might be unpleasant to an interviewer.

- Groom your hair nicely. Again, the rules for how to wear one's hair have changed dramatically over the last couple of decades, especially for men. Use your best judgment and follow what you see on the company's web site as a guide. An investment banking company will probably want to see short, conservative hair, while a tech start-up will likely not be bothered by longer or different styles.

- If you are called for a second interview, the best rule of thumb is to dress like your potential employer; this could mean being slightly less formal, but not always. At that point, you should have a good feel for the company in order to understand and integrate the culture.

Considerations for Women

- Some of the same rules apply to women: you should probably wear some kind of suit, either with a skirt or pants. When wearing a skirt to an interview, you should always wear some kind of hose rather than presenting bare legs. Typically, you should avoid open-toed shoes or sandals. Again, do your research and peruse pictures of employees on social media. When in doubt, be more conservative than not.

- Remember to make sure that you are comfortable, and practice seeing how you feel when you are sitting down; an ill-fitting jacket has a tendency to gap when you are seated, and a tight waistband on pants or a skirt will cause discomfort. Most stores offer some sort of minor tailoring to have adjustments made to what you might purchase for an interview. If your budget doesn't allow you to purchase something nice for the interview, seek out local organizations that assist people in gaining employment. There are places that will help you find something appropriate, like the Dress for Success program.

- As with the advice for men, wear something that is darker in color, avoiding bright or flashy colors and embellishments, for the most part. A dark suit with a lighter blouse is considered the standard. Never wear low-cut blouses or sheer fabrics of any kind, and make sure the length of your skirt, if wearing one, is appropriate. Conservative interviewers often complain about the length of skirts; too short is inappropriate, while too long isn't professional. Stick to roughly knee-length skirts for interview occasions.

- If you must accessorize, then be judicious: don't cover your hands in rings or wear stacks of bracelets or long, chunky necklaces and earrings. Accessories are your chance to shine, really, if you employ them properly. With a conservative suit, one nice pendant or pair of pretty earrings can really pop and make you stand out.

- The same ideas above also apply to hair and make-up: be relatively conservative. Don't wear heavy eye make-up or drastically dark lipstick; these looks aren't considered wholly professional. With hair, keep it neat and tidy—be yourself, of course—and avoid overly stylized or trendy looks (such as lavender hair or faux beehive dos). Nails should be groomed, but avoid long, overly decorated nails, especially of the trendy press-on type. Not only do these appear flashy and lack professionalism, but they get in the way of your ability to execute daily business tasks.

- When it comes to shoes, avoid the kind of shoe you'd wear out on a weekend. Keep the heel to a minimum, and be sure that the shoes are closed both at the toe and the back. A basic pump style is always available, and these comfortable yet smart shoes will virtually never go out of style. It's a good one-time investment in a neutral color, such as brown or black.

- Match your hose to your skin color, rather than wearing colorful or graphically printed tights.

Remember that the goal is to draw attention to your skills, not your style.

- Obviously, you want to be neat and clean for the interview, and be sure to avoid heavy perfumes or other scents that may be overpowering for others in an interview. Don't smoke right before the interview if you can avoid it as smelling of smoke can be a negative trigger for many.

- As with the advice above for men, the guidelines for what constitutes professional dress have shifted and broadened over the last couple of decades. This is why doing your research into the company is important for you to have a clear sense of what would be the most appropriate attire. Still, it is doubtless best to err on the side of caution rather than flamboyance for an interview.

- If called for a second interview, follow the cues that you picked up while at the first. Dress like your boss, perhaps a touch more conservatively, and you should be in line with what is expected.

Some Considerations for All

- While your abilities and skill set are vastly more relevant to whether or not you can do the job you're trying to procure, your image says a lot about how you view yourself. It projects that you have a solid work ethic—enough that you care about how you are perceived by others in the professional space. These guidelines aren't to satisfy some bland, generic standard; they are a way for you to meet expectations while projecting a sense of responsibility and maturity.

- Looking "good" and feeling "good" are reciprocal ideas: if you look good, then you will feel good—and vice versa. The same goes for professionalism: if you look like a professional, then you are more likely to act like a professional.

- It also follows that feeling good is instrumental in performing well and looking professional. That is, take care of yourself by eating well, drinking lots of water, exercising, getting adequate sleep, and applying some of the stress reducers discussed in the previous chapter. Taking care of yourself is a first, big step toward looking and feeling good and professional.

- How you are dressed telegraphs a message about who you are: think about that before your interview and beyond your professional life. What kind of message do you want to send about your persona, your capacities, and your intelligence? This should serve as a constant baseline for checking in on your workplace look.

- Always, when in doubt (or when thrown into an unfamiliar professional situation), overdress rather than underdress. It is far better to show up to a conference in a comfortable business suit when everyone is in khakis and button-ups than it is to show up in jeans and a t-shirt when everyone is wearing a business suit. Better to be the more polished the candidate than a diamond in the (too) rough.

- Keep your sense of personal style without overdoing it. You are an individual, after all, and the way in which you present yourself to the world is part of your identity. Just be clear that your identity should also express a sense of teamwork to your potential employer. Dressing in a standard professional way indicates you are willing to play by the rules, as it were, and be a member of a larger team.

- Finally, remember that looking professionally is, at the base, a way of showing respect for your interviewer and for the company at which you wish to be hired. It is also a way of showing respect for yourself, presenting yourself as a confident, capable, and courteous potential employee.

421

Chapter 8: Interview Skill 2: Acting Professional

Not only do you need to dress for success, as it were, but you also need to put your best foot forward when attending your interview. Acting professionally consists of any number of minor behaviors and skills of etiquette. As anyone who has worked with others in any capacity before well knows, the attitude one displays and the behavior one engages in speaks volumes about personal character and professional capacity. When embarking on an interview, it is understandable to be intimated by strangers who have some sort of control over your potential future. However, now that you have snagged the interview with your sharp resume and descriptive cover letter, you need only to look— and act—the part. The following tips should help you develop your professional etiquette for the interview and beyond.

Professional Interview Etiquette

- Remember that one of the crucial tests you must pass when attending a job interview is the litmus test of whether you will fit into the culture of the company. In general terms, this means that you need to demonstrate professional etiquette and respect not only to your interviewer but toward anyone else you may encounter (other employees, like a receptionist or secretary or colleagues in your department or group). Your skills are rendered irrelevant if your behavior is boorish and rude.

- Consider your first impression; you must not only look the part but also act the part. A first impression can never be retracted, so it is important not to begin an interview on the wrong foot. From the moment you arrive at the company, be on your most professional behavior: for all you know, the person you greet in the hallway or ride in the elevator with may be your future boss or colleague. Be enthusiastic and look happy—rather than apprehensive—to be there. Make eye contact and introduce yourself politely when appropriate, extending a handshake in most cases. When entering the interview space, be sure to accept instructions politely and strike an open—rather than defensive—posture.

- As mentioned in the previous chapter, be sure that the outfit you've chosen to wear for the interview is appropriate and professional, but also be aware of how it will appear when you are seated. You want to avoid the proverbial wardrobe malfunction (gaping blouse, popped button, overly hiked pants). Typically, you will be seated for most of the interview, so that's how you should test the comforts and utility of your chosen attire.

- Always remember to smile and appear interested in what the interviewer is saying. A smile (or, conversely, a frown) can speak volumes. If you appear smiling and approachable, then you are perceived as a team player with valuable character attributes as well as professional skills to bring to the company. A frown, on the other hand, can fluster or annoy the interviewer; it is difficult to know how to interpret the facial expression. Are you angry, annoyed, bored, frustrated, or otherwise unimpressed? This is not the impression you want to convey. Remind yourself that this experience, while somewhat nerve-racking, should be an amicable way in which to showcase your considerable talents and value. This would bring a smile to anyone's face.

- Body language, in general, reveals a lot about a person's feelings and character. Crossing your arms against your chest looks defensive, even hostile, while a lazy slump indicates a lack of interest or disrespect. Keeping your hands folded in your lap throughout the interview can have the effect of implying childlike anxiety. "Man-spreading" can look aggressive or arrogant. Again, maintain eye contact when answering questions, and avoid sweeping hand gestures. You can hold a pen or pencil in your hand if it helps to center you, and this can come in handy should you wish to jot anything down. Basically, your body language should indicate that you are engaged and open, enthusiastic and polite.

- When greeting others, be sure that you have a solid handshake, somewhere between limp and crushing. A firm handshake reveals self-confidence and a courteous understanding of overall business etiquette. When meeting someone for the first time, it is considered polite to use an honorific, such as Dr. or Ms. or Mr. If the company for which you are interviewed is owned or operated by foreign nationals, then it would behoove you to do some research into the basic etiquette of the other country. Personal space is defined differently in different cultures, in addition to attitudes about how men and women behave.

- Addressing someone by their name is also a powerful piece of business etiquette that you can employ to curry respect. Everyone likes to be noticed and remembered, so try your best to remember and repeat the names of people that you meet. Should you be called in for a further interview, this considerate formality will inevitably be noticed. Still, don't sound sycophantic: continuously repeating the interviewer's name throughout the interview—"now, that's an interesting question, Dr. Jones. Let me see how I can answer that fully, Dr. Jones. Thank you, Dr. Jones"— can be annoying and patronizing.

- As you are seated for your interview—which you should be invited to do, rather than simply plopping down—place your personal items beside or underneath your chair. For everyone's sanity and to preserve your dignity, turn off your cell phone and any other device you may have carried with you. Have your resume and cover letter, along with a notepad or folder for notes, at the ready.

- If for some disastrous reason, your phone should ring during an interview, you will be called upon to do some swift damage control. Do not dare look at the phone to check (unless you truly have a life-and-death situation on your hands); simply turn it off and apologize to the interviewer. You would have to be an excellent candidate to overcome this most egregious of etiquette breaches. It's better not to take your phone in with you if you have a habit of forgetting to switch it off. And off means *off*, not silent.

- When leaving the interview, be sure to restate your interest in the job and your pleasure at having met everyone. Shake hands again and repeat names, when appropriate. Be sure to thank the receptionist who showed you in, if relevant. Basically, just show proper manners on your way out the door.

- After the interview, it is customary to write a "thank you" note of some sort to the interviewer or interviewers to acknowledge their time and your opportunity. More on that will be covered in Chapter 12.

Professional Etiquette beyond the Interview

The following are some professional skills that will help you to develop into the most productive and respected employee that you can be. These skills are useful in many aspects of life, from job interviews to employee and customer interactions to any other business scenario.

- Relying on a personal set of ethics and integrity will always serve you well in the workplace. Loyalty and commitment help to cement your value as a team member, as well.

- Continuous learning increases your value over time; the more skills you are able to master, the more important (and financially valuable) of an employee you become.

- Sharing your own broad knowledge with your colleagues and others in the workplace will reveal your generosity and positive attitude.
- Be sure always to be reliable and consistent: even if you don't have the most skills or the highest creative thinking, dependability and constancy are absolutely crucial aspects to becoming a long-term employee.
- Try to stay positive, even in the face of adversity. If you do make a mistake in the workplace (or elsewhere in life), take ownership of your faults and make attempts to learn from it. Nobody is perfect, of course, but the most likable and flexible of employees admit when he or she could do better, then strives to make it so.
- A skill not to be overlooked is that of proactive engagement. Instead of waiting for others to confront a gap or fix a problem, engage with issues yourself. Noticing problem areas and dealing with them saves colleagues and superiors a lot of time and potentially wasted effort. This is the kind of engagement that earns promotions and other accolades.
- Keep up with your workload with diligence and enthusiasm. Maintain your self-discipline: prioritizing

and focusing on the most important work at hand is crucial to keeping a workplace organized and productive. Avoiding distractions (like random internet time) will serve you and your productivity well.

- Use whatever resources are available to you to develop your personal and professional growth. If you are diligent in your aspirations, then your success will go farther than you thought possible.

- Avoid indulging in ego, especially within team efforts in the workplace. Your role is to support the company and advance company interests. Should your own personal feelings or ethical compass become compromised by those interests, then it is time to reevaluate your position and, perhaps, look to other sources for work. Otherwise, remember that you are a member of something larger than yourself.

- With regard to the above, be generous in your acknowledgments of others' contributions. Give credit where it is due, and strive to recognize the importance of every member within a team—this is especially important if you become a part of management. Keeping morale buoyant and stable is a fundamental part of your job, and that includes maintaining the happiness and equality of those working under you.

- Understand and utilize data that is made available to you on whatever project, whether it be sales reports or customer feedback or employee evaluations. Too often, insightful data is lost amid a desire for quicker turnover or higher productivity. Without attention to the data generated by results, whole departments can lose their efficiency and valence.

- Still, even in light of the above, strive to maximize efficiency within your own work and that of your team's or group's work. If you are able to identify ways in which to save time and/or capital, then you prove yourself to be an invaluable champion of the company as a whole. This role is also one that can lead to advancement.

- Be a willing contributor to any project or effort that is within your capacity. The more you enthusiastically "pitch in" to whatever is being proposed, the more central you make yourself to various efforts to increase productivity and/or visibility.

- Be aware that your voice is important and should be heard: when there are alternatives to an initiative, let your bosses and colleagues know about them. Even if your idea isn't ultimately followed up on, you indicate your willingness to engage with complex issues and develop problem-solving skills.

- If your ideas aren't accepted wholesale, don't complain or indulge in other base emotions. Remind yourself that you are part of a team.

- The above goes for anything that happens to become an obstacle toward success, personally or communally. Start to view events and circumstances not as obstacles but as opportunities for greater future success. Keeping a positive attitude and shifting our viewpoint makes for a consistently positive workplace. Complaining or whining about issues only marks you as a negative presence and does nothing to advance the issue at hand.

- When you face challenges, you reveal the steadfastness of your character. Listen carefully to all points of view when troubleshooting and problem solving. Creating a solution takes time and effort, so demonstrate patience, as well.

- Strive to be transparent in all of your business dealings. Honesty and openness will only make you a stronger employee (and person) and will always help you to avoid problems down the line. Getting caught in obfuscation always leaves a dark mark on your performance history.

- Keep yourself and your team organized and focused. Utilize tools such as calendars and vision boards to maintain motivation and to stay on track. An organized team that has a clear goal in mind is almost always more productive.

- Finally, communication is key to all good working relationships—to all relationships, really—so be sure to keep open communication with colleagues, management, and other valuable team members at all times.

434

Chapter 9: Interview Skill 3: Preparing for the Interview Part I

Now that you've secured the interview and have reviewed your professional etiquette, start thinking about the specific logistics of the interview itself. There are numerous practical and psychological issues that you should anticipate before attending the interview and getting started. First, not only should you arrive on time and looking professional, but you should also anticipate practical preparations. Second, you should review your willingness to take on the job, as well as what that role entails. Third, before you show up for your interview, spend some time thinking about potential questions and practicing your proficient answers.

Practical Preparations

Besides looking at your best and arriving on time, there are a few other practical considerations for how to function at your best at a job interview. As the old canard goes, nothing beats preparation in order to elicit a good performance. The better prepared you are, the more confident you will be, and the job you desire will be well within your reach.

- **Bring your resume and cover letter** with you to the interview. You will want to have a copy for yourself, as well as additional copies for the interviewer or interviewers. This is just in case you need to reference something in the course of the interview, or if additional interviewers end up coming to the session unbeknownst to you. This can also assist in future interviews so that others who might end up being involved in your hiring have copies of your credentials. Of course, the company can make additional copies, but it looks professional and organized if you happen to have a few extra copies on hand. Also be sure to have a pen or pencil with you, examples of any materials that might be relevant to the position (portfolios, for example), and copies of a printed **list of references** with names, titles, company and contact information. Most often, you don't need to provide this information with your resume, but if you get the interview, make sure to have this ready. Also, as mentioned before, *turn off your cell phone* before you go into the interview. Don't just silence it, turn it completely off.

- **Review your resume, cover letter, and job description** before the interview. While you will have a copy of at least two of those things on hand, you should be prepared enough not to have to reference them frequently or at all. If you're not absolutely clear on your employment history and duties that you have

437

listed on your resume, then it comes across as inept (or even potentially inflated or false). Your cover letter should have included at least one or two more personal statements about your employment history, business ethics, or mission statement: be prepared to elaborate on anything that you have discussed there. As well, review the original job description that you used to respond so that you are clearly able to anticipate how to answer questions that match your experience and skill set to what the company originally advertised.

- **Clean out your purse and/or bag** before you go to the interview. You don't want to waste time or to seem disorganized rooting around through your bag in order to locate any items you may need. Also, think about anything that you might need in the course of an interview for practical use—tissues, hand sanitizer, breath mints, eye drops, or other emergency toiletries—before or during the interview. It is always better to be prepared than not.

- **Use the product or otherwise familiarize yourself with what the company does/makes** prior to the interview. Get as much practical, hands-on experience as you can with what the company does overall, in addition to what you yourself have applied to do specifically. Understanding the product will allow you to be able to take the first steps toward learning how your role can enhance that product's viability or marketability. An interview isn't time for a critique, of course, but it is a time to show that you are aware of the product value and how your skills can contribute.

Job Requirements and Skill Review

Aside from the practical considerations of what to bring and what to ask before the interview, you will also need to prepare some information that will undoubtedly come up during the interview. Being ready with these answers helps you to feel calm, confident, and fully prepared even before any questions are asked.

- **Know the job inside and out** before you arrive. That is, you should understand as fully as possible what the job requirements are for the position. If you have only a short description from the original advertisement, see if you can find out more detailed information from the company web site, social media, or a contact within the company. The more you understand what the ins and outs of the job entail, the better able you are to think about how to match your skillset to those requirements. Also, think about why it is that you *want* the job; that is, think about why you are best for the position, of course, but it is advantageous to display some enthusiasm about why it is that you are truly excited about the prospect of working in this particular capacity for this particular company. A little bit of genuine enthusiasm goes a long way.

- **Know your audience** before you come to the interview, if at all possible. Find out who will be interviewing you and do some specific research on them, if available. The more you know about your interviewer(s), the better equipped you will be to anticipate what kinds of questions they will ask and what kind of expertise they are looking for. This information should give your confidence a boost, knowing (at least to a degree) what you are walking into.

- **Ask about the interview**, as different companies will employ different kinds of interviews: it could be a one-on-one interview with a boss or a human resources manager—knowing which it will be should help you know how to prepare. A direct supervisor will likely want to know more specific details on your specific skill set, while a human resources interviewer will likely ask more general questions about your fitness for the company culture and team structure.

Other companies will employ committees or teams to interview you, which means that you should be prepared to answer a wide range of questions. Finally, it is completely fair to ask what kinds of questions might be addressed at the interview (see more on that below), so that you can be prepared with some potential answers in advance.

- **Review your skills** and be sure that you know how to elaborate on their applicability to the particular position. Be sure that you can adequately explain how a particular skill—effective communication, for example, or past leadership experience—connects with a specific job requirement. As with resumes and cover letters, throwing out these timeworn phrases is ultimately meaningless if you don't have any idea how they will connect with the real-time, practical demands of the job. For example, you might suggest that your effective communication skills will serve you in leading a team via clear, concise and consistent email threads or will assist you in creating newsletters or memos for the department or will be crucial to your ability to generate efficient reports for management. Each skill that you listed on your resume should be applicable to a particular facet of the position for which you are interviewing. Those practical connections show that your skills have concrete value and make you a more memorable candidate.

Potential Questions, Proficient Answers

Other than researching the company and outlining some stories for your interview, you should also spend some time anticipating potential questions and devising proficient answers. There are several kinds of questions that interviewers might ask and being prepared, in some form or fashion, for each type of potential question will mean that you are not unpleasantly surprised or unprepared for anything. For an in-depth look at interviewing techniques, types of questions, and how to prepare proficient answers, see my book *Job Interview Q&A*. For a brief explanation of this part of the interview process, see below.

- **Be prepared to respond to the inevitable "tell me about yourself"** opener. Generally speaking, one of the first responses that interviewers might prompt is an open-ended dissertation on yourself. This question is a kind of litmus test, an ice breaker, and a jumping-off point all in one. First, it reveals whether or not you are comfortable and prepared. Second, it functions to allow everyone to settle in a bit and relax before getting into the specific nitty-gritty of the interview. Third, it is a chance for the interviewer to discover

442

something about you that he or she might wish to follow up on. Thus, this seemingly off-hand prompt is actually an important initial component to many interviews; have an answer ready to go, focusing on the aspects of yourself that relate to the job position, as well as being genuine and interesting.

- **Credential questions** will ask you to elaborate on your educational experience, any certifications or other licenses you may have acquired during the course of your previous experience, or positions of leadership you may have held. You should be prepared to discuss specific aspects of your credentials, such as classes taken or conferences attended—anything relevant to how you achieved the degrees, certificates, licenses, or other accolades that you have earned. This is not about work experience, but about your diligence and perseverance in gaining the accreditation needed to fulfill the expectations of certain positions.

- **Experience questions** will ask you to elaborate upon your past work (or volunteer or intern) experience. These kinds of questions prompt you to think about how you interact with others, how readily you respond to expectations and/or pressure, how well you organize and communicate, or how effectively you produce and/or work with a team. This is where you want to come up with a story or two about overcoming obstacles, solving problems, increasing productivity, or otherwise initiating innovation in your past experience. It also sometimes gives you a chance to discuss a passion project that you've undertaken in the past, either via work, interning or volunteering.

- **Opinion questions** will ask just that: your opinion on either an abstract issue or a concrete fact/problem/event. These kinds of questions ask you to comment on issues within your industry or regarding your past work experience. They often require you to make ethical judgments and to explain how you might respond in a given situation. These questions are both an opportunity to reveal something significant about your overall character, as well as how you might respond to difficulties or pressure.

- **Behavior questions** will ask what you would do in particular scenarios, as well as prompting you to provide an overarching template of how you operate in a professional setting. These kinds of questions might ask how you would solve a particular problem or how you worked to reach a specific goal. Conversely, these might ask you to describe how you overcame a stressful situation at work or how you responded to a setback. This would be an opportunity for you to indicate how one or more of the items listed in your skillset would be applicable to a real-time situation in the workplace.

- **Case studies questions** are usually particular to one specific interview, wherein the interviewer(s) will present a scenario to the potential candidate, then allow the candidate time to study the case before performing an analysis of the situation and projecting results or offering advice on how to render the best possible outcome. This is the kind of interview you would usually be informed about in advance.

- **Brain teasers questions** are quick-fire questions that test specific skills or analytical abilities. In certain cases, you might be asked to perform mathematical problems or solve logic puzzles. In other cases, you might be asked to demonstrate proficiency in a task associated with the industry. For example, before an interview as an editor, you may be asked to take a grammatical test or review a sample submission using editorial marks.

- **Also, you should prepare some questions of your own** prior to the interview. You might have some questions with regard to company practices and policies, product research and development, the

445

logistics of your department, or salary and benefits. Prepare a list of these in advance, as most interviewers will allow some time in the end for your questions. Be cautious with regard to questions of salary and benefit, especially if not dealing with a direct superior. They may only have enough information to give you ranges or broad ideas. In addition, the question might come back to you, so be prepared to present a range, from the baseline of what you will accept to the high end of what you desire. Also, think of how badly you want the job: if you will only accept the job if it comes with a certain salary and benefits, make this clear upfront.

- **Finally, a bit of practice** prior to the interview. Practicing your answers aloud in front of a mirror gives you some idea of how ready you are to respond, or you can practice with mock interviews, should you have friends or family who'd be willing to help you out. If you plan to throw out specific information for any of your answers—numbers, dates, statistics, examples— be sure to memorize these. Jot down notes on an interview preparation sheet for you to review.

Checklist

- [x] _____
- [x] _____
- [x] _____
- [x] _____
- [x] _____
- [x] _____
- [x] _____

Chapter 10: Interview Skill 4: Preparing for the Interview Part II

Not only will you need to think about your own skills and qualifications for the position, but you will also need to be prepared for what others might expect from you. This is why the research recommended previously in this guide is so important. Additionally, in the end, you want to approach the interview with genuineness and honesty, as personality and character are crucial components of what interviewer(s) are ultimately looking for in a candidate. Finally, there are some common pitfalls that you will want to avoid when participating in the interview; a partial list of these below should help you anticipate these and sidestep them when necessary.

Understanding Expectations

Not only should you review your own skills and qualifications, but you should also consider what hiring managers often have in mind when interviewing candidates. Understanding these expectations can help you generate potential responses that hit the mark for what management is looking for.

- First of all, consider the position itself: what managers will expect depends largely on the nature of the job and the experience and skill set needed to fulfill that job. Thus, if you are looking at an entry-level position, then the expectations for lengthy job experience or leadership roles will be lower. In this case, it is likely that you are just embarking on your career, and so other parts of your resume will be more significant, such as educational accomplishments and other extracurricular achievements. If you are looking for a job in management or a highly technical or specialized field, then you can expect that interviewers will be looking for specific details on your abilities and accomplishments within that particular field. The position for which you are interviewing plays some role itself in understanding the expectations that hiring managers will have of you.

- Following on the above, however, employers looking to hire new workers will be much more interested in how they have demonstrated effectiveness in past work experience, rather than in educational achievements—unless you are seeking a truly entry-level position. So, emphasizing your experience, especially with regard to some of the top skills that employers are looking for (see the following chapter for more on that), will be the most significant way to impress upon them that you will be a smart choice.

- Also, remember that you are likely competing with several other candidates for the job: think about what in your past work experience makes you stand out. You'll want to be sure to prepare at least a couple of answers that demonstrate your unique abilities and how they are applicable to the current position being offered. Basically, you need to sell yourself as the best applicant for the job.

- Within that set of unique skills that you are presenting, you want to emphasize what managers might call "hard" skills: these are the particular technical skills that are required for the job, whether it be in teaching or tech development. "Soft" skills, such as effective communication and a team-building attitude, should be on display during the interview, as well, of course. But what might set you apart from the other candidates is a surplus of expertise in a particular arena (for a teacher, say, you might have published case studies in your field; for a graphic designer, say, you may have developed new software that enables easier manipulation of features).

Conducting Yourself with Authenticity and Honesty

No amount of technical expertise or an enthusiastic report will guarantee you any job if you are not conducting yourself with integrity. If you lie on your resume or exaggerate your accomplishments, then you are likely to be exposed in the course of the interview itself—or once you're on the job, which could lead to an embarrassing and impactful dismissal or demotion. It is imperative that you come across as genuine and honest in all your professional dealings.

- The conundrum of how honest to be during the application and interview process is a fraught one: some advice out there suggests that you be honest . . . but not *too* honest, that it's acceptable to bend the truth a bit in the service of your ideal job search. Other advice suggests that managers and employers are truly seeking the most honest and forthcoming individuals for their positions. So, which advice is best? Certainly, the old canard "honesty is the best policy" applies to just about everything you do in life; the consequences of getting caught up in falsehoods could do more damage than even the "harmless" fib you peddled in the first place might. It reveals volumes about a person's integrity when lies are exposed, even if they are minor ones—sometimes *especially* if they are minor ones ("why would she lie about something so minor? What's wrong with her?"). Thus, it is always best to err on the side of truthfulness than not. However, that doesn't always indicate that you have to reveal every single thing about your work history or experience: everyone makes mistakes, and if you have learned from them, it might be an advantage to bring such issues to light in an interview (indeed, many interviewers will ask outright to talk about past mistakes and how you dealt with them). But, everyone also deserves to be defined by aspects of their life besides their mistakes: a particularly damaging or difficult time need not be put on the table unless it becomes highly significant to the conversation or position. Know the difference between revealing that you were fired for a mistake that you've since rectified and keeping quiet over an incident with office politics that might be misinterpreted outside the culture of your former company.

- Nevertheless, it is never appropriate to list a certification, license, or other accomplishments that have subsequently been revoked for some reason. Even if the accomplishment in question isn't relevant for the position to which you applied, it is still unwise to elide the full truth. It is likely that the most casual search will reveal your "lie of omission," which will almost certainly knock you out of the running for the job. Additionally, claiming licensure for certain positions that you no longer have is considered a criminal act in many cases.

- Another simple reason not to elide the truth when discussing your history, your achievements, or your personal qualities is that it can lead to dissatisfaction in the job should you get it. For example, if you claim that you enjoy working with teams and emphasize your past experience with groups, but you really would rather work on your own as an individual, then obtaining a position wherein you are required to work with others regularly would be unpleasant at best. In addition, if you are hired based on the fact that you indicated that you truly enjoyed the success that comes out of hard, meaningful work, then realize that your work-life balance is being compromised, management might see quickly that you aren't actually a good fit for the job. Emphasize the character qualities and work skills that you actually possess and are positive about—this ensures that you get the job that you want and become the employee that managers need. Sometimes you might not get an offer by presenting your work style and achievements honestly; however, it is certain that you will, ultimately, get the job that is the best fit for you.

- Some common areas in which candidates elide the truth are actually opportunities to show what an exceptional employee they can eventually be. For example, when asked about "weaknesses" in the workplace, you might get uncomfortable, not wanting to reveal your shortcomings in your desire to present yourself as the best candidate. However, revealing your vulnerabilities can often make you seem more relatable and open: clearly, nobody is perfect and pretending you don't have weaknesses looks aloof and arrogant; interviewers like to see that you are self-aware and willing to improve. For another example, when asked about how you handled a difficult situation at work offers you the opportunity to show how you actually work through adversity: instead of telling the interviewer that you handled everything with smooth aplomb, revealing what was challenging for you in the scenario and how you overcame those challenges shows that you are a problem-solver and a determined employee. For a final example, the touchy subject of why you were fired always seems like a landmine, but it can be another opportunity to reveal something positive about yourself overall: if you take the attitude that "nothing was my fault," this shows you to be potentially immune to critique and perhaps difficult to work with. If you admit and accept at least some of the responsibility for what occurred, then you reveal that you can overcome difficult situations and are resilient enough to learn from bad experiences and become a better future employee. Thus, there are numerous occasions when honesty—however painful—might indeed give you an advantage.

When Interviews Go Wrong

In any stressful situation, there are bound to be impediments toward pulling off perfection. A job interview is filled with a plethora of potential to make little mistakes that might harm your prospects overall. Many of these minor landmines can be avoided with just a little bit of insight, preparation, and self-awareness, as we have discussed in the previous chapters. However, you are not the only participant in the job search prospect, and an interview might reveal some troubling "red flags" about your potential employer, as well. Securing the ideal job is as much about finding the right position at the right organization as it is about being prepared and skilled. When you attend your interview, also be on the lookout for certain signals that indicate that this company may not be the one for you. After all, with this guide to assist you—your professional resume, concise cover letter, and interview preparation techniques—the ideal job is just around the corner—and it isn't about settling. Keep looking (assuming you have the resources to do so) should you encounter some of the following issues.

- If your interviewer doesn't seem to be perfectly clear on what the position entails or what your responsibilities might be, then this is a clear sign that there is some miscommunication or disorganization within the company itself.

- If your research prior to the interview reveals a rosy public image with satisfied employees and customers, but your experience at the company and during the interview seems at odds with that, then perhaps you should reconsider. The public image of a company might not always live up to its actual culture; this is a time for you to use your best judgment about what's in your best interests.

- If your interviewer doesn't seem engaged with your answers or asks only a repetitive set of generic questions, then it is likely the case that either the company has already determined who they will hire (hint: it's not you) or the position is a redundant one, mostly unimportant to the workings of the company.

This might indicate that prospects for advancement are low or non-existent.

- If the research you conduct on the company indicates that leadership is in flux, is floundering, or has a high rate of turnover, then this is a clear red flag that something is wrong at the core of the company itself. You don't want to chain yourself to a sinking ship, as it were.

- The same consideration applies to your understanding of the company's mission statement. If their mission seems unclear or contradictory, then that's an indication that the company is in trouble or in a rut.

- If your interviewer seems unprepared, then you should reconsider, as well. Again, this reveals a lack of organization and clarity within the company; or, if the interviewer will be your direct supervisor, it reveals an indication of their habitual work practices— and that might be frustrating for you in the end.

- Finally, if the process of interviewing feels too drawn out—it's taken months to get from resume to interview to follow-up interview—then it's another red flag that indicates disorganization, indecision, or other core problem.

459

Chapter 11: Interview Skill 5: Demonstrating the Top Skills

If you are working on your resume, cover letter, and interview preparation, then you will definitely want to know what employers are looking for the most. While each individual job will have its own special set of requirements and unique attributes, there are certain kinds of skills that every employer seeks in just about every employee. This isn't to say that you have to possess each and every one of these skills—that would be nigh impossible—but it is to give you some guidelines to see what employers are typically expecting and how you can showcase your experience and skillset to best meet those expectations. Usually, skills are broken down into soft skills—the kind of skills that any employee regardless of training or experience will have to some degree—and hard skills, which are the specific technical and professional expertise necessary to perform particular kinds of jobs. Additionally, there are some extraneous skills that aren't necessarily categorized as "soft" or "hard," but they are skills that will set you above many other candidates. See below for details on the top skills for which companies and managers are searching.

Soft Skills

These skills are the character attributes and personal qualities that a candidate brings with them to the position. These personality traits and behavioral standards are what allow an employee who has standard hard skills to gain an advantage over other candidates. Managers look for soft skills because no matter how good you are at executing tasks or effectively producing if your interpersonal or communication skills are lacking, then you are likely not the best person for the job. Soft skills are also transferrable skills, appropriate in any workplace scenario, meaning that an employee with excellent soft skills is flexible and useful in almost any position. These skills are gained not through formal training, by and large, but via personal experience and self-awareness; because they are gained over time, the employee with solid soft skills adds value to a company beyond their basic functions. Soft skills demonstrate diversity and broadness of experience, as well as attention to detail and openness to others.

- **Adaptability** is crucial to being able to work in any environment with diverse personalities, changing responsibilities, and varying production requirements. The more an employee is able to adapt to shifting scenarios, the more valuable she provers herself.

- **Attitude** cannot be understated. Employees who are able to demonstrate positive attitudes and determination, even when faced with challenges, are clearly not only valuable in what they can offer in production but also in how they can create a comfortable, calm, and welcoming environment.

- **Communication** skills are crucial to any job that you might encounter, including oral, nonverbal, written, and aural. Your ability to communicate effectively can make you an invaluable part of any group of companies. Your communication style should be empathetic, open-minded, respectful, and precise, depending on the situation. Listening is just as important as speaking in a communication situation. Understanding your audience also determines how you approach communication; how you speak to a customer is different than how you might speak to a colleague or a boss. And, even in an increasingly technological age, written communication skills are valuable, for emails, interoffice memos, marketing purposes, reports, production schedules, and so on. Learning to write correctly and concisely makes you a better candidate.

- **Conflict Resolution** can be an extremely important skill to possess, particularly in companies wherein employees work closely together in teams. This skill implies a variety of attributes that allow you to resolve issues as they arise, including mediation, empathy, facilitation, creative problem-solving, and accountability. There are even entire positions within organizations that are dedicated to conflict resolution capabilities, but this is a valuable skill for any employee.

- **Creative Thinking** is another broad soft skill that includes a variety of attributes, such as analytical abilities and effective communication. Creative thinking also requires an open mind to see problems and opportunities from different angles, as well as organizational and leadership skills to see them through.

- **Critical Thinking** is distinct, though not completely different, than creative thinking. Critical thinking skills imply the ability to make unbiased observations; provide appropriate analyses and interpretations; process issues through reflection and evaluation; inference underlying subtext; offer explanations, and employ problem solving and decision-making skills. An employee should also be able to apply critical thinking skills independent of direct guidance. Critical thinking is applicable to any and all scenarios in your professional and personal life. The ability to think critically is vital to success.

- **Decision Making** is a key component of critical thinking overall and reveals an independent, well-informed, and decisive employee. Good decision-making skills indicate that a candidate is knowledgeable and authoritative.

- **Flexibility** makes an employee more valuable because he can accept more responsibilities, accomplish a wider variety of tasks, and generally contribute to a larger degree in the workplace as a whole. Flexibility requires both a diversification of skills and an attitude of openness.

- **Interpersonal** skills are crucial to communication, of course, and show an employee's ability and willingness to interact with others. This includes high degrees of empathy and tolerance, as well as emotional intelligence and a sense of self-awareness.

- **Leadership** reveals an ability not only to perform required tasks but to step up and take on roles of greater responsibility. Showing leadership requires effective communication (including, crucially, the ability to listen to feedback), a high level of motivation to take on more responsibility, and the ability to organize and delegate tasks and functions. Leaders are also generally trustworthy and creative, with strong interpersonal skills.

- **Motivation** is inherent to leadership, of course, as well as to success in everyday working situations. Motivation is a highly interior attribute, as external motivations such as praise or financial reward often don't last beyond the initial payoff. Motivation constitutes an internal desire to do better and be more effective. Highly successful people are nearly always highly motivated by personal goals and ideals.

- **Networking** is part of our interpersonal skill set, but it is distinct in a couple of ways. It requires an ability to observe and foster connections between disparate groups of people or organizations—seeing patterns and how these interact—as well as an extroverted ability to connect to strangers and promote your interests.

- **Problem Solving** employs a variety of soft skills. It includes the ability to analyze a situation, generate possible responses, evaluate which response will be most effective, implement a coherent plan, and assess final results.

- **Teamwork** is both an interpersonal skill and a hallmark of attitude. It requires effective communication skills, including respectful listening, reliability within the team itself, and conflict resolution attributes.

- **Time Management** is important to any professional or personal set of tasks. Deadlines and goals may not quite be the same thing, but without the boundaries of time, not much gets done. The ability to prioritize, set a schedule, keep organized, and maintain a balance between work and rest is absolutely crucial to any employee.
- **Work Ethic** implies that you have the ability to be self-directed and motivated to be on time, be prepared, and be willing to get the work done when and as it needs to be done.

Hard Skills

In order to be successful at any job, an employee needs to demonstrate a combination of soft skills, as detailed above, and hard skills. Hard skills are the technical and professional skills that are gained through specific education and training. This is the expertise you have gained through formal education and hands-on experience, specific to each particular field or job. This includes not only formal education and technical training, but also apprenticeships, internships, continuing education, certification or licensing programs, and on-the-job experience. Hard skills are easily evaluated through objective definition and measurement. Some hard skills that are used in particular professions are listed below.

- Accounting
- Administrative
- Analytics
- Automotive
- Banking
- Carpentry
- Computer
- Construction
- Data
- Design
- Editing
- Electrical
- Engineering
- Financial
- Hardware
- Healthcare
- Information Technology
- Languages
- Legal
- Manufacturing
- Math

- Mechanical
- Medical
- Nursing
- Optimization
- Pharmaceutical
- Pipefitter
- Plumbing
- Project Management
- Programming
- Research
- Reporting
- Science
- Software
- Spreadsheets
- Teaching
- Technology
- Testing
- Translation
- Transcription
- Word Processing
- Writing

Other Skills

Besides the categories of soft and hard skills, employers are often looking for some miscellaneous skills that can be integrated into your responsibilities to ensure that you are a more efficient and productive employee. These additional skills highlight your ability to diversity within the workplace, adding value to whatever department in which you work. Most of these skills are technologically oriented, though not all.

- Obviously, basic computer skills are a requirement of virtually every job in today's workplace environment. In fact, listing "computer skills" on a resume is a virtually meaningless act, given that the wide range and level of expertise within the broad category of computer skills is vast and nearly indefinable. Still, indicating that you have proficiency with particular computer skills is valuable to any employer and should be mentioned at some point in the hiring process. Should you possess particular, higher-level computer skills, this may warrant mentioning on a resume. Computer skills can be broken down into some basic attendant categories:
    - Productivity software: this includes the Microsoft Office suite of programs, which any employee should be able to maneuver at least at a basic level (Word, Excel, and PowerPoint). You should also know how to utilize and manage

email, as well as digital calendars (often included within email platforms). Digital message, video conferencing, and cloud management software are other forms of productivity software that you might be called upon to use. Again, there is no need to mention these skills on a resume; wait until you are asked about them.

- o Digital marketing: this runs the gamut from web site design and maintenance to social media campaigns and has become integral to most modern companies wishing to grow a customer base. These skills include web site design, social media management, CMS and CSS knowledge, familiarity with digital media marketing and search engine optimization, as well as web site analytics. If you possess any of these specific skills and they are relevant to your position, do mention them on your resume.
- o Computer programming skills are in high demand, as well. If you are well-versed in such computer languages as HTML and JavaScript, then you should most definitely mention this. Other programs include C++, Python, and

knowledge of open source software such as Linux and Unix.

- o Graphic design is another computer skill that adds value to an employee in this technological age. Familiarity with the Adobe suite of products, desktop publishing, or video creation software should be mentioned on a resume, as well.

- o There is also a demand for people with IT troubleshooting skills, though this expertise would likely be required for specific jobs rather than general application. Systems administration, server maintenance, and help desk abilities, along with various other tech support capabilities, are in great demand.

- o Cybersecurity skills are a rapidly growing field, as well, though again is mostly specialized. An understanding of malware, data encryption technologies, and virus protection software is also in high demand.

- Social media skills, as distinct from general computer skills, are becoming more and more intertwined with business needs. Like computing skills, social media skills cover a broad range of particular abilities and expertise. Social media skills can also refer to more traditional means of disseminating information and conducting marketing.

o Writing concise, correct, and engaging copy is a social media skill that is useful from blogging to web site content to marketing campaigns and beyond. Technical savvy with enormous platforms like Facebook and Twitter can be advantageous to any small company or start-up.

o Content creators need not be only writers: candidates with graphic design abilities or video creation skills are also needed to maintain a viable social media presence. Both writing and visual content creation require good editing skills.

o Public speaking is a valuable skill for many employees: being able to present a report or deliver a motivational speech can be an excellent resource for your company.

o Customer service skills also require social networking and interpersonal skills that can be crucial to the success of product-oriented companies. If you have spent time honing your customer service capacities, then you should definitely make note of that.

- Language ability is another valuable skill that can showcase your flexibility as an employee. Spanish language skills are probably the most valuable in general terms, while other languages may be important in particular fields or for multinational corporations.

Chapter 12: Interview Skill 6: Listening and Follow Up

While most of any job interview will be primarily focused on you and what you have to say, don't make the mistake of forgetting that listening is also an important part of the process. You are also in the process of gathering information from the interviewer and from the company itself while you are vying for the position. Listening can be just as valuable as speaking, ultimately. In addition, when the actual interview is finally over, this doesn't mean that you are completely finished with the hiring process. There are important guidelines to meet when following up with the interviewer and potential employer, as you will discover here.

The Art of Listening

It is potentially the case that listening is one of the most underestimated skills that are necessary for a job interview. Showcasing solid listening skills will make you appear empathetic, engaged, intelligent, and enthusiastic. While you should certainly practice your answers to potential questions as detailed earlier in this guide, you should avoid spouting off practiced answers without truly listening to what the interviewer is requesting. An interview should have an ebb and flow like a conversation, and while much of it will be focused on you, be sure to allow yourself time and space to listen and absorb what is going on at the other side of the equation.

- Coming with a list of prepared answers and follow up questions just isn't quite enough. As stated above, be sure you are responding to the specific questions asked during the interview, rather than trying to force your prepared answers to work on the spot. With regard to your list of prepared questions, be aware that this offers you an important opportunity to engage with your interviewer about what is in your best interest. When the interviewer(s) ask about your own set of questions, don't simply reel them off like a quick checklist. Ask a clear question and really listen to the answer, jotting down notes and reactions as you go. Oftentimes, a response to your question will lead you to a follow-up question or raise a concern or cement a positive assumption. In addition, the kinds of questions that an interviewer asks might give you ample opportunity to ask a relevant follow-up question. For example, if an interviewer seems focused on how long you intend to stay with the company and in what capacity, you might want to ask about retention and standards for promotion: the interviewer might be signaling, on the one hand, that employee turnover rates are quite high (a red flag) or promotional opportunities are there for the taking (a positive incentive).

- Be sure to use your listening skills to perceive information that may be somewhat implicit rather than explicit. If an interviewer consistently asks about your ability to handle stressful situations, then you might rightly deduce that this is a high-pressure workplace. If an interviewer seems interested in your future professional development plans, this might signal that you are a candidate for a higher-level position. In any case, the interviewer will consciously or incidentally reveal a lot about the company. Listening to what is said will give you ample opportunity and ammunition to ask pertinent questions and make smart decisions.

- There are specific ways in which you can hone your listening skills. Let's face facts: many of us, particularly when faced with being put on the spot in a stressful situation such as a job interview, will tune out what is going on around us. Diligent observation and listening skills take some practice.

- Practice listening with a friend or family member. Ask them to tell you an unfamiliar story, then try to relay the details back to them a few hours later. Or, simply let your support group know that, in preparation for the interview, you'd like to be made aware of when you are accidentally zoning out. As long as you leave personal feelings aside, you'll likely learn a lot about how carefully you listen—or not.
- Prepare for the interview thoroughly, both in terms of practical preparation and in terms of psychological preparation. Have everything ready to go the night before (outfit, materials, travel plans), as well as conduct stress-relieving activities the day before and get a good night's sleep. The more prepared you are, the better able you are to relax enough to be a good listener.
- Keep your materials as organized and simple as possible, so you can avoid accidental distractions. It's likely you'll miss something important if you're rooting around in your bag for a pen, for example. And remember to *turn off your cell phone*. One quick buzz or ring can

ruin an entire interview, much less your ability to focus and listen.

- o Your body language will indicate to the interviewer how well you are listening. Show engagement by leaning toward the interviewer when he or she is speaking; nod when appropriate other such items avoid interruption. All of these silent signals reveal that you are a good listener—a boon to you during the interview process itself, and a boon to any employer who wishes to hire an employee with excellent communication skills.

- o Repeat back to the interviewer what he or she is saying in order to be certain that you have the most important details clear. This is a method by which you clearly indicate that you have been respectfully listening.

- o Don't worry if you have to ask the interviewer to repeat a question or explain something more thoroughly. Nobody is a perfect listener and that kind of diligence can prevent misunderstanding.

Steps for Follow Up

While it may appear that the process of applying for and securing your dream job is complete when the interview is over, there is still one more important step up: you should follow up appropriately. When you follow up in appropriate ways, it can have the added benefit of reminding the potential employer of why you are a strong candidate in the first place; it shows respect and attention to detail, as well as allowing you to pursue answers of your own. Here are some details about how to conduct a proper follow-up protocol.

- When should you follow up? There are two distinct answers to this: the first is that you should follow up immediately with some kind of thank you note (more on that below); the second is that you should allow an appropriate amount of time to pass before nudging the interviewer to give you some specific results. At the end of the interview itself, find an opportunity to ask when you might hear back from the company if you haven't already been told. If you don't hear back from them in the allotted time period, wait two or three more days before you send a polite email or place a polite phone call. If you aren't sure when you'll hear back, wait at least a week before checking back in. As with listening skills, a polite and professional follow up note can remind a potential employer of your qualifications, abilities, and attributes.

- How should you follow up? This, of course, will depend upon the nature of the interview and job position. It is rare, however, that you should ever follow up in person. The most common ways to follow up are with an email or a phone call, and which you choose depends on your level of confidence in speaking extemporaneously or needing to script a response. A follow-up email gives you the opportunity to compose your (concise!) thoughts before sending, though it doesn't always provide the kind of immediate gratification that you may want or need. If you decide to call the interviewer or hiring manager, be sure to jot down what you'd like to say beforehand. In either case, be sure that your tone is friendly and that you keep your remarks concise. You can also ask if they require any further materials from you in your follow up—this might be especially relevant if you are concerned that the interview did not go as well as you would have hoped or if you remembered some important information that you weren't able to convey at the time of the original interview.

- Regardless of whether you eventually need to follow up further, you should *always* write a quick note of thanks after the interview. While some might suggest that this is rather old-fashioned, it is still very much the case that this practice is routinely followed and clearly appreciated. The more thoughtful the note, the more successful the results. Here are some things to consider when writing that crucial thank you note:

- o Be sure to write and send a thank-you note within 24 hours of the interview—any longer and it becomes a moot point. Today, most thank you notes are sent via email, but one sent via mail can garner special attention; just be sure that it is sent promptly so that you aren't forgotten in the interim. Typically, an email is a better choice because of the short time-lapse, but if you are physically close enough to stop by with a handwritten note, then that might be the best choice.

- o Address the thank you to everyone who played a role in your application process, from all the interviewers to the recruiter, when applicable. In some cases, it may be applicable to send a quick note to another employee who participated in some form, as well. In many cases, you will be directing your thank you to one specific interviewer. In other cases, if you are interviewed by a few people, then you might want to send a quick note to all involved, especially if their capacities or responsibilities in the interview differed. If you are interviewed by a full panel of people, then you might consider writing one overarching note to the person in charge, and Cc-ing everyone else.

- o A thank you note should contain a friendly and respectful greeting, using the person's name and honorific (Dr., Ms., Director, etc.), with a short paragraph expressing your appreciation for their time and effort, closing with a professional "sincerely" and your name. If you can think of specific detail from the interview that was especially striking, then you might briefly mention it in your paragraph in order to remind them of you. You also might throw in a compliment if it is sincere.

- o Essentially, your tone should be professional yet personable. Avoid emojis of any kind, and don't pepper the note with exclamation points or overly excitable adjectives and adverbs. There are numerous templates available online should you wish to review some.

- Finally, know when to move on: if you have sent a thank you note and have made two attempts at follow up without response, then it is time to start preparing for your next interview. Be patient, however, and space out your follow up over the course of a couple of weeks: thank you note immediately, follow up within a few days of when a response was anticipated, and one final follow up a week or so after that. If there is no response within a month, then your time and energy are best spent moving on.

Chapter 13: Overview and Checklist

So, you have read through this entire guide and followed the steps toward securing and successfully navigating a high stakes job interview. This final chapter will give you a quick overview and checklist to follow once you have absorbed the details that have been proffered throughout the book. Use this to literally mark off each step in the process as you go, and note that you can utilize for each and every application and interview you secure.

13.   Personalize your resume and cover letter for each and every job to which you apply. Keep a master list of applications sent, including names of the company, names of directors or hiring managers, job descriptions, and dates application sent and interview scheduled. This provides you with a long-term template toward tracking your success—or lack thereof—and changing your approach as necessary.

14.   As soon as you find out that you have gotten an interview, begin your research and preparation. Study like you might have once studied for a final exam. Do diligent research on the company, as detailed in Chapter 4, and brush up on your own resume and cover letter prior to the interview. You might also want to study up on specific skills that are outlined in

the job description, especially if you haven't utilized these particular skills for a while or are applying for something that is a bit outside your previous job experience. While you cannot expect to master a new skill within a few days, you can certainly wind up with a more thorough understanding of what you might be asked to do.

15.   Remember to prepare for potential interview questions and rehearse potential answers, as detailed in Chapter 9, and prepare your own set of questions that you would like answered in the course of the interview itself. Outline a couple of stories, as discussed in Chapter 5, so that you are ready to respond to personal and professional questions in a cohesive and coherent manner. Reach out to other employees at the company, if appropriate, or to others working in the industry for some deeper insight into the company culture and managerial expectations. You can also utilize databases that compile real-life interview experiences, such as Glassdoor.

16.   Remember to review the job description before going to the interview, as well: note specific keywords that you might use when outlining your story or

practicing your potential answers. Do practice out loud, as it will help both memory and confidence.

17.   If you discover a gap in your skillset, be sure to be prepared to provide a satisfactory answer as to why and/or how you can remedy such a gap. Remember to be honest and authentic when pitching your experience and attributes in a resume, cover letter, and interview.

18.   Be sure to practice stress relief, especially the night before the interview, and schedule your time wisely so that you get enough rest. Eat a healthy dinner the night before and a decent breakfast the morning of the interview. Spend some time with positive visualization or meditation before you leave for the interview; see tips and techniques in Chapter 6. The goal in the 24 hours leading up to the interview is to be as prepared but relaxed as possible.

19.   Remember to dress professionally but comfortably; follow the tips provided in Chapter 7 for a full complement of what to consider when preparing your interview look. Brush up on professional etiquette, as well, so that your behavior matches your polished and professional appearance.

20.   Give yourself a pep talk before the interview: remind yourself that you were skilled enough to get

the interview and worthy of the job offer. Don't forget to make eye contact and to practice a firm handshake. Walk into the building with confidence and enthusiasm.

21.   Check that you have everything you need before you leave for the interview. Copies of your resume and cover letter, writing utensils, and a pad of paper or other such items for taking notes. Make sure your bag is uncluttered and organized and (as has been repeated throughout this guide) *turn off your cell phone*.

22.   Throughout the process, it might be worth your while to keep a journal of your preparations and experience. Each interview provides an opportunity to learn something new and valuable to take with you into the job itself or onto the next interview. Be sure to debrief yourself directly after the interview, taking down notes as to what you thought was particularly successful and what you felt could be improved upon. This might prove to be the most beneficial use of your interview preparation time in the long run.

23.   Be sure to follow up, as detailed in Chapter 12: write a concise and professional thank you note within 24 hours of the interview and check-in about results in a patient and polite manner. Even if you did not get

the job, you might indicate that you would be willing to listen to suggestions for how you might be a better candidate in the future. Always avoid burning bridges: you never know when another, more fitting opportunity might arise. You should always be prepared and professional for any chance to shine.

CHECKLIST

Conclusion

A job interview is potentially a life-altering event. You have been searching for your ideal job, amassing skills and experience along the way to help you secure what you need for professional success and personal satisfaction. While an excellent resume and cover letter will enable you to secure a foot in the door, the interview itself also requires a particular set of skills and some significant amount of practice for it to be as successful as possible. Employers often consider the interview a litmus test not only for how an employee will be productive and valuable at specific work-related tasks but also for how an employee will fit in with the corporate culture and be a productive team member beyond the technical skills they bring.

As such, you should treat the job interview as a process much like an educational or training opportunity. It requires research and knowledge, experiential training, and practice to be good at job interviews. This guide has provided you with a plethora of tools you can utilize in order to become the most attractive candidate out of many. Not only have you honed your resume and cover letter writing skills, but you have also learned how to research a company, outline your story, and reduce the stress associated with the intense process of securing your dream job. From looking and acting professionally to being thoroughly prepared for any style of interview, any kind of question, you know now how to demonstrate that you have both the hard and soft skills that will make you a valuable employee to any industry or company.

Ultimately, the importance of a job interview really cannot be overstated: this simple act is the culmination of your years of hard work, focus, and energy. You may have paid tens of thousands of dollars for a higher education or special training just to get to this point; you may have spent your entire life dreaming of this particular job in this particular field; you may have an inkling that this job might be able to propel you to success and security in ways you have heretofore only dreamed of. The job interview is one way in which to gain entry into whatever elite group of which you've always wanted to be a part.

Winning Interview

A Detailed Guide for a Winning Approach to Job Interview. Learn the Best Strategy for Conquering the Interview Process and Get Your Dream Job.

unless express consent of the Publisher is provided beforehand. Any additional rights reserved.

Furthermore, the information that can be found within the pages described forthwith shall be considered both accurate and truthful when it comes to the recounting of facts. As such, any use, correct or incorrect, of the provided information will render the Publisher free of responsibility as to the actions taken outside of their direct purview. Regardless, there are zero scenarios where the original author or the Publisher can be deemed liable in any fashion for any damages or hardships that may result from any of the information discussed herein.

Additionally, the information in the following pages is intended only for informational purposes and should thus be thought of as universal. As befitting its nature, it is presented without assurance regarding its prolonged validity or interim quality. Trademarks that are mentioned are done without written consent and can in no way be considered an endorsement from the trademark holder.

Introduction

One of the most significant parts of our professional lives is what we do *before* we actually get the job: prepare for and conduct a job interview. As we spend time and money obtaining educational degrees and/or technical training, not to mention professional experience in lower level jobs, internships, and volunteer work, we imagine that the reward for investing our personal resources in all of this is, ultimately, to secure that ideal job in a career of our choosing. The final barrier to obtaining that dream is to secure an interview—and employment—with the right company. Here you will find suggestions on how to conduct a winning interview, the kind that will garner you that ideal job.

From learning how to put together the best resume and cover letter to understanding and preparing for the most common interview questions, this guide will take you step by step through the process of obtaining and successfully completing a job interview. You will also learn how to do important research on a company prior to the interview, as well as how to maintain professional standards at the highest level. The guide will also take detailed look at the most important categories of skills that employers are looking for in their prospective employees, as well as review some common mistakes to avoid.

Now is your chance to secure the job of your dreams. With some careful planning, preparation, and practice, you are well on your way to accomplishing the best job search and interview possible. Use this detailed guide for a winning approach to your upcoming job interviews, learning the strategies for how to conquer even the toughest parts of the interview process.

Chapter 1: The Importance of an Interview: Getting Your Dream Job

The process of securing and performing well in a job interview can be challenging, but it is ultimately one of the most rewarding endeavors on which you can embark: securing your ideal job is one way in which to gain entry into whatever elite group you've always wanted to be a part of. While there is no truly typical job interview—the experience encompasses too many variables (candidate, employer, field, and so on) to be wholly predictable—there are some common elements that occur in most interview situations. Understanding the basics of interviewer's categories of questions, as well as honing your ability to answer clearly and cleverly, can give you a significant advantage in the interview process. The importance of a job interview really cannot be overstated: this simple act is the culmination of your years of hard work, focus, and energy. You may have paid tens of thousands of dollars for a higher education or special training just to get to this point; you may have spent your entire life dreaming of this particular job in this particular field; you may have an inkling that this job might be able to propel you to success and security in ways you have heretofore only dreamed of.

The job interview is also a very complicated endeavor, from the pre-interview preparation to the interview itself to the post-interview follow-up. You have to remember that you are, essentially, in the process of selling yourself: you are trying to get the employer to buy your certain set of skills, both hard and soft (which will be discussed later in the book), as well as your enthusiasm and personality. The guidelines that you will review throughout the course of this book will give you the best advice on how best to sell your particular set of experiences, skills, and personality.

A job interview isn't merely a moment in time wherein you are asked some questions and demonstrate some skills: it can potentially alter the course of your life, getting the job of your dreams. Thus, it should be approached with care and thoroughness: you should prepare for a job interview the same way in which you would prepare for a great athletic event or a major performance. That is, you should not only hone your skills and learn from your experiences, but you should also practice and practice well. To show up for a job interview without fully undertaking some considered practice is to show up for the big game without any warm up at all. Your livelihood and your future depend on your career, to some extent; treat it with care and precision, as you would other facets of your life.

One of the first ways in which you can prepare adequately for an interview is to start thinking about what kinds of questions the interviewer may ask, and preparing some possible answers to potential questions. There are many standard questions that interviewers will ask, in various ways, and going over these and understanding what is being asked, as well as how best to answer is one of the most important parts of any interview preparation. The kinds of questions asked range from verification and experience questions to opinion and behavior questions, among others, and they require different kinds of in-depth preparation (see my book *Job Interview Q&A* for a more thorough overview of the many kinds of questions and possible answers, along with some ideas for practice). Using the STAR answering method—focusing on situation, task, action, and result—will likely net you the best responses. Much of this will be covered later in this guide.

Always be sure to bring your cover letter and resume to the interview with you, in case you need to reference something specific from your past experience or current explanations of skills. Jotting down a separate list of specific skills that you have is also a good idea to have with you, particularly if you tend to get anxious in an interview: these lifelines can help you regain your footing should you get a little nervous.

Still, the best way in which to combat nerves is to prepare thoroughly, so be sure also to review both your resume and your cover letter before you come to the job. Make notes on your copies that will remind you of particular stories you might wish to tell in the context of an interviewer's question. Additionally, it is a good idea to bring a few extra clean copies of your resume and cover letter, in case there are more than one interviewer or in case the interviewer wants to pass on your information to someone higher up in the company. The same should be prepared in the case of a reference list, as well.

Also spend some time reviewing the job advertisement, so that you are as clear as you can possibly be regarding the expectations and duties of the job itself. You should be able to connect your skills and experiences directly to what is asked of in the original request for employment. Or, in the case of a career transition or promotional position, you should be able to explain how your skill set will translate to a new set of responsibilities and tasks. Find out as much as you can from as many sources are available as to what the job itself will entail; the more specifically you can address what the employer needs, the better a choice you make yourself. Show how your energy and enthusiasm to tackle new challenges will make you the best candidate.

In addition to looking at the job itself, do some research on the company itself, its culture and its accomplishments. You should have a clear idea of the company's history, its mission statement and goals, its management structure, and its products and/or services. You are not merely selling yourself as an individual, but you are also working to sell your ability to fit into a larger corporate culture and structure. This will also give you material for questions that you might have at the end of the interview; the more you know, the more prepared you are to make the best decision for yourself. To that end, you should be prepared to find out what kind of potential for growth and promotion there is available in a given position. It would be prudent to understand how this position can translate into future opportunities—this is especially important if you are starting at an entry level position. Not only does it give you valuable information for making your final decision, but it also shows your potential employer that you have ambition and goals to move from one level to the next.

Clearly, it is also prudent to ask about salary and benefits, unless this has been made specifically clear prior to the interview. In many cases, a job advertisement will post a salary range rather than a specific number, and benefits may or may not be listed. Be polite and direct when asking the question and remember to have your own threshold in mind: it is a waste of everyone's time if the salary that will be offered to you is one you will not take. Thus, approaching these things in a professional manner from the beginning is always the best method.

Finally, your attitude and professionalism are perhaps the most important things that you can offer during an interview. If your resume and cover letter have already demonstrated that you have the experience and skills to garner an interview in the first place, then what will put you over the top is your enthusiasm and knowledge of the company, the job, and your own achievements. Be prepared and eager, friendly and professional, and that ideal job is well within your reach.

Chapter 2: Preparation for an Interview: Understanding the Company

Clearly, one of the most important aspects of preparing for the job interview is to understand the fundamental facts and workings of the company for which you are interviewing. It seems intuitive that you would want to find out all you can about the company for which you wish to work; however, many people make the mistake of not reviewing the information thoroughly enough to answer—or be prepared to ask—some basic questions. Certainly, a surefire way in which to ensure that you are one of the best—if not *the* best—candidate for the position is to demonstrate how well you fit with the company and its culture. This requires that you not only understand exactly what the job is requiring (read and re-read that job description) but also what the company as a whole does and how it conducts business as usual. Showing that you know a good deal about the company—its founding and history, its corporate structure, its products and results, its overall culture—lets the interviewer know that you are a serious candidate with enthusiasm for working at this particular company. This is one of the ways you can set yourself apart from other candidates and set yourself up for success. You want to have a clear understanding of the practical workings of the company, as well as a sense of how workers are expected to behave and produce. Here are some strategies that you can follow to ensure that you are the best prepared candidate—and, ultimately, the best fit for this particular company itself.

- Obviously, **review the company's web site** thoroughly. This will reveal many truths about a company, from the most basic information to the mission statement to overarching themes that seem to run throughout the organization. You should know all the basic information about a company, such as its history and size. Be sure to read the "About" page on the web site, as it will give you the bottom line regarding a company, but also pay attention to keywords and phrases that come up throughout the site, which will give you greater insight into the corporate culture and specific goals of this particular organization. In addition, the web site's very structure and organization, as well as the quality of its design and writing, will speak volumes about a company—such as whether clear communication or flashy graphics are more important.
- The same process applies to a company's **social media presence**: a lot can be inferred about a

company based on its presence—or lack thereof—on social media. If there isn't a social media presence, then you can be reasonably confident that the company considers itself traditional or artisanal in some form or fashion. If there is a social media presence, but it is not professionally or consistently run, then you can infer that either the company needs assistance in this area or that its public image is poorly distributed. This is helpful information for you personally, as well as professionally. It would be imprudent to go into an interview with a detailed critique of a company's social media presence, but it might, under cautious circumstances, be a place for you to suggest your worth.

- It is also an incredibly good idea to understand something of the company's financial history and well-being. In particular, do some research on the company's **market position**: understanding how potential consumers see the company's products, services, and/or brand is crucial to understanding its fundamental corporate culture, as well as where it might be headed in the future. This kind of research might also allow you to promote your particular skill set in the strengthening of that market position.

- **LinkedIn**, of course, is the most prominent social media spot for companies and professionals. Do take a glance at that, as well, and if you know the interviewer's name, also be sure to peruse his or her profile in addition. This can give you valuable insight into their specific role within the company and how you can speak directly to that. It can also help with breaking the ice, as well: perhaps you have something in common with the person (school or colleagues, other activities or interests).

- **Glassdoor** is another invaluable site, especially with regard to the interview itself. They offer sets of interview questions and responses that you can peruse, as well as providing reviews from former candidates with information about how interviews were conducted or how companies were operated. These reviews may not always be perfectly accurate—disgruntled employees can certainly vent on this site—but it will allow you to form an overall impression of company culture and practices.

- You can also do a quick Google search (Google News is even more pinpointed) to see what is currently going on in the company at large. This is especially valuable if you are applying to a smaller subsidiary or segment of a larger, international company.

Basically, you are **researching to find out what has been in the news** regarding their development and activities in recent months.

- Once you've conducted some of this practical research, you can start to spend some time **formulating some secondary impressions** of the company to give you a sense of how you will fit in and how important this particular job interview is to you. Occasionally, what you might discover in your research will be disconcerting and you may decide to devote more effort to another position or company armed with that knowledge.

- Barring that, be sure that you feel well-informed about **the company's strengths**. This will be an excellent way to ensure your interviewer that you are enthusiastic about the progress of the company, as well as give you the ability to showcase how your skills dovetail with their strengths.

- Take a minute to discern **how financially healthy a company is**—especially if you are applying to work at a start-up or other emerging company. This allows you to be a better decision-maker, as well as potentially making you an impressive candidate. Knowing some details about the financial dealings of the company can be an advantage in certain cases.

- Reinvestigate social media sites with a different goal in mind: how does the company interact with the larger community? Updates about goals and progress, welcoming new customers or divisions within the company, reports about upcoming promotions and events: all of these things will give you a stronger sense of **how engaged the company is with the local community, with employees, and beyond**. This kind of review can also give you insight into how a company responds to complaints or delays or other problems.

- A way to get to know a company in-depth is to **seek out someone who works there or once worked there**: they will be able to provide direct advice on company culture and goals. Be sure to conduct yourself professionally when undertaking such an attempt—this is for a job interview not for personal gossip—and know who you are talking to. A former employee may not have the most recent, relevant information, and an unhappy employee may not provide the most accurate assessment.

- Do some specific research on the **company's history and its top employees**, such as the CEO, CFO, and other top management. Name-dropping in an interview can be inappropriate, of course, but you may discover an interesting fact or two that fits perfectly with your own experience. On some occasions, interviewers might expect you to have working knowledge of a company's founder or historical development. It can't hurt to come prepared.

- At this point in your research, you should have been able to glean some information regarding **the company's values and how they align with your own**. This becomes important with how you will approach certain topics within the interview or hiring process. For example, the subject of work-life balance is always an important one but a sensitive one that should be handled with care. If you notice that the company's values are skewed toward production and shareholders, then you must be willing and ready to put in a long and devoted work week. If the company is devoted to sustainability, then you should be aware of how you present yourself (plastic straws are probably frowned upon). Basically, when you agree to work at a particular company, you are implicitly agreeing with the company's values; be sure that you feel comfortable with and knowledgeable about these core concerns.

- While you may not be able to bring up everything you discover in an interview, doing company research has the benefit of preparing you for what to expect not only during the interview but also when you are successfully hired. Certainly, **be prepared to talk about a company's history, mission, and major players, as well as any significant achievements that have recently been made**. The more that you can present yourself as an already well-informed employee, the better you demonstrate how well you fit into the company culture and its overarching goals.

- Last, it also makes perfect sense to spend a little time **researching the industry as a whole**: knowing what the competition is doing and how they operate can offer ideas as to how you might be able to position yourself as the ideal employee with a breadth of industry-wide knowledge. It can also significantly impress an interviewer if you gain some insight into how your company is responding to particular competition and how you see your presence in that initiative.

Chapter 3: Preparation for an Interview: Understanding Your Skills

Clearly, one of the most important parts of the interview is the showcasing of your skills and experience—these are the reason that you were able to get the interview in the first place. It is also important, however, to understand which of your skills is the most marketable, valued by employers, as well as how to emphasize those skills within an interview. Essentially, skills can be broken down into two specific categories: hard skills and soft skills. Hard skills are the technical and profession-related skills that you have learned via education and/or training; these skills prepare you for the specific field and/or industry in which you will be working and, as such, are not necessarily transferrable from one job to the next. For example, if you are trained as an accountant, this wouldn't assist you in getting a job as a teacher. Therefore, in most job interviews, the hiring manager is more interested in hearing about your soft skills: these skills are the ones that you develop over time and through experience—such as interpersonal skills, effective communication, leadership, and teamwork—that will transfer readily from one position to the next. Soft skills are the skills that will move you from entry level to management, for example, and make you a more attractive candidate, in general. In Chapters 6 through 12, the most significant of these skills will be explored in depth, helping you to showcase them in an interview setting. In addition, there are some extraneous skills that aren't necessarily categorized as "soft" or "hard," but they are skills that will set you above many other candidates.

Here you will find a general overview of the kinds of skills that you will be called upon to demonstrate in a job interview and in subsequent employment. This isn't to say that you have to possess each and every one of these skills—that would be nigh impossible—but it is to give you some guidelines to see what employers are typically expecting and how you can showcase your experience and skill set to best meet those expectations.

Hard Skills

Hard skills are the primary skills that you develop through technical training and other educational experiences; combined with soft skills, these make up your complete profile as a potential employee. This is not just your formal education or degrees or technical certifications, but also includes such things as professional development through continuing education, internships for companies or other entities, apprenticeships of the same ilk, different kinds of licensure or certification programs. Review all of the training you have had to understand the kinds of hard skills you have to offer to potential employers. Hard skills are things that can be easily evaluated through objective definition and clear measurement. A grouping of the kinds of hard skills that can be gained through educational or other training is listed below.

These can be mathematical skills, such as those used in accounting, banking, financial industries, and many computer positions. These can be specific technical skills, such as those applied to analytics, design, electrical, mechanical and other kinds of engineering, information technology, manufacturing, software or hardware programming, data entry, the use of spreadsheets and other technical office skills, and general technology training. Hard skills also describe the specialized fields in which people work, which require particular degrees and other licensures or certifications: this includes administrative work, any number of healthcare jobs (medical specialties, nursing, pharmaceutical), legal professions, teaching at just about any level (especially university), translation and other high level clerical work (as in courts), and transcription. Industries that may not necessarily require a university degree will often require particular hard skills that need licensure or apprenticeships, such as automotive, carpentry, construction, pipefitter, plumber, electrician, and other skilled technical work. Hard skills also include general expertise in such things as languages and translation, research and reporting, writing and editing, and the many and various scientific fields.

Soft Skills

Soft skills, on the other hand, are skills that we learn over time and through experience and intellectual or emotional development. These personality traits and behavioral standards are what allow an employee who has standard hard skills to gain an advantage over other candidates. Managers look for soft skills because no matter how good you are at executing tasks or effectively producing, if your interpersonal or communication skills are lacking, then you are likely not the best person for the job. Soft skills are also transferrable skills, appropriate in any workplace scenario, meaning that an employee with excellent soft skills is flexible and useful in almost any position. These skills are gained not through formal training, by and large, but via personal experience and self-awareness; because they are gained over time, the employee with solid soft skills adds value to a company beyond their basic functions. Soft skills demonstrate diversity and broadness of experience, as well as attention to detail and openness to others.

- **Adaptability** shows that you are able to work in various employment situations, as well as being able to shift focus with ease and work with others. You will be valuable in virtually any professional scenario if you are able to adapt with swiftness and ease.
- **Attitude** is that ineffable quality which separates a solid worker from a valuable employee: you can work hard and get the job done, but if you do so with enthusiasm and positivity, then you are both a better employee and a more valuable one. This soft skill is crucial in interviews, as well.
- **Communication** skills are necessary to any professional endeavor you will ever undertake; this includes oral, nonverbal, written, and aural. You must demonstrate an ability to effectively communicate with managers, colleagues, customers, and others; clear and concise written skills, and interpersonal abilities are a key component to any job. You must also learn how to listen, an underrated but equally important part of the communication equation. Learn to understand and read your audience for the best results; how you speak to a customer is different than

how you might speak to a colleague or a boss. Written skills are also still yet an important part of our professional life; you will undoubtedly be called upon to compose such things as emails, interoffice memos, marketing purposes, reports, production schedules, and so on. Honing your writing abilities will make you a better candidate and more valuable employee.

- **Conflict Resolution** is a necessary skill, especially in a company that is dedicated to working in teams or is highly collaborative. Indeed, many companies have entire departments or teams dedicated to just such issues as conflict resolution, to make a company stronger and more enmeshed. You have to be able to resolve differences among co-workers and team members in order to meet deadlines and produce effective results.

- **Creative Thinking** asks that you be able to review various problems through different and innovative lenses. This shows you not only to be an effective problem solver, but someone who is capable of thinking beyond the status quo, who might make the difference in a mildly successful product or service and a wildly successful, unique one.

- **Critical Thinking** reveals our ability to analyze logically, observe without bias, and make judgments based on available concrete evidence. Critical thinking skills are invaluable in assessing problems, proposing solutions, and producing clear results. These skills are revealed in nearly every task you execute as an employee, so they are crucial to long-term success.

- **Decision Making** is a part of critical thinking that shows that you are fair-minded, independent, and decisive. Your ability to observe a scenario, come up with various logical solutions, and choose the best to achieve the best result is absolutely important to most professional scenarios.

- **Flexibility and Dependability** make an employee more valuable because he can accept more responsibilities, accomplish a wider variety of tasks, and generally contribute to a larger degree in the workplace as a whole. Flexibility requires both a diversification of skills and an attitude of openness, while dependability shows maturity and commitment.

- **Goal Oriented** skills show that you are willing to learn and are motivated to meet deadlines, improve skill sets, and move beyond the basics of the position. These skills are intimately bound to organization and time management skills, as well as the ability to be self-motivated and dedicated.

- **Integrity and Intelligence** are also soft skills that many employers are looking for, though they are hard to measure. Integrity implies an ethical commitment to a particular set of standards, as well as a willingness to demonstrate loyalty (within reason) to a company and its mission. Intelligence reveals a candidate who can analyze and solve problems, as well as respond positively to a wide variety of tasks with self-direction.

- **Interpersonal** skills show how you are able to interact with others, using empathy, effective communication, and openness. Being a good employee goes beyond the technical expertise you bring to the job; you must also be able to work well with others, foster good relationships with clients, and otherwise contribute a personable, friendly, and professional persona to the company.

- **Leadership** shows that you can take on more than the most basic of tasks and work to achieve a greater level of success, inspiring others to work harder and better. Candidates with strong leadership qualities reveal an independence of mind and excellent interpersonal skills to reach out to others.

- **Networking** asks us to employ our communication and interpersonal skills to develop professional relationships over time and space in order to enhance the company's professional standing, as well as your personal reputation. In today's business environment, networking can mean the difference between expanding success and contracting.

- **Organization** skills are crucial to the continuing and consistent success of an employee. Without the ability to manage and prioritize tasks and deadlines, an employee risks sacrificing productivity and sabotaging teamwork. Keeping calendars and being punctual and prepared for meetings, among many other abilities, reveals good organizational skills.

- **Problem Solving** is a subset of critical thinking skills, asking that you be able to analyze a given situation with impartial logic, come up with various responses, and choose the best response to generate the best result.

- **Teamwork** reveals your ability to work well with other, requiring strong interpersonal skills as well as a positive and flexible attitude. In certain work scenarios, teamwork is more important than independent leadership skills or other individually focused skills.

- **Time Management** is a crucial component of our busy lives in general, and in a professional situation, time management skill show that you are able to prioritize tasks and execute them effectively, while meeting production goals in a timely fashion.

- **Work Ethic** underlies every successful employee: this is someone who gets to work on time, organizes work effectively in order to produce consistently, shows a positive attitude and a willingness to work hard to get the job done, no matter what the circumstance.

Other Skills

There a variety of miscellaneous skills that are also important to many contemporary jobs; these can be categorized as specialized hard skills, in part, but they are also general technical skills that most employees will utilize on the job, regardless of their field or individual experience. These skills are transferrable across a wide variety of employment opportunities and encompass the kinds of modern developments in the 21st century workplace. These are, ideally, listed in a separate column on your resume to show your expertise in viable contemporary tasks.

- You need **basic computer skills** for any professional level career available in today's marketplace. These need not be listed on your resume—any potential employer will expect you know how to use email or word processing software—though there are some specialized categories that you may want to mention beyond simple productivity software such as Microsoft Office suite and so on: a familiarity with digital calendars on different platforms, for example, or extensive experience with video conferencing or cloud management software might also be considered more specialized skills that an employer might be looking for, depending on the position.

- There is also the burgeoning field of **digital marketing**: from web site design to social media campaigns, contemporary companies often depend on this trend for their continued viability and success. So, if you have experience with web site design, social media management, CMS and CSS knowledge, or a solid familiarity with digital media marketing and search engine optimization, you would do well to list this prominently on your resume. This applies to **computer programming skills**, as well. If you are well-versed in such computer languages as HTML and Java script, then you should most definitely mention this. Other programs include C++, Python, and knowledge of open source software such as Linux and Unix. **Graphic design** is another set of specialized computer skills that would be wise to mention on a resume, such as familiarity with the Adobe suite of products, desktop publishing, or video creation software.

- There is also a growing need for employees who have **IT troubleshooting skills**, such as experience with systems administration, server maintenance, and help desk abilities, along with various other tech support capabilities. This would probably apply to a specific job rather than a general resume, but if you have any passing familiarity with these skills, do mention it. **Cybersecurity skills** is a related and growing field that is in increasingly high demand. An understanding of malware, data encryption technologies, and virus protection software is also in high demand.

- **Social media skills** are now a field distinct from general computer skills and imply an ability to engage with social media in a variety of technical and marketing-specific ways. They include such as abilities as the writing of correct, concise, and engaging copy (for company web sites, as well as Facebook profiles, LinkedIn or Glassdoor information, even Twitter); graphic design or video creation skills are also necessary for a viable social media presence; and other online networking skills.

- **Public speaking** is still a valuable skill to nurture and develop for any employee: from presenting reports to engaging with local or national media, an employee with solid public speaking abilities can add value to their candidacy.

- **Customer service skills** are crucially important to particular industries that sell a specific product or service. They require strong interpersonal skills and an affable personality.

- **Language ability** is always valuable to nearly any industry and certain industries or employers require some basic language skills in order to interact with customers and/or clients. Depending on the industry, Spanish-speaking ability might be important to the customer base, for example, or Chinese language ability might be useful in attracting investors.

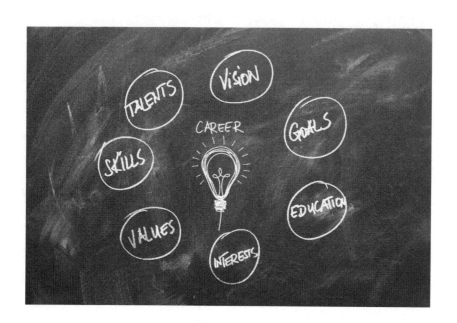

Chapter 4: Preparation for an Interview: Common Q&A Strategies

In addition to identifying skills and researching the company, you will actually need to prepare yourself for the specific interview. One of the most important ways in which you can prepare is to identify common questions in job interviews and prepare specific answers to these. This means you must spend some time anticipating potential questions and devising proficient answers. There are several kinds of questions that interviewers might ask and being prepared, in some form or fashion, for each type of potential question will mean that you are not unpleasantly surprised or unprepared for anything. For an in-depth look at interviewing techniques, types of questions, and how to prepare proficient answers, see my book *Job Interview Q&A*. For a brief explanation of this part of the interview process, see below.

Basic Q&A Strategies

- **Be prepared to respond to the inevitable "tell me about yourself"** opener. Generally speaking, one of the first responses that interviewers might prompt is an open-ended dissertation on yourself. This question is a kind of litmus test, an ice breaker, and a jumping off point all in one. First, it reveals whether or not you are comfortable and prepared. Second, it functions to allow everyone to settle in a bit and relax before getting into the specific nitty-gritty of the interview. Third, it is a chance for the interviewer to discover something about you that he or she might wish to follow up on. Thus, this seemingly off-hand prompt is actually an important initial component to many interviews; have an answer ready to go, focusing on the aspects of yourself that relate to the job position, as well as being genuine and interesting.

- **Credential questions** will ask you to elaborate on your educational experience, any certifications or other licenses you may have acquired during the course of your previous experience, or positions of leadership you may have held. You should be prepared to discuss specific aspects of your credentials, such as classes taken or conferences attended—anything relevant to how you achieved the degrees, certificates, licenses, or other accolades that you have earned. This is not about work experience, but about your diligence and perseverance in gaining the accreditation needed to fulfill the expectations of certain positions.

- **Experience questions** will ask you to elaborate upon your past work (or volunteer or intern) experience. These kinds of questions prompt you to think about how you interact with others, how readily you respond to expectations and/or pressure, how well you organize and communicate, or how effectively you produce and/or work with a team. This is where you want to come up with a story or two about overcoming obstacles, solving problems, increasing productivity, or otherwise initiating innovation in your past experience. It also sometimes gives you a chance to discuss a passion project that you've undertaken in the past, either via work, interning, or volunteering.

- **Opinion questions** will ask just that: your opinion on either an abstract issue or a concrete fact/problem/event. These kinds of questions ask you to comment about issues within your industry or regarding your past work experience. They often require you to make ethical judgments and to explain how you might respond in a given situation. These questions are both an opportunity to reveal something significant about your overall character, as well as how you might respond to difficulties or pressure.

- **Behavior questions** will ask what you would do in particular scenarios, as well as prompting you to provide an overarching template of how you operate in a professional setting. These kinds of questions might ask how you would solve a particular problem or how you worked to reach a specific goal. Conversely, these might ask you to describe how you overcame a stressful situation at work or how you responded to a setback. This would be an opportunity for you to indicate how one or more of the items listed in your skill set would be applicable to a real-time situation in the workplace.

- **Case studies questions** are usually particular to one specific interview, wherein the interviewer(s) will present a scenario to the potential candidate, then allow the candidate time to study the case before performing an analysis of the situation and projecting results or offering advice on how to render the best possible outcome. This is the kind of interview you would usually be informed about in advance.

- **Brain teasers questions** are quick-fire questions that test specific skills or analytical abilities. In certain cases, you might be asked to perform mathematical problems or solve logic puzzles. In other cases, you might be asked to demonstrate proficiency in a task associated with the industry. For example, before an interview as an editor, you may be asked to take a grammatical test or review a sample submission using editorial marks.

- **Also, you should prepare some questions of your own** prior to the interview. You might have some questions with regard to company practices and policies, product research and development, the logistics of your department, or salary and benefits. Prepare a list of these in advance, as most interviewers will allow some time at the end for your questions. Be cautious with regard to questions of salary and benefit, especially if not dealing with a direct superior. They may only have enough information to give you ranges or broad ideas. In addition, the question might come back to you, so be prepared to present a range, from the baseline of what you will accept to the high end of what you desire. Also, think of how badly you want the job: if you will only accept the job if it comes with a certain salary and benefits, make this clear up front.

- **Finally, a bit of practice** prior to the interview. Practicing your answers aloud in front of a mirror gives you some idea of how ready you are to respond, or you can practice with mock interviews, should you have friends or family who'd be willing to help you out. If you plan to throw out specific information for any of your answers—numbers, dates, statistics, examples—be sure to memorize these. Jot down notes on an interview preparation sheet for you to review.

Answering Techniques: STAR Method

There are many different ways in which you can answer interview questions, but one technique in particular has been utilized successfully in job interviews for many years: the STAR technique gives you specific guidelines for how to respond to the most common types of interview questions, by giving you the basic outline for how to put together the most concrete, detailed but concise answer that you can. STAR stands for situation, task, action(s) and result(s); each element should be addressed within your answer. Using the STAR technique to outline particular answers to potential questions is one of the most effective ways in which you can prepare yourself for a job interview.

Situation

With regard to the interview itself, the STAR method indicates a path by which you construct your answers to any variety of questions, and the first thing you should do—besides taking a moment to ponder the question—is to lay out the **situation** in your answer. In general, the STAR technique is primarily focused on the kinds of answers that you would give to behavioral questions (though most questions posed in an interview could readily be behavioral questions). As such, when you are asked a question about past experiences or actions, the first thing to do is to illustrate the situation: essentially, you are describing the situation in which the relevant event was taking place. This context could be anything from working on a team project to dealing with a difficult colleague. **Situation** lays down the groundwork from which you build the edifice of your answer, one story at a time. Beware of providing too much background and instead focus on the most relevant parts of the situation: you want to underscore the complexity or depth of the situation so that your resolution seems that much stronger, but you don't want to dwell on details that have nothing to do with your part in the process (an interviewer doesn't need to know that the client had been with the company for three years, for example, just that a client in good standing had an issue that you were able to resolve). Two or three sentences to set up the **situation** is really all that is needed. Remember, there will be plenty more questions to come. Think back to the "five Ws," as your high school English teacher might have said: what, who, where, when, and why.

Still, even if an interview question isn't a clear behavioral question, the STAR method can be applied. Character questions (what are your strengths/weaknesses?), experience questions (what were your previous job responsibilities?), and opinion questions (what do you value in a co-worker?) can all be more effectively answered with a story set up in STAR format. It will give you specific details and concrete actions that more precisely reveal your hard and soft skills.

Task

The **task** portion of your answer details the specific responsibilities you were given in the situation described. These are the tasks that you review before you decide on your course of action, which will be detailed in the following chapter. Tasks allow you to identify concrete details of objectives that will reveal your attendant skill set. You have already relayed the background in the situation part of your answer; now show what particular tasks were your responsibilities in dealing with the situation. As with situation, listing task should be brief, but it is crucially important that the tasks be concrete and familiar to the interviewer. If you are discussing tasks that a personnel manager might not understand, then you aren't really illuminating your skill set. Be aware of your audience before you determine what kind of tasks would best suit an interview question. An interviewer who has deep knowledge of your technical expertise would be better able to relate to highly specialized tasks.

In preparing for any interview, it is an excellent idea to compile a list of skills to which you can refer. These skills should be both soft skills—attitude, communication, conflict resolution, teamwork, flexibility, leadership, problem solving—and hard skills, the technical expertise or educational qualifications that you possess. When preparing a STAR answer, refer to your list of skills and be sure that you can relate a particular skill or (better yet) several skills to the tasks you relay in your answer. Being able to show the connection between task designated and skill used to respond is a key component in a strong interview.

Action(s)

When answering behavioral questions during the interview, **action** is where you detail the specific steps you took to reach a goal or solve a problem. This part of your answer is the place to showcase the wide range and depth of your skills, and it requires attention to detail and a concrete sense of how you determined a course of action that led to positive results. The more specifically you can convey exactly what actions you took indicate to the interviewer that you possess higher level soft skills as well as the hard skills to execute results. You should also consider preparing several examples of specific actions you have taken in a variety of different professional experiences; be sure to use examples that showcase different strengths, rather than repeating the same one or two. Show that your skill set has breadth as well as depth.

Make sure that you have a written list of your skills and start to think of specific examples using concrete detail that show how you have put these skills into action. It is not enough to suggest that you have "effective communication skills"—anyone can claim that—you must come up with actual examples that reveal how your actions put your effective communication skills to work, producing real, desirable results.

Result(s)

The last part of your answer during an interview should focus on the **results** that your previous actions brought about; you want to emphasize the positive aspects of those results, of course, in addition to any innovative impacts that your actions might have had. Certainly, no interview story should end with, "because my ideas were so radical, I was ultimately let go." This is not a story to be telling at an interview. You want to highlight the successes you've had in past work experience (or educational, though most employers want to see something directly related to work, even if it's volunteer or internship work). Even if you are talking about a past experience that might have been negative—a time you failed, for example, or a challenge that seemed insurmountable—you should always endeavor to end on the most positive note you can. This might lead to **results** that reveal how much you learned and changed after a negative experience, or how you developed professionally in the face of difficult circumstances. Don't fall into the trap of telling a story that ends flatly, with no positive trajectory out of the negative experience.

Other questions will inherently emphasize the positive, so you should have no trouble iterating **results** that matter: an interviewer doesn't just want to hear about what your responsibilities were or which actions were taken; they want to hear about why those decisions and actions ultimately *mattered*. If these results are measurable, all the better: if your results are quantifiable—sales numbers grew by X percentage, or productivity rose by a factor of X, or customer interest soared by X-fold—then you demonstrate the concrete nature of how you produce positive results out of decisive and skilled actions.

Also note that, oftentimes, when an interviewer asks a behavioral question, he or she will not necessarily ask you to recount what the results were. However, this is implicit in the question itself, so be sure to go beyond just recounting the situation encountered and the actions taken; an interviewer will want to know what the results, ultimately, were.

Chapter 5: The Interview: First Impressions

Making a memorably positive first impression is one of your most crucial tasks in an interview setting: first impressions can never be re-done or taken back, so it is imperative that you have a full understanding of what it entails to engage in professional etiquette from the moment you begin the interview—even prior to that actual beginning—to the moment you follow up.

An ideal first impression is initially informed by how we look, in particular, in how we are dressed and groomed prior to the interview. In recent years, the standards for what constitutes "business" dress have been changed and, for the most part, expanded. Still, a job interview is more than likely more formal than typical employee dress standards (especially when considering the proliferation of "casual Fridays" and tech start-ups jeans and t-shirts). Whatever the company for which you are interviewing, you should follow some basic guidelines to ensure that you are looking professional and making a smart first impression.

Professional Presentation: Looking the Part

- In doing your company research, you should have some broader knowledge of company culture, including how employees are supposed to present themselves in the workplace. Use that knowledge to base your understanding of how to present yourself at an interview: as stated above, an interview is likely a more formal affair than an everyday work look, but it gives you a starting point. Be sure to peruse any company photos, especially on social media, to get an idea of how employees dress when they are representing the company.

- While you are trying to look your best—professional and poised—you should also take into consideration your comfort level. That is, don't wear something that is too tight, too bulky, or too warm to an interview. The more comfortable you are in your professional attire, the more confidence you project. Be sure to take the seasons into occasion, and wear layers if you tend to get warm during an interview; you can take off a jacket should you need to, if you are wearing a nice dress shirt or blouse underneath.

- Avoid wearing anything that is revealing, such as a sun dress or low-cut blouse. This guideline doesn't at first appear to relate to men, but a vee-necked shirt or lack of socks might fall along these lines for men. The idea is not to look like you're going out with friends, but they you are representing yourself professionally for a company.

- Be certain that your clothes are recently cleaned, especially if you plan to wear a suit or other truly formal attire, and check for stains, tears, or other signs of distress. If you do not have an appropriate outfit for an interview and lack the financial ability to purchase one quickly, there are many resources in communities, like Dress for Success, that will help you find something appropriate at a reasonable price—or for free.

- Lay or set out your clothes the night before the interview. This ensures that you make a good inspection of everything (if you have pets, be sure to give yourself a quick roll before you leave the house) and that you don't have any last minute delays. One of the worst things you can do is to show up late for an interview: give yourself plenty of time to get ready and to get there on time.

- Don't second guess yourself or overthink it. If you feel reasonably comfortable and have chosen a clean, pressed outfit that seems to meet the standards of the company, then you are probably going to be just fine.

- While your abilities and skill set are vastly more relevant to whether or not you can do the job you're trying to procure, your image says a lot about how you view yourself. It projects that you have a solid work ethic—enough that you care about how you are perceived by others in the professional space. These guidelines aren't to satisfy some bland, generic standard; they are a way for you to meet expectations while projecting a sense of responsibility and maturity.
- Looking "good" and feeling "good" are reciprocal ideas: if you look good, then you will feel good—and vice versa. The same goes for professionalism: if you look like a professional, then you are more likely to act like a professional.
- It also follows that feeling good is instrumental to performing well and looking professional. That is, take care of yourself by eating well, drinking lots of water, exercising, getting adequate sleep, and applying some of the stress reducers discussed in the previous chapter. Taking care of yourself is a first, big step toward looking and feeling good and professional.
- How you are dressed telegraphs a message about who you are: think about that before your interview and

beyond your professional life. What kind of message do you want to send about your persona, your capacities, and your intelligence? This should serve as a constant baseline for checking in on your workplace look.

- Always, when in doubt (or when thrown into an unfamiliar professional situation), overdress rather than underdress. It is far better to show up to a conference in a comfortable business suit when everyone is in khakis and button-ups than it is to show up in jeans and a t-shirt when everyone is wearing a business suit. Better to be the more polished the candidate than a diamond in the (too) rough.

- Keep your sense of personal style without overdoing it. You are an individual, after all, and the way in which you present yourself to the world is part of your identity. Just be clear that your identity should also express a sense of teamwork to your potential employer. Dressing in a standard professional way indicates you are willing to play by the rules, as it were, and be a member of a larger team.

- Finally, remember that looking professionally is, at base, a way of showing respect for your interviewer and for the company at which you wish to be hired. It is also a way of showing respect for yourself, presenting yourself as a confident, capable, and courteous potential employee.

Professional Presentation: Acting the Part

Acting professionally consists of any number of minor behaviors and skills of etiquette. As anyone who has worked with others in any capacity before well knows, the attitude one displays and the behavior one engages in speaks volumes about personal character and professional capacity. When embarking on an interview, it is understandable to be intimated by strangers who have some sort of control over your potential future. However, now that you have snagged the interview with your sharp resume and descriptive cover letter, you need only to look—and act—the part. The following tips should help you develop your professional etiquette for the interview. See the next chapter for some other tips on how to put your best foot forward for any job scenario.

- Remember that one of the crucial tests you must pass when attending a job interview is the litmus test of whether you will fit into the culture of the company. In general terms, this means that you need to demonstrate professional etiquette and respect not only to your interviewer but toward anyone else you may encounter (other employees, like a receptionist or secretary or colleagues in your department or group). Your skills are rendered irrelevant if your behavior is boorish and rude.

- Consider your first impression; you must not only look the part but also act the part. A first impression can never be retracted, so it is important not to begin an interview on the wrong foot. From the moment you arrive at the company, be on your most professional behavior: for all you know, the person you greet in the hallway or ride in the elevator with may be your future boss or colleague. Be enthusiastic and look happy—rather than apprehensive—to be there. Make eye contact and introduce yourself politely when appropriate, extending a handshake in most cases. When entering the interview space, be sure to accept instructions politely and strike an open—rather than defensive—posture.

- As mentioned above, be sure that the outfit you've chosen to wear for the interview is appropriate and professional, but also be aware of how it will appear when you are seated. You want to avoid the proverbial wardrobe malfunction (gaping blouse, popped button, overly hiked pants). Typically, you will be seated for most of the interview, so that's how you should test the comforts and utility of your chosen attire.

- Always remember to smile and appear interested in what the interviewer is saying. A smile (or, conversely, a frown) can speak volumes. If you appear smiling and approachable, then you are perceived as a team player with valuable character attributes as well as professional skills to bring to the company. A frown, on the other hand, can fluster or annoy the interviewer; it is difficult to know how to interpret the facial expression. Are you angry, annoyed, bored, frustrated, or otherwise unimpressed? This is not the impression you want to convey. Remind yourself that this experience, while somewhat nerve-racking, should be an amiable way in which to showcase your considerable talents and value. This would bring a smile to anyone's face.

- Body language, in general, reveals a lot about a person's feelings and character. Crossing your arms against your chest looks defensive, even hostile, while a lazy slump indicates a lack of interest or disrespect. Keeping your hands folded in your lap throughout the interview can have the effect of implying childlike anxiety. "Man-spreading" can look aggressive or arrogant. Again, maintain eye contact when answering questions, and avoid sweeping hand gestures. You can hold a pen or pencil in your hand if it helps to center you, and this can come in handy should you wish to jot anything down. Basically, your body language should indicate that you are engaged and open, enthusiastic and polite.

- When greeting others, be sure that you have a solid handshake, somewhere between limp and crushing. A firm handshake reveals self-confidence and a courteous understanding of overall business etiquette. When meeting someone for the first time, it is considered polite to use an honorific, such as Dr. or Ms. or Mr. If the company for which you are interviewed is owned or operated by foreign nationals, then it would behoove you to do some research into the basic etiquette of the other country. Personal space is defined differently in different cultures, in addition to attitudes about how men and women behave.
- Addressing someone by their name is also a powerful piece of business etiquette that you can employ to curry respect. Everyone likes to be noticed and remembered, so try your best to remember and repeat the names of people that you meet. Should you be called in for a further interview, this

considerate formality will inevitably be noticed. Still, don't sound sycophantic: continuously repeating the interviewer's name throughout the interview—"now, that's an interesting question, Dr. Jones. Let me see how I can answer that fully, Dr. Jones. Thank you, Dr. Jones"—can be annoying and patronizing.

- As you are seated for your interview—which you should be invited to do, rather than simply plopping down—place your personal items beside or underneath your chair. For everyone's sanity and to preserve your dignity, turn off your cell phone and any other device you may have carried with you. Have your resume and cover letter, along with a notepad or folder for notes, at the ready.

- If, for some disastrous reason, your phone should ring during an interview, you will be called upon to do some swift damage control. Do not dare look at the phone to check (unless you truly have a life-and-death situation on your hands); simply turn it off and apologize to the interviewer. You would have to be an excellent candidate to overcome this most egregious of etiquette breaches. It's better not to take your phone in with you if you have a habit of forgetting to switch it off. And off means *off*, not silent.

- When leaving the interview, be sure to restate your interest in the job and your pleasure at having met everyone. Shake hands again and repeat names, when appropriate. Be sure to thank the receptionist who showed you in, if relevant. Basically, just show proper manners on your way out the door.
- After the interview, it is customary to write a "thank you" note of some sort to the interviewer or interviewers to acknowledge their time and your opportunity.

Chapter 6: The Interview: Communication Skills

Obviously, possessing effective communication skills is crucial to any interview or professional position: you must have basic writing abilities, effective oral communication strategies, as well as acceptable interpersonal skills. In addition, listening skills are an oft-forgotten, yet equally crucial, component in effective communication. These skills are in display from the beginning of any job search: your resume and cover letter will reveal how well you communicate in writing, while the job interview itself will showcase how effectively you communicate orally, as well as how attuned you are to good listening. See below for a refresher review of the basic components of effective communication skills.

Writing Abilities

- Obviously, the first piece of information that you must create before you even attempt getting the job interview is the **resume**. After you have acquired the skills, education, and experience necessary to secure your ideal job, you have to be able to put them into a professional, easily readable, and impressive compilation that is called the resume. Think about how each and every one of your experiences can apply to something in the job that you are applying to—and, yes, you should customize your resume for each job for which you apply. If you don't necessarily have a lot of working experience—say, you are a recent college graduate—then you need to show how other activities you have done (volunteering, interning, hobbies) will translate well into the professional arena.

- To get started, seek out sample resumes from across the internet or from other job platforms. You need not worry about building a great resume from scratch; there are any number of templates available at many different sites that can get you started. Be sure to match the template with your field, as you don't want an academic curriculum vitae if you are applying for a standard job in business, and vice versa (just for one example).

- Once you find a template that you think is right for your particular set of skills and your field, then be sure to spend adequate time customizing it. You don't want such a generic resume that you won't stand out in the field of other candidates. Also think about your own personal style and how you can show that—

within reason and with professionalism—on your particular resume.

- Also consider how you organize your resume, for there are many different ways in which you can relay the material. Most often, resumes are organized chronological, listing educational and professional achievements and positions in the order at which they occurred, from most recent on down. But you could also create a different type of resume, if you have a different set of skills and experience: a functional resume, for instance, lists skills and abilities with relevant examples, instead of listing them in chronological order (this might be a good idea if your work experience is limited); a targeted resume will have you specifically "target" your abilities and past experience to the exact job that you want, following closely on the original request for employment. And, of course, a combination resume puts these different methods together. Think about what is the best fit for you and for this particular job.

- The resume itself should be simple and easy to read: most hiring managers will merely skim a resume, rather than read it thoroughly, so the more able you are to make the most important information the most prominent, that better serves your purpose. Some basic formatting tips and techniques are as follows:

- o use a basic font, as discussed above;
- o don't justify your margins, which creates odd gaps in formatting;
- o keep dates and other numbers aligned to the right;
- o use digits when employing numbers (10, rather than ten);
- o avoid centering any information;
- o use boldface to highlight either the company for whom you worked or your respective roles at previous workplaces, but not both;
- o avoid all caps;
- o when using bullet points, keep it to two lines or less;
- o employ a separate section for skills, so prospective employers can read through quickly;
- o and be consistent in formatting throughout your resume, leaving some white space for ease of reading.
- There is no need to include a list of references on your resume itself; if you get the job interview, the

interviewer will expect that you have references, and you should be prepared to provide them.

- Next, your writing abilities will be showcased in your **cover letter**, of course. Not all jobs require a cover letter, but most skilled professional jobs do. Even if you're not asked to provide a cover letter, a brief and well-written expression of interest in and qualification for the job would not be misplaced.

- While this may not be the advice that many applicants wish to hear, it is the best possible advice: you should craft an individual and specific cover letter for each position to which you apply. In a typical three paragraph letter, this would mean changing details in the first paragraph regarding the position itself, and writing your second paragraph—the bulk of the cover letter—about your skills, qualifications, experiences, and enthusiasm for this particular job. Address the cover letter personally and professionally to your interviewer, hiring manager, or potential employer, when possible. You should also do some research into the company itself, so that you have some idea of the bigger picture; this is addressed later in this book.

- There are always templates available online, as with resumes, so don't hesitate to use one of these, or at least review some of them to get a better idea of how to begin and develop your cover letter. When opening the letter, try to move beyond the intentionally generic "I am writing to apply for X position with X company"—this is dull and reveals a potential lack of enthusiasm on your part.

- While "To Whom It May Concern" is still a standard in the annals of writing to someone you don't personally know, when addressing a cover letter, strive to make it somewhat more specific, such as "Dear Hiring Manager" or "To the Department of X at Company X." This simply shows that you aren't recycling a rehashed letter for multiple jobs.

- Use the cover letter to review more of your work history and experience than what is revealed in your resume; that is, be careful to simply repeat what is already listed on your resume. Start thinking, instead, about particular activities in which you participated in a professional capacity that reveal something special about you as an employee. Illustrate what skills this task asked you to utilize, talk about what was accomplished as a result, and think about what soft skills you were also called upon to use. Getting down to this specific level will not only make you a stronger candidate, but will also serve to help you begin to prepare for the interview itself.

- Avoid the pitfall of talking about how much this job would mean to you—sure, that's in your self-interest, but your potential employer doesn't necessarily care. Instead, focus on what you would bring to the job and to the larger company as a whole. The intention is to show how well you would fit into a particular position at this specific company.

- This is also the place where you can make a case for the fact that you would be an ideal fit for the position—even if your work history doesn't necessarily reveal that. This is especially important in a cover letter that you write for a job that takes you off your beaten career path, or if you are writing a cover letter for your first big job out of graduation. You need to be able to show how your training and skills and personality are equal to the task of whatever this job might have on hand. That said, link any experience directly to the job, when at all possible.

- You also want to strike a balance in your tone. Of course, a cover letter should be succinct and professional, but it shouldn't be overly stiff or formal. You want some part of your personality to show, as well. When you are excessively formal, you appear stiff and distant, while too much conversational personality can appear flippant and inappropriate.

You want to both approachable while maintaining a professional demeanor.

- You should also employ the research you have done on the company in the cover letter itself, using key words and other lingo that will reflect your knowledge of the company at large. Peruse the web site and social media for the company and employ some of the key words and/or phrases used there; don't overdo, of course, or you risk sounding too sycophantic.

- Finally, you *must* EDIT your cover letter carefully and thoroughly; have an English savvy friend or colleague help you out if necessary. Cover letters with grammatical or syntactical difficulties undermine any good they can possibly do. One bit of advice for any writing you may do in your professional career: READ IT ALOUD before you conduct a final edit and turn it in. Reading aloud can help you capture the tone (is it too stiff and formal? Too conversational?) and flow (is it too rambling? well organized?), as well as alert you to mistakes (if you're gasping for breath at the end of a sentence, then it probably needs some editing). When you enter the interview space, you should know your cover letter as well as you know yourself—indeed, because that is what it is, a reflection of yourself—and be prepared to elaborate on in material within it.

- For more detailed guidelines to the resume and cover letter part of the job interview process, see my book *Job Interview Preparation*.

Effective Oral Communication

- Clearly, the interview itself is designed for you to showcase your oral communication skills. One of the best ways that you can ensure that you are revealing your skills in the most effective manner possible is to **prepare and practice** for the interview, following the tips and techniques as outlined in Chapter 4. You can also find more in-depth guidelines to how to prepare for interview questions and answers in my book, *Interview Q&A*.

- Another way in which you can demonstrate effective oral communication is in how you manage yourself: **body language and other non-verbal cues** fill in the blanks in any interview (or, really, any) situation. See the guidelines for how to conduct yourself professionally to understand how to telegraph the correct cues during an interview.

- You will also want to learn how to manage your stress levels. A lot of people's greatest fear is that they will

say the wrong thing. To avoid this pitfall, remind yourself that this is actually quite a simple stressor to overcome. Keep it simple: avoid profanity or offensive language and just be yourself. That's really all the advice you need to conquer that particular fear.

- While in the interview, if you need a moment to **compose yourself**, then take it. Ask the interviewer to repeat a question, or rephrase the question back to him or her to give you a chance to think about it before answering; take a sip of water; check in with the interviewer that you've fully answered a given question. There's nothing wrong with allowing yourself a moment of time to think. It's perfectly acceptable to say, "That is a really good question. Let me think about that for a moment."

- Also remember that almost all questions offer you the opportunity to **reveal something positive about yourself**, in addition to the obstacle of inadvertently showcasing something negative about yourself. If you are asked about your strengths, then you should obviously address particular skills, either hard or soft, that you have demonstrated in specific and concrete ways in the past. It is not enough to say that you have "very effective communication skills"; you need to be able to reveal how you have specifically used those skills in past positions: "I think that one of my greatest strengths is my effective communication skills, which I demonstrated in writing the annual report and providing press releases to the media." Or, "My effective communication skills led to a role within the team as mediator in solving problems and conflicts." With regard to a hard skill, you might show how your facility with programming led to a specific promotion or a coveted position on a high level team; in this case, describe the specific project and your role in it. Still, displaying one's strengths takes some humility and finesse: if you come across as a braggart—"I was the best salesperson the company had ever seen"—then you are effectively undermining your candidacy.

Interpersonal Skills

- Professionally speaking, interpersonal skills reveal how an employee engages and interacts with those around her, and they are a sign of **emotional intelligence and the ability to communicate effectively**. While not always directly related to written, oral, or aural skills, the ways in which these interpersonal skills are relayed is through these communication outlets. Interpersonal skills show how an employee is motivated and how he or she uses knowledge and analysis to get the best results in a given professional situation.

- Specifically, interpersonal skills consist of **several elements**: displaying self-confidence; maintaining a strong work ethic; fostering the ability to work well with others; sustaining dependability; demonstrating openness to others and to feedback; collaborating well with others; and showing appreciation and positivity.

- Again, a great deal of interpersonal skills is covered by **maintaining a professional etiquette** as discussed in Chapter 5.

The Importance of Listening

- It is potentially the case that listening is one of the most underestimated skills that is necessary for a job interview. Showcasing solid listening skills will make you appear **empathetic, engaged, intelligent, and enthusiastic**. While you should certainly practice your answers to potential questions as detailed earlier in this guide, you should avoid spouting off practiced answers without truly listening to what the interviewer is requesting. An interview should have an ebb and flow like a conversation, and while much of it will be focused on you, be sure to allow yourself time and space to listen and absorb what is going on at the other side of the equation.

- Be sure to use your listening skills to **perceive information that may be somewhat implicit rather than explicit**. If an interviewer consistently asks about your ability to handle stressful situations, then you might rightly deduce that this is a high pressure workplace. If an interviewer seems interested in your future professional development plans, this might signal that you are a candidate for a higher level position. In any case, the interviewer will consciously or incidentally reveal a lot about the company. Listening to what is said will give you ample opportunity and ammunition to ask pertinent questions and make smart decisions.

- There are specific ways in which you can **hone your listening skills**. Let's face facts: many of us, particularly when faced with being put on the spot in a stressful situation such as a job interview, will tune out what is going on around us. Diligent observation and listening skills take some practice.

  - Practice listening with a friend or family member. Ask them to tell you an unfamiliar story, then try to relay the details back to them a few hours later. Or, simply let your support group know that, in preparation for the interview, you'd like to be made aware of when you are accidentally zoning out. As long as you leave personal feelings aside, you'll likely learn a lot about how carefully you listen—or not.

o Prepare for the interview thoroughly, both in terms of practical preparation and in terms of psychological preparation. Have everything ready to go the night before (outfit, materials, travel plans), as well as conduct stress relieving activities the day before and get a good night's sleep. The more prepared you are, the better able you are to relax enough to be a good listener.

o Keep your materials as organized and simple as possible, so you can avoid accidental distractions. It's likely you'll miss something important if you're rooting around in your bag for a pen, for example. And remember to *turn off your cell phone*. One quick buzz or ring can ruin an entire interview, much less your ability to focus and listen.

o Your body language will indicate to the interviewer how well you are listening. Show engagement by leaning toward the interviewer when he or she is speaking; nod when appropriate; and avoid interruption. All of these silent signals reveal that you are a good listener—a boon to you during the interview process itself, and a boon to any employer who wishes to hire an employee with excellent communication skills.

o Repeat back to the interviewer what he or she is saying in order to be certain that you have the most important details clear. This is a method by which you clearly indicate that you have been respectfully listening.

Chapter 7: The Interview: Positive Attitude

There is no substitute for enthusiasm and positivity, especially in what amounts to a stressful situation and litmus test for personality. In a job interview, it is important to remember that the attitude that you present is almost as crucial as the credentials you bring with you. All the education, training, and experience in your given industry will not make up for a lack of interest and energy. This is not only important to the interview itself, but it is undeniably important to the employment to follow—perhaps, arguably, a positive attitude is one of the keys to a successful and satisfying life, in general. In any event, this "soft" skill remains one of the most potent skills that you can bring with you to an interview and to employment overall. Below is a handy reference for the kinds of positivity that you want to bring with you to work each and every day, followed by some specific ways in which you can use your positive attitude within the job interview itself.

Working Positive

- Always remember to **use positive language**, especially in potentially disheartening situations. When a project is late or revenues are down, try to see the opportunity in the obstacle, rather than dwell on the negative. Avoid profanity in your professional life, as well; while it may not be disturbing to everyone (indeed, in some professions, profanity is rampant), it diminishes your professional stature and comes across as negative or even aggressive to many.

- When dealing with others at work, **avoid directly criticizing**. There is an enormous difference between constructive suggestions and overly critical attack. If someone on your team is consistently late for meetings or misses deadlines, then approach them with kindness and genuine concern: what's going on? How can we help? Also remember to always approach others in private when discussing sensitive matters. A compassionate and open approach is always more successful than a scathing, negative dressing down. Keeping an open and constructive feedback loop is crucial to the smooth success of any workplace environment.

- Speaking of working well with others, always endeavor to **put teamwork first**. This isn't limited to difficult situations, of course: if someone has done excellent work, then be sure to acknowledge their contributions. If things are not going well with a team, then be sure to include everyone in a brainstorming session about how to come up with solutions. If you start to recognize that every obstacle is actually an opportunity, then you are on the best track toward promoting positive teamwork.

- Another way to keep the workplace positive is to **avoid gossip**. This kind of backbiting undermines any sense of team spirit and serves to make you a potential target of retribution and anger. Keep the workplace professional; the personal is truly none of your actual business.

- Finally, while not every day at your job can be a wonderful day—we've all had those Mondays—try to **avoid complaining**. If you or your team are having a particularly bad day, use humor to try to shake things up and shake off the bad vibes. If that isn't appropriate in the circumstances, then keep things positive with a word or two of encouragement, a reminder that the only way to go from here is up. Your positivity is positively contagious!

Interview Techniques

- Within the job interview itself, **maintaining a positive attitude** is crucial to your success: if you don't seem enthusiastic and energetic at the interview, then your performance as an employee is immediately suspect.

- Part of the process to showing a positive attitude is how you utilize your **professional etiquette**. Be friendly and professional with everyone you meet, from the security guard to the secretary to the interviewer. Make eye contact, shake hands firmly, and remember to smile.

- Also remember that it is the interviewer's task to test you a bit, and this will often take the form of asking questions that focus on the negative; it is your task within the interview to always **give your answers a positive spin**:

  o Common to most interviews, the **question about weakness** will inevitably be asked, in some form or another. "What critical feedback do you receive most often?" is just another version of the same kind of question. This kind of question poses a pitfall because it asks you to reveal something negative about yourself, which certainly leaves us feeling vulnerable, especially in an interview situation. It also poses a pitfall in that you might either avoid the question or forget to steer into positive territory. In the first instance, a candidate

586

might respond by suggesting that the critical feedback he's ever received has been inconsequential; this comes across as arrogant and/or lacking in self-awareness. In the second instance, you reveal a flaw without indicating that you are working on it. The best answer acknowledges that you have a weakness—this indicates self-awareness and humility—and reveals specific and concrete actions that you have been taking to improve—focusing and ending on the positive.

o In a similar vein, potential employers will also often ask about an **obstacle that you have overcome** in the past. This, again, invites the uncomfortable proposition that you reveal something difficult and/or negative from your past. Nevertheless, if you are prepared with a STAR ready answer (see Chapter 4), providing details about the situation, tasks, actions, and results that shows how you ultimately overcame said obstacle, then you are actually telling an inspiring story about both your professional abilities and your personal attributes. Telling a story that combines the use of your hard skills and soft skills is the strongest way to approach this kind of question.

- Because stress is a component of every professional experience, employers will often want to test your facility for handling it, so you should expect a question about **how you deal with stress or pressure**. Again, don't make the mistake of suggesting that you never get stressed out or that you deal with stress just fine. This is clearly skirting the truth, and the employer knows it. Rather, construct a specific example wherein you acknowledge that you felt enormous pressure (of deadline, on your skill set, or other) but took steps to deal with that stress to overcome it. Make sure that you reveal the results (STAR method, again) of your process: showing that even though you almost buckled under stress but ended up figuring out a way to deal with it and overcome it—to positive ends—is a satisfying and inspiring story.

- Another potential pitfall are questions that ask you to comment about your **personal experience with management or colleagues**. An interviewer might ask what your worst experience was or to describe a conflict that happened in your previous experience. Certainly, you should approach the question with honesty—but also with a healthy dose of tact. An employer wants to know what kind of person and/or management style you work best with, of course, but he or she doesn't really want to know that about past squabbles or the personal foibles of others. Avoid any personal references, names, or other information that might tip the interviewer off to a particular person about whom you might be discussing. Indeed, it is best not to discuss others when answering the question, in general. Instead, come up with a specific example wherein a negative experience—a clash of personalities, or a conflict of interests—created a temporarily difficult working situation, emphasis on the *temporary*. You want to end the story with how it was resolved in as positive a manner as possible.

o If you are currently employed by another company within the industry, then you will most likely be asked about **why you are leaving your current job**. This question proffers a

589

possible landmine of inappropriate responses, just as with the above question. This is not the time to get personal or to use the interview as a chance to complain about another company, boss, or colleague. Instead, it is the opportunity for you to offer your potential employer an honest assessment of what wasn't working for you in your current position that encouraged you to seek a job elsewhere. Tactful honesty is the best policy here, as well. Try to frame your response in the most positive terms available: "I have thoroughly enjoyed my work with X Company, but at this time, professional growth opportunities are few. I wanted to begin thinking about career advancement at this moment in my professional life, so this job offered me the chance to best use my many skills."

○ Another difficult question you might get is to talk about your **greatest regrets and/or your greatest achievements**: as with questions about weaknesses and strengths, be sure you have a ready answer prepared that doesn't swing too hard to the negative or dwell too much on the arrogance. Showing an ability to learn from regrets is the best approach in that scenario, while relaying one specific achievement in the context of your professional life is the best way to show success without arrogance. Stick to one example that is specific to one past experience.

- For more detailed advice on specific interview questions and answer techniques, see my book, *Job Interview Q&A*.

Chapter 8: The Interview: Demonstrating Teamwork

One of the other vital skills that you will want to demonstrate both in the interview and on the job is teamwork. In an increasingly collaborative environment, most professional industries prize an employee's ability to work well in a team, which both increases production and requires a host of "soft" skills, such as effective communication and conflict resolution. Be prepared in your interview to talk about ways in which you have demonstrated teamwork in the past and your willingness to join this particular team in the future. Below are some questions that you might be asked, along with some suggestions as to how to respond during your interview.

- Some very basic questions or prompts that a hiring manager may give you are "give me some specific examples of your previous experience with teamwork" or "how do you feel about working on a team?" What the interviewer really wants to know is if you **enjoy working with a team and how, specifically, can you demonstrate these skills**. This requires specific answers with concrete details and particular examples, not merely a recitation of the merits of working with others. Be sure to prepare a story, using the STAR method (situation, task, actions, results), to describe a specific instance of when you worked on a team and how well that experience went. Ideally, this experience will come out of a previous work assignment; however, if you don't have a lot of work experience, in general, or are potentially new to a collaborative workplace, then you can use experiences that you may have had in recreational sports or volunteer coordination or other extracurricular activity wherein you worked in a team. The important idea here is to make sure that you provide an actual example with specific examples of how you managed to communicate effectively and respond within a team.

- Another kind of experience verification question will ask how you handle difficult situations, in particular how you previously handled **conflict resolution issues**. Conflict resolution is one of those crucial soft skills that employers are looking for, especially in industries that prize teamwork and cross-departmental cooperation. Demonstrating that you have the ability to work with a diverse group of people, with varied skill sets and personality attributes, reveals that you are a valuable asset beyond the actual hard skills that you have been educated or trained to perform. Conflict resolution questions ask that you show a variety of attributes that allow you to resolve issues as they arise, including mediation, empathy, facilitation, creative problem-solving, and accountability. There are even entire positions within organizations that are dedicated to conflict resolution capabilities, but this is a valuable skill for any employee. Be sure to identify, prior to the interview, a particular instance at a specific job wherein you were called upon—or, better yet, simply took up the responsibility without being expressly asked—to resolve conflicts between staff members or between co-workers and management. Showing that you can handle conflict with poise and thoughtfulness reveals a lot about your worth as an employee overall. It also reflects your ability to understand and navigate a complex situation without creating more conflict. Be especially careful not to assign blame to others or to otherwise project negativity; focus on the attributes that you have, as well as the concrete actions you undertook, in order to resolve a difficult matter during a previous work experience.

- Another kind of opinion question asks you to evaluate how **well you work in teams and/or how self-motivated you are** to get things done in a professional and timely manner. As with the above examples, these questions are two sides of the same coin. On the one side, you want to showcase how well you are able to work with others, emphasizing important soft skill such as communication, empathy, and mediation. On the other side, you want to display your ability to get things done without being asked or under constant supervision. Again, make sure that understand the job description and which of these is most important to the employer—they are both important, to be sure, but typically speaking, a position might require more finesse in one than the other. Working in a team environment requires the ability to balance a number of moving parts, both with regard to delegating hard skills and navigating soft skills. If the job to which you are applying requires lots of teamwork, then you likely already have experience in working well with others; find a specific example to relate, as with all questions. Likewise, if you are self-motivated, then find a specific example of how you've applied that skill to your experience; this might be an excellent opportunity for you to talk about your volunteer work or other unpaid experience. Discussing experiences you have had that weren't required or financially rewarded reveals your desire to be productive and/or contribute to your larger community. With regard to specific work experience, you might have an example of how you functioned in a largely unsupervised role: for example, working as teachers or trainers are largely unsupervised on a daily basis, but results can be quantified based on graduation or success rates. This shows that you have strong personal organization skills, as well as a clear ability to meet performance expectations without direct guidance.

- In terms of behavioral questions, an interviewer might ask you about the **roles you have played in team scenarios**. This is similar to the above, in part, but it is distinct in that it requires you to think about your affinity within a team: some people gravitate toward leadership positions, while others are happier being facilitators, and still others are most comfortable executing tasks initiated by others. All types of employees are necessary to make an effective team, so don't try to anticipate what the hiring manager wants you to say; rather, answer honestly using a particular example of what role you played in a team situation and how your role affected the results.

- Another kind of teamwork question—"how are you well suited to company culture?"—strikes a slightly different note. In this instance, you are essentially being asked to evaluate the company for which you are being interviewed to work as a whole: **how are your values and ideas commensurate with those of the company?** This question also provides opportunities and poses pitfalls. On the one hand, you can easily talk about how passionate you are about the company mission and how it falls in line with what you've always wanted to accomplish in your career; or how, during your research, you discovered that the management style here values the particular skill set you have to offer; or, how your past experience has led you to value a different kind of company culture that is clearly on display within this current company. You have the opportunity to emphasize particular skills and experience in order to show how you are a good fit for the company. On the other hand, be careful to avoid the pitfalls of overgeneralizing about company culture—don't talk about what you don't know enough about—or to offer critiques about corporate culture, in general or in particular. Interview questions are designed to reveal something about yourself and your work style and ethic, not to proffer opportunities to expound on your fundamental philosophical beliefs. Answer the question with specific examples of how your abilities and experiences match up to what you have seen of company culture thus far.

- You might also get a question about teamwork that allows you to **showcase your flexibility**. If you are asked about what you would do if the position to which you are applying went from a more self-motivated, individual working style to a more team-oriented approach, then you are actually being asked to talk about your adaptability to new ways of thinking and performing in the workplace. In addition, team-based assignments may involve different kinds of tasks and different groups of people with different skill sets at various times: a potential employer wants to know that you can handle yourself in a variety of situations, not just one particular scenario. In this case, you want to prepare an answer wherein you can talk about a specific work experience that required you to change your mode of working and how you adapted to that. Flexibility and dependability will be discussed further in Chapter 10, but these two qualities are paramount to the development of successful team-building skills, as well.

- Also consider the possibility that you might be asked to **undergo a team interview or participate in a group scenario**. You should feel free to ask prior to the interview if this will be the case, but you should still be prepared to handle these events should they arise without your prior knowledge. In each case, you are really being put to the test as to how you handle various personalities and the stress of performing within a group. Always think of the STAR method when preparing potential answers, and be genuine in terms of participating in a way that showcases your strongest attributes. Be prepared, especially in a group scenario, to evaluate your performance within the group, as well as the group itself. This kind of analysis is crucial to employees who will be required to work with others in creating a productive environment.

- Always remember, too, that part of the interview process is simply to demonstrate that you are **friendly, pleasant, and professional**: utilizing your best workplace etiquette reveals that you are a ready and able team player even before you get offered the job. Keep up the positive attitude, as discussed in the previous chapter, and you will ensure that you reveal yourself a team player.

Chapter 9: The Interview: Goal Oriented

In addition to demonstrating teamwork skills, any solid candidate for a position should be self-motivated and be able to show how and why goals are important. This reveals you to be someone who can think beyond the present and strive for better; it also shows an ability to manage time effectively, organize and prioritize work, and balance daily tasks with broader goals. Basically, demonstrating that you are a goal oriented candidate allows you to highlight a number of soft skills that are valuable to any employer and to any position. The following details some points you may emphasize, some mistakes you might avoid, and some specific questions and potential answers regarding goal oriented behavior you may confront in a typical interview.

- If you can demonstrate that you are a goal oriented candidate, then you show greater focus and resolve. Be sure to prepare some answers that discuss both **short-term and long-term goals**: goals in the short term might reveal what you plan to accomplish within the scope of the particular position for which you are interviewing (implementing a new marketing campaign, for example, or vying for a specific promotion), while goals in the long term might take on what you expect to accomplish within the next five to ten years of your career. Remember that the more specific and concrete the details, the more impressive the answer. Also be sure to distinguish between goals and dreams: goals are realistic milestones that one can achieve through a set of concrete actions, while dreams are desires that require luck or external intervention to succeed.

- A basic kind of behavioral question that you might be asked to answer deals with goals: **how do you show that you are goal oriented**; how do you specifically go about reaching goals. In the first case, your past behavior demonstrates that you are interested in and adept at striving towards productivity and success. In the second case, your story should outline specific and concrete steps that you undertook in order to reach the goals. These kinds of questions can take many forms: "give an example of a goal you set and how you achieved it"; "give an example of a goal that you failed to meet and why"; "why are goals important to your ability to perform?" These are just a few examples of how you might be asked to explain behavior that leads to achieving success and cultivating motivation. Prepare at least two examples of goals that you once had and met to varying degrees: you can showcase how you overcame obstacles or adversity to achieve your goals, for one example, or you can detail how you implement plans in a specific way to pave the way for your accomplishments. In any case, be sure to identify a specific goal that led to a concrete result, focusing on the kinds of skills that you needed in order to reach the goal. This might mean hard skills—you had to learn a new computer skill in order to reach the goal you set—or soft skills—you had to learn greater flexibility in order to overcome the obstacles presented before you can reach your goal. Ideally, you will able to detail both kinds of skills in showing that you are motivated by goals and—most importantly—able to demonstrate behavior that allows you to meet them.

- With regard to the above type of question, you might also be ready to talk about **goals that you have met in different facets of your life**: being a goal oriented person in general is highly predictive of how goal oriented you will be in your professional life. Thus, you might consider discussing personal goals that you have set and met, especially if they show that you are adept at facing challenges and overcoming obstacles. So, preparing a story about goals set and met in your personal life (say, training for and completing a marathon, or raising a set amount of money for a particular charity) can also show you to be a determined and focused candidate with solid follow through behavior. Be aware, though, to always focus on goals that are met through your personal actions, rather than via chance (such as winning the lottery).

- Remember that you should **never hesitate** when asked to discuss your goals or to answer questions regarding goal oriented behavior: this is an immediate red flag to any potential employer, because a candidate who cannot envision a particular future is likely not an employee with a clear sense of how to steer their position or the company itself into a brighter future. Emphasizing goals that are or can be achieved through determination and hard work make you an ideal candidate.

- **Avoid pessimism** when speaking about your future goals; sounding discouraged impedes your ability to project a positive attitude (see Chapter 7), as well as detracts from the larger point of showing that you know how to set reasonable goals and achieve them through specific plans and actions. This also applies when talking about past goals that you have achieved: when discussing any obstacles that may have cropped up while trying to achieve a past goal, always be sure to emphasize that you were able to overcome said obstacle and talk about what you ultimately learned from that experience.

- Behavioral questions will also often involve a description of how you make decisions. **Decision making** is a key component of critical thinking overall and reveals an independent, well-informed, and decisive employee. For example, an interviewer might ask you simply how you make decisions in the workplace, and sometimes they will give you a particular scenario to work through. This requires preparation in terms of reviewing the concrete details of how you came to an important decision in a previous professional context. They might also ask if you have ever made a decision that was either unpopular or, ultimately, ineffective: this is another excellent opportunity to reveal that you are adept at adapting, regrouping, and overcoming obstacles. Remember that it is always best to be honest and that revealing a negative experience can actually reveal some of your best qualities, should you frame the response in the right way. An unpopular decision might ultimately have led to a greater good (think about parenting in this context: what is "popular" to the kids might not be what is actually good for them, but in the long run, they understand it was for the best). A decision that proved a mistake is another way for you to show that you can learn from past behavior and modify your responses to be a better, more effective, and more well-rounded employee. Nobody is immune from making mistakes, and decision making skills are complex skills honed over time; past behavior is both predictive of future results and of flexibility, the ability to learn from stumbles. Good decision making skills indicate that a candidate is knowledgeable and authoritative.

- Behavioral questions will often be focused on **problem solving skills**. Detailing a story in which you successfully confronted and eventually resolved a problem reveals a host of abilities that are applicable in virtually all workplace scenarios. Problem solving includes a variety of soft skills that are necessary to professional success: the ability to analyze a situation showcases your ability to utilize logic and unbiased observation to generate possible responses to a specific issue. It also reveals your ability to evaluate which response will be most effective before implementing a coherent plan and assessing final results. When asked about how you solved a problem, use this formula to create a story regarding one specific instance at a previous workplace wherein you had to apply these important skills. Outline each element and formulate a concise and coherent answer, from identifying and analyzing the problem to generating and evaluating various responses. No matter what the position, problem solving skills touch on virtually all of the most logical and significant of the so-called soft skills. This can allow you to prove that you are quick to respond and intelligent in your reaction.

- Finally, one of the most common—and potentially most dreaded—interview questions is the alarmingly open-ended **"tell me about yourself."** This prompt encourages you to reveal something of your personality as well as professional strengths, often used as an icebreaker to allow both interviewer and candidate to settle into the interview. It is also a way in which the interviewer can gauge how quickly you think in a spontaneous atmosphere and allow you to show how comfortable you are in interpersonal communications. While it may not seem that you need to prepare for this question—after all, you know exactly who you are—it is important to anticipate the question and have some sort of prepared response. If you are thrown off by the question and have no particular idea of where you might focus, then you will inevitably get caught up in a rambling and/or irrelevant response that sets a wobbly tone for the rest of the interview. Instead, think about this question beforehand in light of the position to which you are applying, your relevant past experience and personality traits, and the company culture that you have researched. One simple way to prepare this kind of answer is to give a concise sketch of where you are now, personally and professionally, how you got there, and what you hope to accomplish in the future.

Chapter 10: The Interview: Flexible and Dependable

Another soft skill that employers are always seeking is that of flexibility and dependability. In the contemporary workplace, certain elements of work are changing rapidly (technology being the most obvious arena), and employers want to ensure that their employees are able to adapt to these changes. It is also the case that work is increasingly done remotely, so employers are concerned with their various employees dependability. Obviously, this is important regardless of where or how the work takes place; nevertheless, it is a question to which you will most likely be asked to respond. Following are some suggestions and examples of how to handle questions regarding flexibility and dependability.

- Here are some **probable questions** you might be asked that will give you the opportunity to talk about your flexibility and dependability:
  - "Discuss an experience when you weren't able to finish a task by a deadline or the end of your work day": this prompt allows you to discuss either dependability ("I stayed late in order to get X project complete.") or flexibility ("I was

able to delegate the remaining tasks while negotiating with another group in order to extend the deadline in a way that was acceptable to all.")

- ○ "Discuss a moment when you had an argument with a colleague": how you respond to this allows you to reveal how flexible you are in dealing with others (it also shows effective communication and interpersonal skills), as well as how reliable you are in resolving conflicts and staying dedicated to the work at hand.

- ○ "Discuss a difficult decision you once had to make": your answer should reveal that you remain dependable in the face of pressure, as well as flexible in how you face challenges.

- ○ "Discuss a time when you had to complete a task via instructions you knew to be faulty": your answer should reveal that, regardless of your personal feelings on a manager's instructions, you can be relied upon to carry out a particular task. It can also show that you are flexible in approaching assignments from various points of view. Beware of showing yourself to be argumentative or difficult to work with.

- o "Discuss an experience wherein personal issues interfered with your professional responsibilities": this scenario likely happens to all employees, and your response should show that, no matter how difficult the situation, you remain dependable. Even if your experience reveals that you had to miss work or delay a project, you should be able to relate how you communicated and/or delegated so that others' work was not hampered and productivity was not adversely affected.

- Experience verification questions give you the opportunity to talk about **past accomplishments**, whether they be in the form of increased production and/or revenue, promotions, awards, or unique opportunities that you were able to take advantage of because of your exceptional previous performance. Oftentimes, an interviewer will simply ask you what your greatest accomplishments at a particular job or other experience might be. One effective way to prepare for an interview, in general, would be to keep a copy of your resume, wherein you take notes about particular talking points for each element of the resume: you may not necessarily have the space to list every accomplishment from every position, of course, but if you jot down notes about interesting accomplishments, the interview gives you the space during which to talk about a wider variety of successes than your resume can reveal. For example, if you worked on a particular project that received a significant amount of external attention and you were asked to speak to the media about it, this is an accomplishment that may not merit being listed on your resume but is certainly legitimate and strong enough to discuss in an interview. It reveals not only your **expertise and dedication** to a particular project, but also your effective **communication skills and flexibility** to perform duties beyond the specific tasks required for production.

- Experience verification questions also ask you to expand upon and extrapolate about skills gained from particular experience(s) that occur while on the job. That is, while we are all educated or trained to produce particular results with a set of hard skills (technical expertise, mathematical application, standards for analysis, industry norms), we often **acquire additional skills via the various experiences that we undergo on the job itself**. These kinds of questions ask you to demonstrate that you are a continuing learner, open to new ways of thinking and approaching performance. These kinds of questions might ask about expectations—both the expectations that you had of what your previous position entailed and the expectations that were asked of you and how you fulfilled them (or did not). Basically, this gives you the opportunity either to show how well you handle on-the-job stress and change or to explain why you were only employed for a short time at a particular company (a resume gap). In the first instance, you might tell a story about how you were hired to complete this specific function, say review and update accounting procedures, but as you began to familiarize yourself with the company books, you realized that there were deeper issues that needed to be re-visited. Thus, you became instrumental in a basic restructuring of how disparate teams worked together to meet productivity goals: this shows the interviewer that your experience allowed you to pick up new skills; you should be comfortable sharing that you weren't previously confident in your ability to perform large scale analyses, yet your experience in that particular position imbued you with greater confidence. In the second instance, you might explain how the expectations of a previous position didn't match with the realities of daily experience. For example, you were hired to perform a particular task, such as job training, but ultimately you were asked to intervene in interdepartmental arguments regarding who was responsible for what task; thus, you were thrown into an uncomfortable scenario wherein you had no particular expertise to solve and, therefore, exited the company more quickly than you intended. The expectations that were outlined by the company were violated by actual issues within the company. Either way, these questions reveal that you are quick to learn from experience, as well as resolved to understand your strengths and weaknesses.

- When discussing dependability and flexibility, you are also given the chance to **explain any gaps** in your resume. You will want to discuss—and will probably be directly asked—about any long periods that show you without professional work, or about periods of time wherein you only stayed at a particular job for a short time. In many cases, it is perfectly appropriate to eliminate listing short-term jobs from your resume, though always be honest about whatever questions are asked of you at the interview. Be prepared with an honest and detailed explanation. If you do have significant gaps in employment history, then there are several ways to handle it, depending on circumstances. First, instead of listing specific start and end dates, simply list years employed (2012-2015, for example). Second, if you have several gaps in your employment history, a succinct explanation for each would be appropriate, such as "company closed" or "relocated for spouse's job" or "laid off because of downsizing." Last, if you have a long gap in your employment history, then this is the time to put a summary at the beginning of your resume, which can serve to explain why you are re-entering the work force at this particular time.

Chapter 11: The Interview: Integrity and Intelligence

At the end of the day, most employers greatly value honesty, authenticity, and intelligence—especially emotional intelligence—within an employee. Your resume and past work experience will certainly reveal some aspects of your innate intelligence and abilities, but you will also want to show that you can conduct yourself appropriately and within the boundaries of professional courtesy and understanding. The below sections deal with integrity (and the double-edged sword of honesty) and intelligence, both innate and emotional.

Conducting Yourself with Integrity

No amount of technical expertise or enthusiastic report will guarantee you any job if you are not conducting yourself with integrity. If you lie on your resume or exaggerate your accomplishments, then you are likely to be exposed in the course of the interview itself—or once you're on the job, which could lead to an embarrassing and impactful dismissal or demotion. It is imperative that you come across as genuine and honest in all your professional dealings.

- The conundrum of **how honest to be** during the application and interview process is a fraught one:

some advice out there suggests that you be honest . . . but not *too* honest, that it's acceptable to bend the truth a bit in the service of your ideal job search. Other advice suggests that managers and employers are truly seeking the most honest and forthcoming individuals for their positions. So, which advice is the best? Certainly, the old canard "honesty is the best policy" applies to just about everything you do in life; the consequences of getting caught up in falsehoods could do more damage than even the "harmless" fib you peddled in the first place might. It reveals volumes about a person's integrity when lies are exposed, even if they are minor ones—sometimes *especially* if they are minor ones ("why would she lie about something so minor? What's wrong with her?"). Thus, it is always best to err on the side of truthfulness than not. However, that doesn't always indicate that you have to reveal every single thing about your work history or experience: everyone makes mistakes, and if you have learned from them, it might be an advantage to bring such issues to light in an interview (indeed, many interviewers will ask outright to talk about past mistakes and how you dealt with them). But, everyone also deserves to be defined by aspects of their life besides their mistakes:

a particularly damaging or difficult time need not be put on the table unless it becomes highly significant to the conversation or position. Know the difference between revealing that you were fired for a mistake that you've since rectified and keeping quiet over an incident with office politics that might be misinterpreted outside the culture of your former company.

- Nevertheless, it is **never appropriate** to list a certification, license, or other accomplishment that has subsequently been revoked for some reason. Even if the accomplishment in question isn't relevant for the position to which you applied, it is still unwise to elide the full truth. It is likely that the most casual search will reveal your "lie of omission," which will almost certainly knock you out of the running for the job. Additionally, claiming licensure for certain positions that you no longer have is considered a criminal act in many cases.

- Another simple reason not to elide the truth when discussing your history, your achievements, or your personal qualities is that it can **lead to dissatisfaction in the job should you get it**. For example, if you claim that you enjoy working with teams and emphasize your past experience with groups, but you really would rather work on your own as an individual, then obtaining a position wherein you are required to work with others regularly would be unpleasant at best. In addition, if you are hired based on the fact that you indicated that you truly enjoyed success that comes out of hard, meaningful work, then realize that your work-life balance is being compromised, management might see quickly that you aren't actually a good fit for the job. Emphasize the character qualities and work skills that you actually possess and are positive about—this ensures that you get the job that you want and become the employee that managers need. Sometimes you might not get an offer by presenting your work style and achievements honestly; however, it is certain that you will, ultimately, get the job that is the best fit for you.

- Some common areas in which candidates elide the truth are actually opportunities to show what an exceptional employee they can eventually be. For example, when asked about "weaknesses" in the workplace, you might get uncomfortable, not wanting to reveal your shortcomings in your desire to present yourself as the best candidate. However, **revealing your vulnerabilities can often make you seem more relatable and open**: clearly, nobody is perfect and pretending you don't have weaknesses looks aloof and arrogant; interviewers like to see that you are self-aware and willing to improve. For another example, when asked about how you handled a difficult situation at work offers you the opportunity to show how you actually work through adversity: instead of telling the interviewer that you handled everything with smooth aplomb, revealing what was challenging for you in the scenario and how you overcame those challenges shows that you are a problem-solver and a determined employee. For a final example, the touchy subject of why you were fired always seems like a landmine, but it can be another opportunity to reveal something positive about yourself overall: if you take the attitude that "nothing was my fault," this shows you to be potentially immune to critique and perhaps difficult to work with. If you admit and accept at least some of the responsibility for what occurred, then you reveal that you can overcome difficult situations and are resilient enough to learn from bad experiences and become a better future employee. Thus, there are numerous occasions when honesty—however painful—might indeed give you an advantage.

Understanding Expectations, Demonstrating Intelligence

Not only should you review your own skills and qualifications, but you should also consider what hiring managers often have in mind when interviewing candidates. Understanding these expectations can help you generate potential responses that hit the mark for what management is looking for.

- First of all, **consider the position itself**: what managers will expect depends largely on the nature of the job and the experience and skill set needed to fulfill that job. Thus, if you are looking at an entry level position, then the expectations for lengthy job experience or leadership roles will be lower. In this case, it is likely that you are just embarking on your career, and so other parts of your resume will be more significant, such as educational accomplishments and other extracurricular achievements. If you are looking for a job in management or a highly technical or specialized field, then you can expect that interviewers will be looking for specific details on your abilities and accomplishments within that particular field. The position for which you are interviewing plays some role itself in understanding the expectations that hiring managers will have of you.

- Following on the above, however, employers looking to hire new workers will be much more interested in how they **have demonstrated effectiveness in past work experie**nce, rather than in educational achievements—unless you are seeking a truly entry level position. So, emphasizing your experience, especially with regard to some of the top skills that employers are looking for, will be the most significant way to impress upon them that you will be a smart choice.

- Also remember that you are likely competing with several other candidates for the job: think about **what in your past work experience makes you stand out**. You'll want to be sure to prepare at least a couple of answers that demonstrate your unique abilities and how they are applicable to the current position being offered. Basically, you need to sell yourself as the best applicant for the job.

- Within that set of unique skills that you are presenting, you want to emphasize your "hard" skills: these are the particular technical skills that are required for the job, whether it be in teaching or tech development: what might set you apart from the other candidates is a **surplus of expertise in a particular arena** (for a teacher, say, you might have published case studies in your field; for a graphic designer, say, you may have developed new software that enables easier manipulation of features). This reveals a higher intelligence and dedication.

- In addition to expert intelligence, there is also the arena of **emotional intelligence** that a good candidate should demonstrate. When hiring managers ask questions about emotional intelligence, they want the candidate to demonstrate that they understand their own emotions as well as the emotions of others—and can respond appropriately and professionally. In today's job market, emotional intelligence has become as important, if not more so, than innate intellect. Here are some surefire ways to demonstrate that you have excellent emotional intelligence:

  - **Active listening** effectively demonstrates emotional intelligence, showing that you can engage with others in an appropriate way. For more on effective listening techniques and practice, see Chapter 6.
  - **Don't be afraid to show some emotion**: many candidates become so anxious when

being interviewed that they come across as rote or stiff. Showing some (again, appropriate) sense of humor or a passionate enthusiasm about an experience or opportunity makes you appear more fully human and relatable.

o **Give credit to others when appropriate** for your own accomplishments. This shows you to be a generous team player, as well as displays humility and a corroborative spirit.

o **Talk about how you continue to improve** yourself or your performance. When you reveal a weakness, use it as an opportunity to show that you are self-aware and willing to learn. This kind of open honesty and flexibility is invaluable in any employee.

o **Discussing how you learned from mistakes** is also an effective way in which you reveal your ability to bounce back from failure, showing resilience and determination. Accept responsibility for your part in a project that went wrong or a deadline that was missed, but steer the answer toward how you have improved your skills since then.

o **Be open to talking about conflict** when asked about teamwork or co-workers. Conflict is unavoidable in any workplace and discussing how you were able to confront it and resolve it shows you to be a candidate with high levels of emotional intelligence: the ability to deal with various personalities, adapting to differences of opinion, or communicating difficulties in professional ways.

○ **Ask questions about company values** at the end of an interview. This reveals that you are not only professionally invested in your job but also emotionally aware of how your role fits in with the company as a whole. This kind of question can also reveal to you that the job may or may not be a good fit — handy information to have when making your final decision.

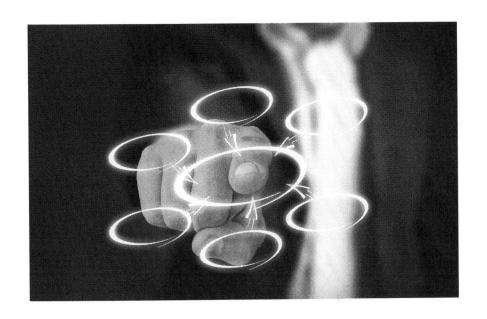

Chapter 12: The Interview: Organizational Skills and Critical and Creative Thinking

Finally, in any job interview, you will be asked questions, directly or indirectly, about your organizational skills and thinking capacity. These soft skills are closely linked in that our ability to organize and our style of organization reveals much about our critical and creative thinking skills. Employers want candidates who are organized enough to meet deadlines and productivity goals while utilizing problem solving and decision making (critical and creative thinking) skills. Below are some examples of the kinds of questions and answers that might be addressed in a typical interview that allow you to discuss these crucial soft skills.

Organizational Style

- With regard to organizational skills, there are any number of ways in which one can successfully maintain an organized professional life; thus, there is no one correct way in which to answer a question based on this. However, you should be prepared to talk about how you organize your work with regard to past experience, using specific details and concrete examples. Essentially, you need to **demonstrate**

that you recognize your own organizational style and be able to relay how it works for you. You must tell a story about a system that works well for both individual goals and team projects.

- In addition to providing specific details on how your organizational system works for you, you should also provide a response that showcases how that organization has **resulted in benefits for others and/or for the company** as a whole. To show that you can meet deadlines as an individual is valuable, but to relate how your ability to move projects along resulted in greater revenue for the quarter is even better. Find an example that demonstrates real time impact.

- You also want to be aware of how your **organizational style can be flexible** so that you are able to adapt to shifting deadlines or changing circumstances. That is, your organizational style shouldn't be so rigid that you cannot work with unexpected challenges.

- Again, be prepared to answer the question about **how you would describe yourself**, in terms of organizational skills. Do you keep detailed calendars, or do you prefer free form journals, or both? Do you use technological tools to help you stay organized and on task? Do you plan your day, your week, your month, or all of the above? How do you respond when your plans are not met? How do you organize within teams? Providing this information with a specific example is, of course, even stronger as an answer.

- Also be prepared to answer questions with regard to your ability to **plan and prioritize**. Behavior questions will ask you to reveal how you prioritize your work and organize your tasks. Your ability to prioritize says a lot about how valuable you can be as an employee, as well as exposes a lot about your decision making skills (or, alas, the lack thereof). For example, imagine that you are a lawyer working on a number of cases at one time: how do you prioritize which case demands the most of your time? You could consider the relative fees that the law firm stands to make in each individual case, focusing your time on those cases which will generate the most revenue. Or, you could determine that the cases with the strongest chance of achieving the desired results (a win, a dismissal, a deal, whatever the desired outcome might be) deserve the largest portion of your time. Or, you could decide that the cases that are most deserving of social or financial justice should take up most of your work day, even if they aren't necessarily financially lucrative or boons to the firm's reputation. Or, you could determine that each case deserves an equal amount of time and prioritize each uniformly. None of these approaches is necessarily wrong or right: they simply reveal a mindset and a work style that you will undoubtedly reveal in your answer to your potential employee. Priorities are strong indicators of employee behavior, in both positive and negative ways. Even if you have the best of intentions in mind, if your priorities do not connect with that of your supervisor or the company, then you are clearly not a good fit for the position. Likewise, if you have a difficult time prioritizing, seeing everything as equal, then you are sometimes unable to discern what is most important in terms of productivity or general results. If an employee feels that interpersonal interactions at work are coequal with time spent on projects, then a company might rightly conclude that their ability to prioritize is not in reasonable proportion. However, if an employee is able to manage a number of tasks with success and on deadline, then it reveals a superior ability to prioritize.

- Part of being able to prioritize effectively is in employing effective organizational skills, of course.

637

Thus, behavior questions will often ask you to describe **how you structure your day, implement a project, or delegate responsibility**. There are some simple ways to respond to questions regarding your organizational skills, such as relaying how you keep track of your work week: using planners, color-coded calendars, reminder alerts, as well as describing your ability to achieve work-life balance are all straightforward if non-specific ways to reveal your organizational abilities. Outlining a story about how some or all of these techniques—or others unique to you—assisted you in completing a project or meeting a deadline is more effective because it shows how your methods influence your behavior. Another way in which an interviewer might get at your style of organization is to ask how you deal with interruptions: your answer will not only show how you effectively organize but it will also demonstrate your flexibility in the demands of a dynamic workplace.

Critical and Creative Thinking

- With regard to critical and creative thinking, you are being asked to verify that you can both **analyze and evaluate a situation in order to get desired results**, as well as that you can do such analysis and problem solving in creative ways. The most common creative thinking question uses the old cliché "how do you think 'outside the box'"? Be prepared to have a story about how your innovative thinking solved particular problems.

- **Competency questions,** as separate from qualification or behavioral questions, are designed to get at underlying levels of ability: it's not just that you've trained in the past or have educational qualifications for the job; it's that you are able to demonstrate that you have an intellectual competency to perform specific tasks and learn new ones. Thus, competency questions are difficult, both to pose and to answer. For the interviewer, competency questions require that they know a great deal about the position to be filled in addition to what the candidate has to offer; competency questions are asked mostly of high level applicants. For the candidate, competency questions probe your fundamental intelligence and abilities independent of past successes or achievements.

- One of the best ways to think about competency questions is to understand what the core competencies of the position are, what core factors are necessary for any applicant to be able to satisfy the requirements of the job. Another way that some business leaders might put it is to consider **the "critical success factors"** for the job, or CSF for short. Depending on the position, these CSFs could be baseline intelligence, risk taking, analytical abilities, strategic planning, tactical skills, overall drive, creativity, ambition, and life balance. The best way to think about competency questions is to think about how to prove—with specific evidence and example—that you have one or more of the aforementioned competencies. For example, if intelligence is a key competency for the job, then you could produce standardized test scores or IQ results. This is an uncommon request, but it is found in jobs that require high levels of education or specialization (think of college professors: they must produce not only proof of degrees—credential verification—but also have passed particular tests and met higher standards for professional inclusion). Sometimes, a competency interview will require you to perform certain tasks to demonstrate competency (to use the professor example again, an applicant may be asked to critique a paper that has been published in their field as a requirement of their hiring). If you are asked to participate in a full competency interview, then there are some specific ways in which you can prepare.

- Think about your competencies and **write out a summary** of what you think they are and how you have been able to demonstrate that you have them. This is a worthwhile exercise even if you have not been called upon to do a full competency interview, as this kind of process will lead to an understanding of your underlying abilities to compete in your filed for any position; these kinds of answers can also be used when responding to behavioral questions, so it is not a waste of time or energy to think about this. You can also consider the ten core critical success factors that most employers are seeking: positive attitude; proficiency in field; oral and written communication skills; basic interpersonal skills; self-confidence and motivation; critical thinking; problem solving; flexibility; leadership; and teamwork. If you can come up with an example of how you have specifically demonstrated at least half of these, then you are coming into an interview with an advantage over other candidates.

Chapter 13: The Interview: Common Mistakes to Avoid and Proper Follow Up

If this is your first time preparing for a professional job or undertaking a broad search, or if it has been a while since you last jumped into the fray, then there are some potential pitfalls that you would be wise to avoid. Likewise, if you have been searching for your dream job for a while now and have yet to be successful, you may accidentally be committing some of these potential pitfalls. It is always a smart idea to review some of the "don'ts" when job seeking; these can ultimately be as important as the "dos." Some of these pitfalls have already been addressed throughout this guide, but here is a handy checklist that you can review immediately prior to the interview, as well as a basic protocol for how to handle post-interview etiquette.

- We often forget how **ubiquitous our internet presence is**; if you fail to consider your online footprint when you apply for professional positions or go to interviews, then you may be ignoring the one barrier between you and your ideal job. It is a good idea not only to maintain a polite and non-controversial social media presence (Facebook and Twitter are now regularly reviewed by human resources departments), but also to avoid participating in forums or other internet outlets wherein you openly discuss your political, social, religious, sexual, or other potentially controversial views—especially avoid doing so when using your own name. When employers view these things, they can—rightly or wrongly—have an oversized impact on whether or not you are hired. If you are comfortable compromising your employment opportunities because you possess strong opinions and views that you feel you must express, then certainly it is your prerogative to do so. Just be aware that there are likely consequences.

- Another common misstep for young interviewees is **not to understand when the interview begins**: the interview begins long before you actually sit down across from a manager or committee. It begins when you turn in a resume and cover letter, when you are called for the interview, and when you arrive at the building (or pick up the phone) itself. That is, you are being assessed based on every bit of information—including behavior—that you present. Thus, *always* be polite to anyone who you encounter in the lead up to the interview: receptionists, secretaries, guards, even people in the hallways or elevators. You don't have any idea who is actually involved in the decision making process—that person you snub in the elevator might just be a colleague or a supervisor. Conduct yourself as if you are in the interview itself at all times.

- **Talking too much** is another potential pitfall about which you should be aware. When asked about yourself, keep the answer short and sweet and, ideally, focused on the position itself. Frame your answer so that it reflects what parts of your personality, skill set, and/or experience are well suited to the job at stake.

- **Don't forget why you are there**: no matter how casual the interviewer may seem or how personal the questions might get, don't make the mistake of thinking that the situation is anything other than a highly professional scenario. Becoming overly comfortable or familiar can ultimately hurt your chances.

- **Always be prepared**: this is why you are reading this guide in the first place. Also check out my other book, *Job Interview Preparation* for more in-depth advice on everything from resumes and cover letters to reducing stress and creating a professional persona.

- **Forgetting or ignoring professional etiquette** can also be an impediment to getting the job. Some advice on how to conduct yourself with the highest professionalism follows:

  - Consider your **first impression**; you must not only look the part but also act the part. A first impression can never be retracted, so it is important not to begin an interview on the wrong foot. Be enthusiastic and look happy—rather than apprehensive—to be there. Make eye contact and introduce yourself politely when appropriate, extending a handshake in most cases. When entering the interview space, be sure to accept instructions politely and strike an open—rather than defensive—posture.

  - Be sure that the **outfit you've chosen to wear** for the interview is appropriate and professional, but also be aware of how it will appear when you are seated. You want to avoid the proverbial wardrobe malfunction (gaping blouse, popped button, overly hiked pants). Typically, you will be seated for most of the interview, so that's how you should test the comforts and utility of your chosen attire.

- Always **remember to smile** and appear interested in what the interviewer is saying. A smile (or, conversely, a frown) can speak volumes. If you appear smiling and approachable, then you are perceived as a team player with valuable character attributes as well as professional skills to bring to the company. A frown, on the other hand, can fluster or annoy the interviewer; it is difficult to know how to interpret the facial expression. Are you angry, annoyed, bored, frustrated, or otherwise unimpressed? This is not the impression you want to convey. Remind yourself that this experience, while somewhat nerve-racking, should be an amiable way in which to showcase your considerable talents and value. This would bring a smile to anyone's face.

- **Body language**, in general, reveals a lot about a person's feelings and character. Crossing your arms against your chest looks defensive, even hostile, while a lazy slump indicates a lack of interest or disrespect. Keeping your hands folded in your lap throughout the interview can have the effect of implying childlike anxiety. "Man-spreading" can look aggressive or arrogant. Again, maintain eye contact when answering questions, and avoid sweeping hand gestures. You can hold a pen or pencil in your hand if it helps to center you, and this can come in handy should you wish to jot anything down. Basically, your body language should indicate that you are engaged and open, enthusiastic and polite.

- When **greeting others**, be sure that you have a solid handshake, somewhere between limp and crushing. A firm handshake reveals self-confidence and a courteous understanding of overall business etiquette. When meeting someone for the first time, it is considered polite to use an honorific, such as Dr. or Ms. or Mr. If the company for which you are interviewed is owned or operated by foreign nationals, then it would behoove you to do some research into the basic etiquette of the other country. Personal space is defined differently in different cultures, in addition to attitudes about how men and women behave.
- **Addressing someone** by their name is also a powerful piece of business etiquette that you can employ to curry respect. Everyone likes to

be noticed and remembered, so try your best to remember and repeat the names of people that you meet. Should you be called in for a further interview, this considerate formality will inevitably be noticed.

o As you are seated for your interview—which you should be invited to do, rather than simply plopping down—place your personal items beside or underneath your chair. For everyone's sanity and to preserve your dignity, **turn off your cell phone** and any other device you may have carried with you. Have your resume and cover letter, along with a notepad or folder for notes, at the ready.

o If, for some disastrous reason, your phone should ring during an interview, you will be called upon to do some swift damage control. *Do not dare look at the phone to check* (unless you truly have a life-and-death situation on your hands); simply turn it off and apologize to the interviewer. You would have to be an excellent candidate to overcome this most egregious of etiquette breaches. It's better not to take your phone in with you if you have a habit of forgetting to switch it off. And off means *off*, not silent.

- ○ When leaving the interview, be sure to **restate your interest** in the job and your pleasure at having met everyone. Shake hands again and repeat names, when appropriate. Be sure to thank the receptionist who showed you in, if relevant. Basically, just show proper manners on your way out the door.

- ○ After the interview, it is customary to write **a "thank you" note** of some sort to the interviewer or interviewers to acknowledge their time and your opportunity. See below for more details on that process.

Proper Follow Up

While it may appear that the process of applying for and securing your dream job is complete when the interview is over, there is still one more important step up: you should follow up appropriately. When you follow up in appropriate ways, it can have the added benefit of reminding the potential employer of why you are a strong candidate in the first place; it shows respect and attention to detail, as well as allowing you to pursue answers of your own. Here are some details about how to conduct a proper follow up protocol.

- **When should you follow up?** There are two distinct answers to this: the first is that you should follow up immediately with some kind of thank you note (more on that below); the second is that you should allow an appropriate amount of time to pass before nudging the interviewer to give you some specific results. At the end of the interview itself, find an opportunity to ask when you might hear back from the company if you haven't already been told. If you don't hear back from them in the allotted time period, wait two or three more days before you send a polite email or place a polite phone call. If you aren't sure when you'll hear back, wait at least a week before checking back in. As with listening skills, a polite and professional follow up note can remind a potential employer of your qualifications, abilities, and attributes.

- **How should you follow up?** This, of course, will depend upon the nature of the interview and job position. It is rare, however, that you should ever follow up in person. The most common ways to follow up are with an email or a phone call, and which you choose depends on your level of confidence in speaking extemporaneously or needing to script a response. A follow up email gives you the opportunity to compose your (concise!) thoughts before sending, though it doesn't always provide the kind of immediate gratification that you may want or need. If you decide to call the interviewer or hiring manager, be sure to jot down what you'd like to say beforehand. In either case, be sure that your tone is friendly and that you keep your remarks concise. You can also ask if they require any further materials from you in your follow up—this might be especially relevant if you are concerned that the interview did not go as well as you would have hoped or if you remembered some important information that you weren't able to convey at the time of the original interview.

- Regardless of whether you eventually need to follow up further, you should *always* write a quick note of thanks after the interview. While some might suggest that this is rather old-fashioned, it is still very much the case that this practice is routinely followed and clearly appreciated. The more thoughtful the note, the more successful the results. Here are some **things to consider when writing that crucial thank you note**:

- o Be sure to write and send a thank you note within 24 hours of the interview—any longer and it becomes a moot point. Today, most thank you notes are sent via email, but one sent via mail can garner special attention; just be sure that it is sent promptly so that you aren't forgotten in the interim. Typically, an email is a better choice because of the short time lapse, but if you are physically close enough to stop by with a handwritten note, then that might be the best choice.

- o Address the thank you to everyone who played a role in your application process, from all the interviewers to the recruiter, when applicable. In some cases, it may be applicable to send a quick note to another employee who participated in some form, as well. In many cases, you will be directing your thank you to one specific interviewer. In other cases, if you are interviewed by a few people, then you might want to send a quick note to all involved, especially if their capacities or responsibilities in the interview differed. If you are interviewed by a full panel of people, then you might consider writing one overarching note to the person in charge, and Cc-ing everyone else.

- A thank you note should contain a friendly and respectful greeting, using the person's name and honorific (Dr., Ms., Director, etc.), with a short paragraph expressing your appreciation for their time and effort, closing with a professional "sincerely" and your name. If you can think of a specific detail from the interview that was especially striking, then you might briefly mention it in your paragraph in order to remind them of you. You also might throw in a compliment if it is sincere.

- Essentially, your tone should be professional yet personable. Avoid emojis of any kind, and don't pepper the note with exclamation points or overly excitable adjectives and adverbs. There are numerous templates available online should you wish to review some.

- Finally, **know when to move on**: if you have sent a thank you note and have made two attempts at follow up without response, then it is time to start preparing for your next interview. Be patient, however, and space out your follow up over the course of a couple of weeks: thank you note immediately, follow up within a few days of when response was anticipated, and one final follow up a week or so after that. If there is no response within a month, then your time and energy is best spent moving on.

Conclusion

Employing a winning strategy for your job interview is a challenging and, ultimately, highly rewarding endeavor. While an excellent resume and cover letter will enable you to secure a foot in the door, the interview itself also requires a particular set of skills and some significant amount of practice for it to be as successful as possible. Employers often consider the interview a litmus test not only for how an employee will be productive and valuable at specific work-related tasks but also for how an employee will fit in with corporate culture and be a productive team member beyond the technical skills they bring.

As such, you should treat the job interview as a process much like an educational or training opportunity: it requires research and knowledge, experiential training and practice to be good at job interviews. This guide has provided you with a plethora of tools you can utilize in order to become the most attractive candidate out of many. Not only have you reviewed the most common types of interview questions, but you have also learned how to answer these with specificity of detail and confidence of form. From looking and acting professionally to being thoroughly prepared for any style of interview, any kind of question, you know now how to demonstrate that you have both the hard and soft skills that will make you a valuable employee to any industry or company.

Ultimately, the importance of a job interview really cannot be overstated: this simple act is the culmination of your years of hard work, focus, and energy. You may have paid tens of thousands of dollars for a higher education or special training just to get to this point; you may have spent your entire life dreaming of this particular job in this particular field; you may have an inkling that this job might be able to propel you to success and security in ways you have heretofore only dreamed of. The job interview is the gateway to embark on the path to success and satisfaction: now you have the knowledge and ability to make it swing wide open. In this detailed guide for a winning approach to job interviews, you have learned the best strategies for conquering the interview process—enjoy your dream job!